Reinventing Public Service Television for the Digital Future

For my mother, Connie

Reinventing Public Service Television for the Digital Future

Mary Debrett

intellect Bristol, UK / Chicago, USA

First published in the UK in 2010 by
Intellect, The Mill, Parnall Road, Fishponds, Bristol, BS16 3JG, UK

First published in the USA in 2010 by
Intellect, The University of Chicago Press, 1427 E. 60th Street,
Chicago, IL 60637, USA

A catalogue record for this book is available from the
British Library.

Cover designer: Holly Rose
Copy-editor: Michael Eckhardt
Typesetting: Mac Style, Beverley, E. Yorkshire

ISBN 978-1-84150-321-9

Printed and bound by Gutenberg Press, Malta.

This publication has been supported by La Trobe University.
http://www.latrobe.edu.au

Contents

Preface

Reinventing Public Service Television for the Digital Future examines the ways in which public service systems are changing as digital technologies transform the media landscape. Exploring the historical evolution of six public service broadcasters taken from across four English-speaking countries – Britain's BBC and Channel Four, Australia's ABC and SBS, America's public television system and New Zealand's TVNZ – this comparative analysis reflects on the diversity and resilience of the public service concept, and its place in the digital era. The book begins with an overview in which I outline the defining characteristics of public service systems, and arguments for intervention, differentiating the concept from the private sector's commercial model, which is discussed from the perspective of its libertarian origins. This leads to an exploration of previous forecasts of public service broadcasting's demise which followed the first wave of 'new media' in the 1980s, when cable and satellite television contributed the multi-channel subscription model, offering what some described as 'consumer sovereignty'. Identifying three drivers of social change that have threatened public service providers – cultural fragmentation, multi-channel technologies and free market ideology – I go on to outline how the digital era has pioneered new solutions. In generating a host of new media formats deliverable across a range of platforms – radio, television, online and mobile – digitalization is greatly enhancing and expanding the capacity of public service broadcasters to accommodate diverse public goals while also maintaining the mainstream presence necessary to justify public funding. The scope for asynchronous interactivity online is facilitating public participation of a kind that brings new accountability and legitimacy to the public service concept, connecting communities of interest and building wider awareness of other public service institutions.

The possibilities for reinvention that public service 'media' are now confronting are explored within each broadcaster's particular historical context, taking the national peculiarities of political and cultural traditions into account. Indeed the variation between the broadcasters is quite considerable, and Chapters Two to Seven, which encapsulate the six case studies, explore each broadcaster in terms of: ethos and goals; audience; funding; and accountability, before finally discussing the transformation wrought by the Internet and the digitalization of the terrestrial transmission system.

In Chapter Two, I examine the BBC as the classic model on which many other public service broadcasters have been based, tracing its capacity for institutional adaptation as social and cultural mores changed and discussing the strategies of various director-generals in accommodating shifting political ideologies. In the new millennium, the BBC took on a new role as a driver of digital take-up, initiating and delivering new services to encourage the public to convert to digital television. A singularly successful public service broadcaster and one of the world's top media 'brands', the BBC is increasingly under threat from a hostile private media sector, which faces declining revenue as advertising budgets are spread more thinly across the expanding array of channels and platforms. As this book was going to print, the BBC's 2010 Strategy Review outlined radical cuts across BBC Online as part of a redefining of the institution's core vision.

Chapter Three explores Channel Four, the publisher broadcaster launched in 1982 as a 'service with a difference', directed to be innovative and to provide a complementary service to that of the BBC. Having pursued an increasingly commercial direction in the 1990s, its channel 'brand' targeting youth – the demographic preferred by advertisers – Channel Four found its hybrid commercial-public service status increasingly criticised by private sector rivals as revenue from advertising dwindled in the expanding media marketplace. Nevertheless Channel Four continues to be an innovator in the digital era, producing some exceptional cross platform projects that deliver public service goals in ways never before imagined. Recently signalling both a desire to reprise the creative risk-taking that won it plaudits in the 1980s, along with aspirations for government funding, the future of this commercial public broadcaster remains uncertain with threatened, privately owned commercial media in attack mode and public finance under stress.

Chapter Four explores Australia's ABC, 'the national broadcaster', which was launched in 1956 as the public sector half of Australia's lopsided dual system, the only public broadcaster in a sea of commercial competitors. Directed to be both a mainstream and minority service, the ABC is at last finding itself able to deliver the requisite 'mix and balance' of its remit in the digital era, as it acquires a portfolio of digital channels. Having survived eleven years of culture wars in which it was regularly under financial and political attack, the ABC has finally received additional funding and government endorsement to expand its services on air and online.

Chapter Five explores the Special Broadcasting Service, SBS, Australia's unique multicultural broadcaster, originally established as a multilingual narrowcast service for Australian migrants. Having been relegated to the UHF frequency with minimal government funding and a tiny audience share, SBS was later allowed to take limited advertising. In recent years, frustrated by revenue limitations, SBS management chose to pursue a more commercial direction chasing ratings and the youth demographic to increase its advertising revenue, angering ethnic groups and other loyal audiences in the process. Having fared less well than the ABC in recent triennial funding, SBS appears to be renewing relationships with traditional audiences and is still awaiting funding to develop its digital channels and online presence, platforms that would enable it to meet its diverse charter objectives more effectively and cost efficiently.

The American public television system, originally established in 1967 as a non-commercial service in contradistinction to the dominant commercial networks, is the focus of Chapter Six. Based on a pre-existing network of educational and community stations the public television system includes over 300 separate local stations linked through two separate national management bodies, the corporation for public broadcasting which funnels federal government funding into the system, and the public broadcasting service, a membership organization that produces a national programme service to which members subscribe. Characterised by its diversity and insecure funding the system poses considerable challenges to anyone seeking to make generalisations about it. Expanding the channel capacity of local stations, digitalization now enables public television to better deliver on its goals of accommodating the interests of unserved and underserved audiences but also exacerbates the problems of inadequate funding. While some stations are pioneering innovative interactive programming others are using their digital channels to increase their income. The absence of financial independence has undermined the development of critical news and current affairs programming, which is generally seen as the major weakness of public television, educational programming generally regarded as its strength. It is a field for which the online era brings special benefits with some stations drawing on community resources, linking activities and programming to build online networks, while others aim to engage viewers in complex topics via sophisticated cross-platform projects.

Chapter Seven details the story of TVNZ, a much restructured state-owned television service with a very uncertain future. From its origins as a public broadcaster with non-commercial days to its current un-reinvented state, following the National Government's removal of its public service charter in 2009, TVNZ has travelled the most troubled path of any of the public broadcasters included in this book. Representing the cash cow model of public broadcasting whereby the government takes a dividend from the profits of onscreen advertising rather than subsidising the service, as is the more usual arrangement, TVNZ nevertheless maintains a public service role in the digital era, albeit a potentially short lived one. The operator of two non-commercial digital channels funded directly by grants under the previous government, TVNZ was cast as a key driver of public take-up of digital television, a role that will disappear after digital switchover. Operating on a predominantly commercial basis since 1989, the New Zealand state broadcaster's profitability continues to make it a target for privatisation, with many observing that the abolition of the charter has removed justifications for maintaining public ownership.

In Chapter Eight I offer a general summation of the new developments arising from the possibilities of the Internet and niche digital channels, drawing on examples from the six case studies. My argument here is that the wide ranging possibilities of interactive, multichannel digital media are not only enabling public service providers to better accommodate the various principles underlying the concept, which is now being recast as public service media, but are also again coming into their own as the leading innovators of cross platform content development and viewer/user participation. Finally, in Chapter Nine I revisit the overall importance of the public system as an institution in which the public invest considerable trust, as evidenced by public opinion surveys. I argue that a trustworthy media has singular importance in contemporary times not least because of the growing lack of trust in commercial media due to conglomeration in ownership, the instability and unreliability of online media and the so-called crisis of professional journalism as the established economic model of newspapers erodes. In the face of increasingly strident protests of unfair competition from the private sector, the ways in which public broadcasters adapt to the digital era have potential ramifications for that trust and may undercut any advantage it offers and ultimately their legitimacy.

Acknowledgements

Research undertaken during Outside Study Program leave from La Trobe University provided the basis for this book. Among those I interviewed I would like firstly to thank Joe Atkinson, who as my Masters supervisor many years ago contributed the encouragement from which this book grew. I would like to acknowledge too, the help I received from Sylvia Harvey who kindly directed me towards other suitable interviewees. Other academics I interviewed to whom I owe a special vote of thanks for sharing their thoughts on the topic of broadcasting futures are Graeme Murdock, whose published research I have also drawn on throughout the book, Robert Beveridge, and Maxine Baker. I also wish to thank: BBC staff – Tony Ageh, Rahul Chakkara, Nick Cohen, Paul Gerhardt, Marc Goodchild, Andrew Owen and David Levy; and staff at Channel Four – Kate Vogel, Adam Gee, and David Booth, who made the time to talk to me. Other interviewees in the United Kingdom to whom I owe thanks are Steve Hewlett, Sarah Thane and Steve Perkins. In the United States my research of the public television system was greatly assisted by Annie Valva, who I would like to thank for kindly directing me towards suitable contacts for this project. Other public television staff I wish to thank are: Nan Rubin, David Liroff, Howard Cutler, Evie Kintzer, Anne Gleason, Tim Olson, Dan Schmidt, Dan Soles and Richard Winefield. Two others who extended my understanding of the particularities of the American public television system are William Hoynes and Scott Sanders. In New Zealand I wish to thank Peter Thompson, who I interviewed and whose published work I have also drawn on. In addition I would like to thank those TVNZ staff who participated in my research – Eric Kearley, David Murphy and Alistair Mathewson – and independent producer, Richard Harman. My research of public service broadcasting in Australia was greatly assisted by the ABC staff I interviewed who I would like to thank for their time and various contributions: Mark Scott, Kim Dalton, Courtney Gibson, Murray Green and Michael Ward. I would also like to thank Georgie McLean and Paul Vincent of SBS for their participation in my research. To those friends and colleagues who kindly read early chapter drafts – Lisa French, Terrie Waddell, Hester Joyce, Gabrielle Murray and Brigid Magner – many thanks. Finally, for all his practical assistance, from navigating the highway between Poughkeepsie and Boston to proof reading the manuscript, I would like to thank my partner, Stuart Kelly who provided support and wise counsel on a host of issues.

Chapter 1

The Need for Reinvention

Introduction

Public service broadcasting has been the focus of pessimistic prophesying for the last 25 years, with the concept's respective merits and shortcomings debated in anticipation of its demise. Michael Tracey's 1998 work, *The Decline and Fall of Public Service Broadcasting,* reflected the gloom permeating this debate. Demise it seemed would just as likely come from institutional withering from within as from commercial competition or ideological opposition from without. Yet in the twenty-first century, as public service broadcasters continue to fight for funding and audience in the fragmenting marketplace, engaging with the possibilities of digital transmission and the World Wide Web, it is evident this system has survived the market liberal reforms of the late twentieth century. Public service broadcasters around the world continue to register considerable public support, and while emerging digital media technologies and platforms bring new challenges they also open new opportunities for delivering the public service remit. Fine tuning their goals and how they deliver them, developing new kinds of audience relationships and, perhaps most controversially, identifying new funding models, public service broadcasters are reinventing themselves for the digital era.

This book examines the process of reinvention through a series of case studies – six public service broadcasters from across four English speaking countries – and illustrates both the flexibility of the public broadcasting concept and the resilience of national cultural differences in the global age. The broadcasters selected represent variously unique qualities that stem from distinctiveness in governance, structure, programming, funding and socio-cultural context. The six broadcasters are Britain's BBC and Channel Four (C4), Australia's Special Broadcasting Service (SBS), and the Australian Broadcasting Corporation (ABC), Television New Zealand (TVNZ), and the public television system in the United States. Re-positioning themselves as media content providers, each of these television broadcasters is reassessing how to deliver and fund the public interest mission in the rapidly evolving on-demand, global, media marketplace.

Why should such adaptations be regarded a reinvention of the system rather than simply symptoms of its decline? What does public service broadcasting (PSB) or public broadcasting (the term now preferred by some commercially funded PSBs) stand for in the on-demand digital era and is it still worth defending? In addressing these questions, this book explores how each of these broadcasters is engaging with new digital media and what they deliver that the market cannot.

When the relevance of public service broadcasting was being questioned in the 1980s – as multi-channel technologies and neoliberal philosophy opened up new user-pays models of distribution – defenders of PSB responded by emphasising the system's broader implications. Universal coverage and access is generally considered most important among these because of the social value of mass audience reach as a public sphere or forum for democratic public discourse. An integral aspect of the civic role associated with the public sphere is the provision of an impartial, non-commercial, national news and current affairs service – independent from the influence of private vested interests. The system's broader civic and cultural functions are also evident in the public service mandate for representing minority interests and for 'quality' programming that reflects and contributes to national culture and identity. Being open to interpretation, 'quality' constitutes a key challenge for public service systems in pluralist society. Pluralist societies are those where the existence of different ethnic, religious or cultural groups is acknowledged and tolerated in the belief that such tolerance is socially beneficial. The concept of pluralist democracy acknowledges that rather than being a homogenous mass, the electorate comprises diverse interest groups. Quality, most frequently interpreted in terms of non-commercial production values – optimising money on screen, investing in research and development, and engaging in innovation and risk-taking – is equally applicable to factual and narrative programming across the full range of popular and high culture genres.

The national status of public service broadcasters has been represented as indicative of their redundancy, of incompatibility with an integrated global communications market, the dominant contemporary vision for the future. In effect, the deregulated communications marketplace has bought unprecedented conglomeration due to the hugely beneficial economies of scale attaching to digital media, thereby further constraining competition. The subsequent dramatic increase in the power of privately owned global media raises issues of political control, access and cultural sovereignty, issues that nationally owned public service broadcasters are best placed to address. Evoking different modes of audience address, two conflicting interpretations of democracy – interventionist and libertarian – underlie the debate about the contemporary relevance of public service broadcasting.

Two Conflicting Visions of Democracy

The public service ethic is grounded in the interventionist conception of democracy which champions individual liberty in the name of the common good. Envisaging society as greater than the sum of its parts, the interventionist view of democracy advocates the individual's right to pursue self-fulfilment through citizenship as a 'positive' freedom that sometimes requires state intervention for its protection. From the interventionist perspective individual liberty entails escape from the narrow bounds of self-interest, enabling individuals to make the best of themselves by participating in a shared way of life and contributing to the common good. Interventionist theory evolved from nineteenth century liberalism, which advocated a more open, pluralist society, and supported universal suffrage and education as the prerequisites for a 'virtuous citizenry'. Concerned that universal suffrage might lead to tyranny by 'collective mediocrity', John Stuart Mill in his famous essay, 'On Liberty', posed the problem of how to universalise a disposition for intelligent self-government. Twelve years later in 1881, T.H. Green's 'Liberal legislation and freedom of contract' argued that government should intervene when necessary to 'maintain the conditions' needed for the 'free exercise of human faculties' (Eccleshall 1984: 52).

The early individualism that accompanied industrialisation fostered new sources of private power and economic inequality never anticipated by 'old' liberals. The main obstacle to freedom was no longer seen as state or aristocratic power, but new structures of social coercion imposed by industrial baronies – glaring inequalities of opportunity in education, health and income. In *Liberalism*, published in 1911, L. T. Hobhouse made a case for redistributive welfare rights on the basis that wealth creation had a social dimension. Thus government was entitled to treat a proportion of individual income as justifiable for taxation to address the needs of the common good. This paternal vision of democracy invoked state intervention in the interests of preserving the rights of all to contribute to the common good.

The libertarian vision of democracy is individualistic and, being grounded in the concerns of early liberals for property rights and freedom from coercion, posits the right to economic freedom for competitive self-advancement as a basic civil liberty. However, the original target of libertarianism – royal absolutism – has long since disappeared and so too, to a large extent, have the original intentions of early liberal thinkers whose claims for civil liberties were motivated by a desire to establish a society free from hereditary privilege and patronage. Instead, libertarian market-liberals now evoke the cause of individual rights to defend the wealth and authority of newly privileged, mainly corporate elites against the state. Libertarian market-liberalism rejects interventionism on both individualistic and utilitarian grounds. One influential libertarian philosopher, Friederich Hayek, relegates the ideals of common social goals and sharing to a tribal past, arguing that modern society is too complex to control and that progress results from individual actions rather than by any social design (Hayek 1960).

In 1987, the comment of former British Prime Minister and market-liberal advocate, Margaret Thatcher, 'There is no such thing as society', reflected a significant attitudinal shift – the rise of asocial individualism and its displacement of the concept of citizenship (*Womens Own* 31 October 1987: 8–10). Signalling obeisance to the principle of user-pays, which is integral to neoliberal free-market economics and now widely subscribed to throughout those countries that call themselves the First World, this ideological position upholds the supremacy of market forces over state intervention. One side effect of the widespread adoption of neoliberalism is that international cooperation in addressing global problems, like climate change and humanitarian and civil rights issues, tends to be disadvantaged.

In the twenty-first century, while threats to the survival of PSB still abound, the importance of independent media in reinvigorating public opinion as a force for social democracy and civic participation is acquiring renewed primacy. Public service broadcasting institutions have been involved in a rear guard action since the 1980s, adapting to the social, economic and technological changes that launched the multi-channel digital era.

One of the greatest threats to public service broadcasting in Britain occurred during the Thatcher era in 1985, with the establishment of the Committee on Financing the BBC (the Peacock Committee), which was widely expected to endorse advertising as a funding model. Balking at the idea of commercialising the BBC, the Committee instead produced a blueprint for public service broadcasting as a market-supplemented, grant-funded model on the margins of the commercial mainstream. This narrow definition neglected what many regarded as the most important characteristics of the public system, its social and cultural foundations. The recommendation of a 'full broadcast market' proved too radical for the times and the Peacock Committee's influence remained largely symbolic, offering subsidised public service content as an alternative to public service broadcasting. New Zealand's Broadcasting Commission, also known as New Zealand on Air (NZoA), is the closest this model has yet come to being realised. During the 1990s, as the provider of contestable public funds for local production on both state-owned and private commercial television, NZoA held sole responsibility for delivering public service goals in a wholly commercial media marketplace. As a non-broadcaster without any editorial powers, the agency's role was effectively reduced to delivering local content rather than addressing public service goals (Debrett 2004). With many different models operating around the world, the absence of any universally accepted definition fuels uncertainties about how exactly public service broadcasting differs from free market systems.

In Europe, and more particularly in Britain, whose broadcasting service has served as a model for many commonwealth countries, the notion of 'public service' governed the manner in which the free-to-air television system developed. Through the public corporation of the BBC, broadcasting was removed from the political arena, granted a monopoly within the specified terms of a charter and licensed to play a leading role in providing education, information and entertainment in the public interest. In the United States, strong traditions of the freedom of the individual enshrined in the First Amendment to the US constitution, acted against government 'interference' in broadcasting, and encouraged the development of a free market system facilitating irreverent popular culture and commercial entertainment.

The two systems differ broadly in their attitudes to freedom and control. The American commercial system with its minimal regulation of broadcasters espouses individual freedom of speech as the ultimate goal of public communications. It posits the free operation of supply according to demand as the best means of providing access for all voices and programming relevant to all consumers. While placing the individual's freedom as the highest public good, the free market system prioritises consumer choice over the rights and duties of citizens as participating members in the collective undertaking of society. Having little or no obligation to ensure programme diversity, free market systems generally cater to the interests of the majority at the expense of minorities, limiting broadcasting's potential to address the inevitable divisions of pluralist society and thereby to contribute to the peaceful resolution of conflict. Individual viewers as consumers are encouraged to accept that life's problems can be resolved through the purchase of commodities.

Opting for more control – and for socially oriented individuality rather than individualism *per se* – the British public service model in its first five decades of broadcasting represented an interventionist approach to the issue of public interest. Over time a set of principles for public service broadcasting was established: universality of coverage; diversity in programming; reflection of national identity and culture; the servicing of minority interests; the provision of an impartial news and current affairs service free from the influence of business or government; and the delivery of innovative, 'quality' programming designed to inform, educate and entertain. At the time of the Peacock Committee in 1985, the BBC Research Unit identified a set of principles based on past practices. Traditionally, through its educative function, public service broadcasting has undertaken a key role in providing the public with information and interpretation of the main arguments and events surrounding important social and political issues thereby empowering viewers, enabling them to make informed judgments and decisions in exercising their rights and duties as citizens, particularly at elections.

In the first four decades of television broadcasting, the kinds of programming shown on each of these two different systems generally reflected their respective relationship with their viewers and also their financial *modus operandi*. Behind the rhetoric of freedom of individual choice lay the prosaic reality that commercial broadcasters sell audiences to advertisers, purchasing programming according to its ratings potential. This means that the majority are well served, while minorities are marginalised – unless they represent a viable niche market and can afford pay TV services. With cost efficiency and reliability, the key factors for programme production and purchase, the free market system has been characterised by adherence to proven formulas and formats, and programming that can be produced as long running series or on a fast turn-around basis. As a result, reality TV, soaps and sitcoms fare better than documentaries and one-off dramas. The pursuit of ratings thus tends to discourage creative risk taking. Although a commercial broadcaster may put a wide range of programming to air, the need to capture and hold the largest possible audience drives the entire schedule. One logical consequence of profit driven systems and a competitive marketplace is the structuring and packaging of news and current affairs according to the strategies of marketing consultants and advertisers, with soft news such as celebrity gossip frequently outranking political information and analysis (Atkinson 1994: 16).

In contrast, public service broadcasting charters generally include requirements for diversity, innovation and quality. Freed from the need to return a profit, the 'classic' PSB system enables greater risk-taking in programme content and form, providing scope for extending the creative boundaries of the medium and thereby also serving industry development. PSB systems generally attribute particular status to news and current affairs programming as a forum for diverse political voices including the often angry and emotional voices of the dispossessed and those in opposition to the powers that be.

The classic BBC model of public service broadcasting was often cast as bureaucratic and remote – being accountable to viewers only indirectly, through the process of licence or charter renewal – in contrast to the direct accountability of commercial broadcastings' transparent response to mass audience taste via ratings. Commonly mistaken as a democratic measure of what viewers want, audience ratings measure only viewers' response to programmes offered, not what they might need or want or grow to appreciate. Ratings also tend to disenfranchise minority interest groups, denying their right to the media representation that legitimises them as a part of the greater whole. Of course public service broadcasters haven't always fulfilled this role effectively either, despite charter commitments to serving diverse interests. This changed at least initially with the establishment of broadcasters with special remits such as Channel 4 (C4) in Britain and the SBS in Australia. Both these channels have an explicit directive to offer an alternative service to that of mainstream public broadcasting, a service originally intended to bring greater authenticity to the representation of minority cultures and greater diversity in television programming. In implementing these distinctive directives, both C4 and SBS developed very distinctive brands which are now being employed to promote a range of media services across various platforms.

Grounded in the now problematic concept of unified nationhood and national culture, public service broadcasting has long been committed to reflecting national identity as part of its role in serving the public sphere. Public service systems have traditionally produced programmes of a distinctly national flavour. With the development of multicultural societies across the West following post-World War Two migration, the concept of national culture acquired a dual meaning as a site of contestation alongside established heritage culture. This dual function can prove problematic for programme makers seeking funding in the marketplace. Programmes challenging conventional representations of national identity may be deemed less likely to win international distribution, posing problems of comprehension for those not well versed in the cultural mores of the country of origin. One outcome of this is 'televisual tourism', the compression of national idiosyncrasies and social realism into more internationally digestible and conventional representations, diminishing television's effectiveness in contributing to wider understanding of contemporary social issues (Murdock 1992: 95).

As global media conglomerates have exploited the commercial opportunities of digital technology and the convergence of broadcasting, telecommunications, entertainment and publishing, programming on commercial television systems has become increasingly transnational. Economic expediency reduces scheduling for global media to repackaging to fit local market variations (Fürisch 2003: 131–53). The resultant tendency to compromise national differences in the interests of international marketability has favoured US programming and formats. US screen culture forms and genres achieved widespread international exposure and acceptance following Hollywood's early lead in feature film distribution during World War One when European film production closed down. The delivery of audiovisual content that is grounded in specific national experience or reflects specific identity issues is thus less likely in the global media marketplace.

Public service broadcast institutions in the past have generally been either national, stand-alone broadcasters with a comprehensive remit or 'market failure' broadcasters licensed to compensate for the most glaring deficiencies of commercial broadcasters. Reflecting the expectations that accompany public funding and universal coverage, the comprehensive schedule incorporates the broadest range of programming, from serious and specific to popular culture forms. This diversification of prime-time programming aims to offer variety of genre and topic in order to serve social and cultural needs in various ways: through argument and analysis of social issues and electoral choice; by representing the viewpoints of divergent interest groups; by catering for the special needs of children; by reflecting unique aspects of national identity and culture; and by providing an outlet for innovative and creative expression. With broadcasting's eclipse by narrowcasting being widely forecast, the comprehensive remit is looking increasingly anachronistic. The dedicated niche channels and electronic programme guides (EPG) facilitated by digital television readily enable viewers to compile their own schedules, which can be comprehensive or focused according to individual interests. While this is undoubtedly an advance in delivering consumer choice, it threatens to undermine one of the primary traditional functions of public service broadcasting, delivering viewers with the resources for citizenship, a key issue for PSB in the digital era.

Three Universal Challenges

The late twentieth century debate about the redundancy and death of PSB centred around three major challenges: cultural fragmentation; new media technologies facilitating multiple channels; and the widespread endorsement of neoliberal policies preferencing market mechanisms – the business ethic. Whilst the social process of cultural fragmentation challenged the efficacy of the comprehensive remit, the development of new media technologies (then satellite and cable delivery systems bringing multi-channel capacity) offered the possibility of specialist niche services for the diverse interest groups within multicultural societies. The most potent challenge, however, was widespread political enthusiasm for the business ethic and 'user-pays' which eroded political will to invest in public broadcasting. As a foundation for understanding how digital's second wave might enhance the future prospects of PSB, these late twentieth century challenges require some further explanation.

Traditional public broadcasting systems were founded on the idea of national culture, a concept that underwent considerable change in the years following World War Two with the emergence of different 'cultural' groups claiming the right to separate representation. This erosion of social consensus came from three different directions: post-war immigration; social rights movements; and new claims to sovereignty. In Britain, the decline of the empire brought former colonial nationals who claimed rights by virtue of British citizenship, while in Australia, the government's post-war immigration programme changed the face of a mono-cultural, ethnocentric society as the European migrants of the 1950s were followed by those from Asia and then the Middle East. In New Zealand, post-war immigration came mainly from the Pacific Island nations, while in the United States immigration has been ongoing since white settlement. Since the 1950s, immigration has generally been followed by calls for multicultural rights. The so-called 'counter culture' accompanying the 'hippy' movement of the 1960s fostered the development of a number of social movements, as diverse groups such as the women's movement, gay rights activists and blacks in the United States made claims for greater and more equitable public acknowledgement of their separate identity. This wave of claims for human rights was followed by resurgence in regional and nationalist movements such as those in Scotland and Wales, and also by demands for cultural sovereignty from indigenous peoples such as the Australian Aborigines and the Maori in New Zealand.

Specific minority needs in the United States were addressed with the establishment of a funding agency to foster a wider range of voices within public television, the Independent Television Service (ITVS); this was similar to the approach initially taken in New Zealand, where in 1993 a proportion of the licence fee revenue was delegated to Te Mangai Paho, an independent Maori funding agency, for funding programming on the mainstream television channels. Te Mangai Paho receives 13 per cent of total licence fee revenue (NZoA 1994–5: 3). Elsewhere, the establishment of specialist television services brought a more substantial approach to the servicing of minority needs. Wales gained SC4, a dedicated Welsh language channel operated in conjunction with Channel Four. In Australia, the SBS was set up in 1980 as a multicultural radio and television broadcaster, and in 2007 the National Indigenous Television service (NITV) catering to Australian Aboriginal was launched. In New Zealand, Maori Television, a dedicated indigenous service broadcasting in Maori and English was established in 2004, and later launched a second Maori language channel, Te Reo, in 2008. Amongst most mainstream public broadcasters, however, the reflection of minority cultures remained difficult since winning high audience ratings came to be seen as the best strategy for disproving the accusations of irrelevance that threatened public funding.

The new media and communications technologies of the 1980s, cable and satellite, enabled multiple channels, and spawned a new industry sector and revenue model – subscription television. Narrowcasting, the provision of dedicated specialist services, appeared to negate one of the original justifications made for public service broadcasting; ensuring that a limited public resource – the electric magnetic spectrum – was managed in the public interest. Narrowcasting indicated to many that public management was redundant since diverse minority interests could be served more effectively through niche services. Repudiating this claim, defenders of PSB argued there were inherent limitations in the commercial management of niche services since user-pays would exclude low-income groups; and as niche markets, only audiences large enough to be considered commercially viable would be serviced. Thus the availability of multiple services would not automatically service diversity or produce plurality of choice. In 1994, the Independent Film Channel and the Sundance Film Channel, 'two of the most daring and progressive film channels' launched on cable systems in the US, were struggling to survive because their 'arty' narrow focus appealed only to sophisticated markets. Despite multi-channel capacity, the mass audience is still the most preferred, and competition for space by niche providers is fierce. Services like the Golf Channel, which offers the added cost benefits of merchandising, are preferred (Gabert 1996: 24). Others noted the shortcomings invoked by specialist subscriptions channels. Commenting on the Discovery Channel's highly successful commercial strategies, Elfreide Fürisch sees its positioning as a global brand for quality reality programming as falling 'short of the central ideas of public broadcasting', which she posits as serving citizenship.

She notes that despite some exceptions of reverse media flow, globally accessible content offers considerable financial advantage over a local focus: 'Discovery relies on a business model of selling its program/channels across borders without adding too many costs for adapting these productions to a local market'. When national broadcasters enter the global market as producers and distributors of documentary, they are competing with Discovery's high profile global reputation for 'reliable product'. This undermines investment in proposals that are innovative or ground breaking in their intent (Fürisch 132: 138).

By the 1980s, widespread adoption of neoliberal economic principles saw policy commitment to public interest criteria displaced by a business ethos promoting the idea that rather than being a public cost, broadcasting should actually yield profitable returns. Mark Fowler, Chairman of the Federal Communications Commission (FCC) from 1981–1987, instigated radical deregulation of broadcasting on the grounds that it was a business like any other (Kellner 1990: 92). Similar changes to broadcasting policy were adopted by the British government from 1984–1990, by New Zealand in 1989 and by the Australian government in 1992. Since the 1990s, a regime of reregulation under the rhetoric of competition policy has seen the implementation of new sets of protocols and mechanisms for ensuring plurality of provision and basic coverage of universal service obligations that have tended to prioritise the interests of the market over those of the public.

Integral to this business ethic, the notion of consumer sovereignty posited user-pays as the most equitable form of media management. In effect, consumer sovereignty actually denies media 'product' to those who refuse to or cannot pay. The business ethic, which increasingly drives broadcasting policy in most Western countries, legitimises reduced state funding for public systems, which in turn increases the pressure on public broadcasters to find alternative sources of revenue thereby compromising the integrity of the public service mission. Faith in the logic of the marketplace has fostered competition across all levels of broadcasting on the assumption that this increases efficiency and responsiveness to public needs.

Reinvention in the Digital Era

While the multi-channel technologies of the 1980s initially prompted debate about the death of PSB, the global digital technologies of the Noughties are sparking a different debate about renewed social relevance, raising new challenges for public providers. What constitutes a fair investment of public money in digital technologies given the existence of the digital divide and its conflict with the principle of universality? Does PSB content provision across a multiplicity of channels and platforms make hybrid commercial funding more compatible with public interest goals? In terms of public investment in local production and the additional returns likely via online global rights, what constitutes a fair ratio of independent to in-house production given the potential revenue to be gained from online royalties? Do free market commercial media have a right to demand that limitations be set for PSB organisations? Consideration of these questions raises others: how should the new potential of both interactive and user-generated content be developed to best serve and extend PSB goals; what is the likely impact of the 'long tail' (online) economy on national media (Anderson 2006); should high definition television (HDTV) be added to free-to-air services, and does the concept of the Third Way – a late 1990s strategy for renewing social democracy – offer any viable alternative pathways for PSB?

Termed 'the digital revolution's second wave', the growing take-up of broadband Internet connection heralds an era of on-demand media and television distribution via the Internet (Internet Protocol TV – IPTV), offering 'always on' availability and global reach (Thompson 2006: 4). Unlike the first phase – the development of digital infrastructure by telephone companies, Internet service providers (ISPs), and governments – the second phase is being driven by content provision and user take-up. Characterised by accessibility across a range of platforms – TV, computer, mobile phone and personal digital assistant (PDA) – and by its utility and versatility being 'searchable, movable and share-able', on-demand content revolutionises the relationship between content provider and viewer/user (Thompson 2006: 5). In the language of corporate media spinners, 'martini media' – anytime, any place, anywhere – is forecast to replace 'appointment viewing'.

Globally available, on-demand media content represents a considerable challenge for national media – both commercial and public service – and for policies intended to protect national culture. Public service media, however, may well gain an advantage here. As trusted media brands renowned for their independence, public service broadcasters acquire new premium in the online environment where unaccredited and unreliable information proliferates. The websites of public service broadcasters rank among the most visited non-commercial portal sites, arguably due to the quality of their content and public trust in the public service brand. Graham Murdock describes the BBC as 'one of the most trusted and widely used Internet sites in Europe' (Murdock 2004). Digital's second phase promises to overcome the threat of redundancy that cable and satellite initially posed for PSB in the 1980s. Given political will, digital terrestrial television (DTT) facilitates the delivery of PSB content across multiple channels and platforms, allowing broadcasters to tailor programming to suit specific niche audience needs while cross-promoting key content of public value or social importance. Another valuable point of intersection for diverse audiences and interest groups is the always-on interface of PSB's portal sites. In this way the underlying ethic of the comprehensive schedule continues to be honoured in a manner that accommodates the complexities of cultural fragmentation and on-demand digital media. The other universal threat to PSB, the Business Ethic, is also changing with Third Way policies reflecting some acknowledgement of the shortcomings of market systems although the impact of these will depend on the political will of successive governments.

By revolutionising the distribution of audiovisual media content online, broadband Internet connection promises huge benefits in cost savings. Added to this the facility of search engines and filters to rationalise a phenomenal abundance of choice is connecting users to relevant content that they would not otherwise have found or known about. The term 'long tail' was coined by Chris Anderson (2006) to describe how these developments are impacting on sales statistics in the online marketplace. Products with mass popularity ('hits', which represent the 'head' of any sales graph) are becoming a smaller and smaller proportion of the market, while niche products – which sell slowly across a longer time frame and represent the 'tail' of any sales graph – are growing and becoming a larger proportion of overall sales. With its speculation of long-term albeit incremental returns on content that previously might have yielded none, the concept has heartened independent producers.

For public broadcasters long resigned to the fragmentation of the mass audience, the growth in niche markets online brings hope of audience renewal in the on-demand environment; the long tail economy also signals the prospect of legitimate new revenue streams making content from back catalogues and archives accessible to non-nationals online. This expansion in global online distribution also makes the negotiation of programme rights between broadcasters and independent programme makers more complex, arguably enhancing (for the public) the value of in-house production – where all royalties are returned to the broadcaster – and the benefits of a mixed production system over the publisher-broadcaster model.

Democratisation of the tools of production is nominated the 'first force of the long tail' by Anderson, and media organisations are intent on harnessing the growing popularity of user-generated content and social networking evident in websites such as YouTube and MySpace (Anderson 2006: 178). The challenge for PSBs is to develop different and more substantial social frameworks for this activity, something the BBC's Creative Archive project offered with plans to open up as much BBC content as rights allow for public use. The kinds of relationships public service broadcasters build with their respective independent sectors will have important ramifications for the survival of local, audiovisual production industries. Here again the distinctive qualities of PSB brands have much to offer by way of promoting national cultural product in the global marketplace.

In the past, technological changes prompted calls for public service systems to be redirected towards remedying areas of market failure, an approach that marginalises and limits a broadcaster's capacity to serve the public sphere. Public television in the United States is an example of this system. Another model of PSB, the broadcaster publisher model, out-sources programme production, simultaneously addressing particular social needs, delivering diversity and reducing public cost by making funding contestable. Channel Four (C4) in Britain and the SBS in Australia are examples of this publisher-broadcaster model.

Partial commercialisation is another response to reduced public funding. New Zealand's TVNZ (now a Crown Owned Company) represents a commercialised state broadcaster expected to deliver public service goals (from 2003 to 2009), while also operating as a successful commercial business returning dividends to government. Also a very successful commercial public broadcaster, Britain's C4 functions without any public funding but reinvests all commercial revenue in station operations and production. The hybrid-funding model represents a potential Third Way solution for PSB but creates tensions by driving broadcasters towards popular entertainment programming in the quest for audience ratings. Even minimal commercialisation such as online advertising can be deemed a threat to editorial independence and thus to the integrity of news and current affairs services. With the multiple distribution systems available in the digital era, possibilities for commercial revenue streams abound. The challenge for PSBs wanting to exploit these possibilities is to identify ways of keeping the separation of commercial and public ventures watertight to secure the integrity of public services.

Gaining widespread interest following its adoption by the governments of both Tony Blair in Britain and Bill Clinton in the United States, the Third Way ostensibly seeks to sustain social democracy by charting a middle path between two conflicting ideologies, 'old-style social democracy and neoliberalism' (Giddens 1999: 26). The concept has proven controversial with one key outcome of the Third Way's mix of market and interventionist strategies, Public Private Partnerships (PPPs), drawing criticism for conceding too much to the market, leaving public investors short-changed. PPPs' potential for hiding debt rather than serving public interest has been identified as an attractive benefit for governments investing in them (Ewins 2006: 1). While accepting that political exigencies are likely to see public rather than private interests compromised in joint partnerships, this book treats the Third Way as a framework for exploring the efficacy of hybrid funding models and suitable mechanisms for PSB governance and accountability in the marketised media sphere. Given widespread neoliberal opposition to PSB expansion, a Third Way compromise – a hybrid funding model – often appeared the best option for sustaining local content on television. Of the six case studies of public service broadcasters discussed in the following chapters, four have distinctive hybrid funding systems which developed in response to different national circumstances.

That the special status of PSB still resonates in the multi-channel reality of the digital age is evidenced by the 2006 renewal of the BBC charter and licence fee following several years of public debate. In its 2005 digital strategy programme, *Building Public Value*, the BBC undertook responsibility for driving 'digital Britain' and launched a range of initiatives intended to make broadband Internet connection more attractive. Much television content is now available on an on-demand basis across a range of platforms, a development that is also seen as serving civic education, making news and current affairs content more attractive to younger viewers. Other new developments are local television, the Creative Archive Project, mentioned earlier, and involvement in a range of infrastructure developments. These include a free digital satellite, digital radio, BBC iPlayer – a digital rights management (DRM) software application by which licence fee payers will access BBC media online on an on-demand basis – and Canvas, an IPTV protocol being jointly developed with the two British commercial broadcasters, ITV and Five. Alongside national services, the BBC will continue to exploit the global value of its brand, operating eleven commercial ventures through BBC Commercial Holdings Limited, the profits of which are reinvested in the public broadcaster. The commercial ventures include the 24-hour global news channel, BBC World, and BBC Worldwide, which oversees seven operating businesses. The BBC's commercial businesses are operated according to its Fair Trading Guidelines which are governed by three principles: (i) Commercial activities must be consistent with, and supportive of, the BBC's purpose as a public service broadcaster; (ii) the BBC must always trade fairly; (iii) the reputation of the BBC brand must not be undermined (BBC 2007c).

As the pre-eminent public broadcaster of the English-speaking world, the BBC inspired many clones. However, global recognition of the BBC brand, which draws on the unique cultural status of the public institution, means this source of funding is less relevant to PSBs elsewhere. On the opposite side of the globe, TVNZ highlights the perils of market pressures when institutional reinvention is undertaken as part of industry deregulation. The state owned broadcaster's adoption of the business ethic, initially taken as an interim step to privatisation, has since been married to a charter of public interest goals to accommodate the Clark Labour government's 1999 election promise to revive public service broadcasting. The broadcaster's hybrid funding, however, is unchanged. Operating with a dual remit, a directive to pay a dividend to government alongside the public interest goals of the charter from 2003 until 2009 (when the National Government of John Key abolished it), TVNZ's reinvented PSB form seemed set up to fail being uncomfortably dependent on the good intentions of government in meeting its chartered goals. The Clark Labour Government's commitment of six years of funding towards two non-commercial free-to-air digital channels, TVNZ 6 and TVNZ 7, will allow TVNZ to more readily provide public service content alongside the commercial fare its dual remit requires, at least until the money runs out. In a country accustomed to radical overhauls of the state broadcaster, New Zealand governments face relatively little opposition to changes of direction (Debrett 2005; Comrie & Fountaine 2005).

In stark contrast, Australia's ABC retains greater public service purity being funded solely from the public purse. Despite its national broadcaster status, two decades of budget cuts and increasingly intrusive political intervention since the mid Nineties have constrained the nature and scale of the ABC's digital reinvention. Legislative restrictions and limited funding restricted the ABC to just one additional digital channel, ABC2, which initially screened largely repeats or catch-up from the main channel. Since 2009, funding for a children's channel, ABC3, and plans for a 24-hour news channel for mid 2010 have expanded the ABC's digital services. Now offering television content on-demand for broadband users, along with a wide range of complementary information and services for various user groups, ABC Online reflects the PSB directives to be innovative and a creative risk taker.

Unencumbered by the need to reach a mass audience, television broadcasters providing complementary services – American Public Television, Channel Four (until 1992) and SBS

– have arguably been better insulated from commercial forces and better placed to serve the pluralist public in diverse ways, extending diversity of choice within prime-time. American public television developed within an entrenched commercial environment that endorsed the free market system as the best means of serving public needs. The notion of public culture that underlay the public service ethos was at odds with American commercialised popular culture forms. Conflicting with liberal individualist traditions, public service systems were viewed simply as state owned. Defined more narrowly as a non-commercial system, public television was relegated to addressing specific areas of market failure but was handicapped in its interpretation of these by dependence on annual government funding. Implanted onto an existing network of educational stations, the decentralised federalist structure of public television faces internal tensions between national goals and local needs, which undermine its ability to meet the challenge of competition from niche subscription services. The absence of assured public finance continues to pose practical and ethical dilemmas, obstructing the system's capacity to provide independent news and current affairs programming.

Given these shortcomings, public television has focused on its educational services and on building connections with its audience at the local level via the Internet. Having developed in a commercial environment against government commitment to free market systems, public television drew strength from a specific, democratic purpose grounded in federalist traditions and a decentralised structure. In the new millennium, despite the financial fragility endemic in public television, the system's membership arm, the Public Broadcasting Service (PBS), and its bigger city stations are exploiting the cost effectiveness of online delivery and the interactive potential of digital media in order to reinvent and thereby reaffirm two key components of the system, localism and education. PBS online means the system now has a national presence, something unavailable in the past.

In the twenty-first century the matter of audience renewal is a critical issue for PSBs, with a generation raised in the era of interactive media rejecting parental viewing habits. The pursuit of this younger audience, also the audience of choice for commercial broadcasters, is clearly evident at both C4 and SBS, and sits in tension with PSB directives to serve diversity. Conceived in an environment of strong public service traditions, Britain's C4 was largely a response to cultural fragmentation and public perceptions that existing broadcast institutions were elitist. It was established as a complementary service, representing a diverse range of viewpoints that was distinctively different in content or presentation to that of other broadcasters. Originally funded on the principle of assured finance, C4 represented a uniquely successful compromise of commercial funding and public interest goals until given responsibility for selling its own advertising in 1990. A period of intense commercial expansion in 1997–2001 and diversification across different media platforms sought to 'renew the audience for C4's vision of PSB' (Born 2003: 779–82). Subsequent efforts to re-focus C4 as a public broadcaster afforded prominence to news and current affairs and documentaries, while still enjoying commercial success largely through the reality series *Big Brother*. In attempting this balancing act, C4 now draws on a portfolio of digital narrowcast channels – available on Britain's free-to-air digital platform, Freeview. A major commissioner of documentaries and seedbed for emergent talent, C4's commitment to innovation is also visible in its negotiation of a viable space for British, independent audiovisual-producers in the long tail digital economy.

In Australia, SBS television developed within a dual system where the ABC, as the national public service broadcaster, served as both ally and threat in a limited competitive market. Originally a response to the ethnic community's exclusion from mainstream media, SBS television (SBS TV) combined specific minority and national interest goals by endeavouring to unite the conflicting causes of social justice and social harmony under the umbrella of multiculturalism. With minimal public funding and limited commercial revenue, poverty has been elemental in SBS TV's innovative scheduling style. The arrival of subscription services via cable and satellite in Australia in 1996 brought further competition, accompanied by cuts to public funding. In 2003, announcement of a drive to attract the youth demographic drew criticism that ethnic audiences were being abandoned. Whether motivated by a need for advertising revenue or generational renewal, the youth strategy signals a shift in station focus away from serving a general multicultural or cosmopolitan audience towards a general youth audience (albeit a diverse one). This also represents a strategic repositioning for SBS TV away from its original narrowcaster role towards a stronger broadcaster brand for the multiplatform media era. In 2005, SBS TV introduced spot advertising in anticipation of increasing overall advertising revenue by AU$10 million, countering public opposition with claims that audience drop-off between programmes was a disincentive for advertisers, and the promise that revenue would be reinvested in local programming.

In order to clarify the origins and better define the traditional role of public service broadcasting and the comprehensive remit, the following chapter outlines the development and structure of the BBC, detailing its adaptations to technological and economic change. Later chapters explore how the five other broadcasters have fared in their interpretation of the public service remit, detailing their respective responses to digital media. The final two chapters assess the impact of the Internet, digitalization and broadband on the delivery of public service goals, with reference to the contemporary experience of each of the broadcasters covered, and to the way in which these developments are changing relationships between broadcasters and the public, before engaging with the place of PSBs in building public trust. The reinvention of these public institutions is most visible online where their portal sites serve as grand, central stations for mainstream and niche media services, exposing niche and mass audiences to the full range of media possibilities and viewpoints, thereby addressing the social risks of fragmentation whilst serving the need for minority representation. The expansion of media channels in the digital era means that dedicated services are now a more viable option for the delivery of content of specific interest to discrete minority groups, albeit often on a user-pays basis. However, the remaining issue regarding servicing minority interests is their representation within the mainstream which, as mooted earlier, has important implications for pluralist democracy and social harmony.

The ways in which public broadcasters are responding to the challenges and opportunities of digital television and broadband inevitably reflect differences in national circumstance.

From the global perspective, however, the challenges confronting PSBs are less testing in the new millennium than they were in the last two decades of the twentieth century. While no guarantee of survival, reinvention is revealing a new purpose for PSBs, one that is displacing past claims of the system's redundancy. With the second wave of digital media technologies – characterised by mobile platforms, always-on access and global reach – PSB's usual gradual adjustment has been overtaken by a need for reinvention as critical issues of definition have risen to the fore. Reinvention refers to a re-interpretation of public service goals to accommodate and exploit the facility of digital media: online archiving, user generated content, interactive content and online distribution. While reinvention may not bring any special new solution to the funding woes of PSB, the argument presented here is that this digital reinterpretation nevertheless means that claims of the system's irrelevance and redundancy no longer hold water, and that PSBs as cross-platform media organisations are equipped to serve the public good in ways no others can.

Chapter 2

The BBC – 'The Cornerstone of National Culture'

Introduction

Britain's distinctive solution for the management and control of broadcasting was not simply an expedient response to spectrum scarcity, but built upon an established tradition of public culture. While many Europeans feared the growth of mass society and universal enfranchisement as an uncivilising force, the British remained relatively optimistic. Faith in the uplifting qualities of culture through mass education was reflected in the writings of social theorists like Herbert Spencer and Matthew Arnold. Echoed in the literature of the late nineteenth century, these ideas found institutional form in public libraries, art galleries and museums. As Anthony Smith observes, 'the idea of serving the public by forcing it to confront the frontiers of its own taste was a powerful one' (Smith 1976: 63). In Britain, the issue of how broadcasting should be managed was not whether the government should control it but how this should be done. An immediate concern for the founders of broadcasting was the abasement of the press by its use for state propaganda during World War One. Wariness of direct governmental control preoccupied early decisions, and institutional independence became a distinguishing feature and strength of the BBC along with centrality to national culture.

Critics of the BBC have come from both the left (decrying it as elitist and paternalistic) and from the right (decrying it for inefficiency and for interfering with market forces). Attacks on the credibility of journalists and the competence of BBC management in the 1980s were accompanied by industry deregulation, bringing increasing competition and reductions in public funding. While the licence fee funding system has survived the radical reforms mooted by the Thatcher Government's Peacock Committee in 1986, and the political and market pressures of the digital era, there have nevertheless been substantive changes to the BBC's role and to its institutional governance. Relating the circumstances that gave rise to the BBC in its pre-eminent form, this discussion will explore how the BBC's institutional culture and goals have evolved over time, how the relationship with the public has changed as services and coverage have expanded, and what all this means for the future of the BBC's public service mission in the digital multichannel media environment.

Interpreting the Public Interest

Broadcasting policy in Britain has been informed by numerous committees of enquiry; established as events required, these have invoked public debate about the social role of broadcasting. The first such committee, held in 1923 and chaired by Sir Frederick Sykes, recommended that 'control of such a potential power over public opinion and the life of the nation ought to remain within the state', establishing both the form and significance broadcasting was to have in Britain. However, it was the conviction of the BBC's first general manager, John Reith, that broadcasting should be a public service independent from government that influenced the constitutional form the BBC was to take. Adopting many of his ideas, the second committee of enquiry into broadcasting in 1926, chaired by the Earl of Crawford and Balcarres, called for the termination of the privately operated British Broadcasting Company, advising that broadcasting 'should be conducted by a public corporation as trustee for the national interest'. In 1927, the BBC became a corporation constituted under a ten-year Royal Charter funded by a national receiving license fee (MacDonald 1993: 4).

Convinced of the medium's potential for informing and educating citizens, Reith, who became the BBC's founding director-general, argued that broadcasting should operate as a public service with high standards and a strong sense of social responsibility. He fought to maintain the BBC's monopoly for 'unity of control' which he saw as being in the public interest, noting, 'few people know what they want, fewer what they need' (McDonald 1993: 4). Reith believed the educative value of broadcasting could help to consolidate the nation at a time of great social change (Madge 1989: 57; 185). His ideas were formalised in operating practice and BBC programme-making decisions came to be governed by set goals: to cater for the majority of the time (75 per cent) to the majority of the public, though without forgetting the needs of the minorities; to keep programming on the upper side of public taste and to avoid giving offence; and to provide a forum for public debate which would be impartial and free from governmental interference (McDonnell 1991: 12). Through coverage of official events, patronage of the arts, its domestic and short wave services during World War Two, and links with the residue of empire via the World Service, the BBC projected a cohesive version of the various fragments of British public life. The high moral tone and educative role Reith had set – to inform, educate and entertain – reinforced 'quality' as a hallmark of the institution's integrity.

Quality was defined in terms of its difference to the products of commercial services, and closely connected with the mission to support national culture and raise the level of public taste. Although the open paternalism of Reith was later discarded, esteem for culture and quality continued. When Sir Ian Jacob, as director-general in 1954, incorporated popular music into radio schedules, he explained, 'A public service broadcasting service must set as its aim the best available in every field' (McDonnell 1991: 36). The change was not a mere reaction to mass audience taste but an acknowledgement of an emerging pluralist audience, and that maintaining quality of service required increased diversity and innovation.

Quality was also applied to news and current affairs through the principle of impartiality, and the seriousness with which the BBC maintained a stance of editorial neutrality (Mulgan 1990). Quality was evident in the practice of investigative journalism and in the dedication to giving 'full ventilation of the facts', for taking 'responsibility to explain and examine the great questions of the day', and for ensuring that interviews are 'tough and rigorous, testing each side of the debate' (BBC 1996: 53).

Even when commercial television arrived, protection of programme quality remained a paramount consideration with those who valued the role of broadcasting in national culture lobbying for government regulation of commercial broadcasters. The subsequent structure placed commercial interests under close scrutiny and endeavoured to harness market forces for service in the public interest. The 1954 Television Act implemented commercial television in Britain as a unique system of private enterprise under public control, with the Independent Television Authority (ITA) instituted as a regulatory public body responsible to parliament. The ITA's power to set advertising costs eliminated advertisers' potential bargaining power and opportunities for influencing the schedule's content and style. The 1963 Television Act, which extended the life of the ITA for another twelve years, described it as a public service and applied the same programme standards as those of the BBC; between 1963 and 1979, the two corporations functioned as a public service duopoly (McDonnell 1991: 45).

References to quality and culture remain foremost in the BBC's role as defined by the BBC Trust's six commitments and the six public purposes outlined in the Charter and Agreement (BBC 2009b; 2009a). Quality, in its varied interpretations (high culture, diversity, impartiality, professionalism, and serving the public interest), signals the prioritising of the wider public good over individual consumer wants. Any future structural changes to public funding or the BBC's commercial arm, BBC Worldwide, are likely to affect how quality is defined in practice. The BBC's performance on delivering quality is assessed across the range of programme genres via audience surveys administered by the BBC Trust and reported on annually (BBC 2009b: 15). Quality is articulated as a goal throughout the Royal Charter, with providing 'journalism of the highest quality' nominated as the first priority for Public Purpose One – 'sustaining citizenship and civil society' (BBC 2009c).

The BBC's independence from government was achieved in the first years of radio broadcasting through an idiosyncratic constitutional structure and established codes of practice, mediated by prominent directors general and chairmen. The first director-general played a particularly critical role in winning institutional autonomy in the general strike of 1926. Resisting the efforts of the Conservative Government led by Prime Minister Stanley Baldwin to commandeer the BBC as an instrument for propaganda, Reith drew a bottom line for independence (BBC 2005). Nevertheless, the BBC's refusal to give airtime to opposition leader Ramsay MacDonald and Labour supporters reflected vulnerability to government pressure. In 1928, Reith successfully requested withdrawal of the ban on the broadcasting of controversy, 'one of the two general prohibitions' initially enforced under the licence by the Postmaster-General – the other forbad the BBC from expressing any opinions of its own (Haley 1949: 110; Coatman 1951: 291). But political crises have tested the BBC's independence throughout its history. Triumphs include the stand taken during the 1956 Suez crisis when the Labour Party was allowed to voice its dissent over the World Service, and the decision to broadcast *The Question of Ulster: An Enquiry into the Future* in 1972, which aired dissenting Irish viewpoints despite the Home Secretary's bid to have it banned. During the Thatcher era, capitulations to government criticism threatened the BBC's reputation for impartiality (Sparks 1995: 154). These are discussed later in the section on accountability. Incidents of such pressure have, however, come from both sides of politics. In 2004, BBC susceptibility to government influence arose during the Hutton Enquiry into the suicide of Dr David Kelly, a nuclear munitions expert in the Ministry of Defence identified as a source for a BBC report on the Blair Government's dossier of reasons for invading Iraq. The BBC report drew government ire because of implications the government had 'sexed up' the dossier from British Intelligence (Hutton 2004). Following the Hutton enquiry, the journalist Andrew Gilligan left the BBC while its chairman, Gavyn Davies, and director-general, Greg Dyke, were both pressured to resign.

The BBC's reputation for independence also faces increasing pressure from the corporation's collaborative commercial ventures through BBC Worldwide Limited, its international commercial arm, where the web of cost-benefits that binds co-production deals and business relationships sits uncomfortably alongside public service values – a topic covered in more detail in the discussion on accountability.

Another fundamental principle of British public service broadcasting, that of universal coverage across the nation, assumed a mass audience, a concept that has diminishing relevance in the era of on-demand digital media. In the 1980s, satellite and cable subscription services, where the user pays only for what he or she views, were promoted as more democratic than public service broadcasters, where viewers pay regardless of their use of the service. Defenders of public service broadcasting (PSB) countered that this apparently democratic solution, based on individual viewer/consumer rights, actually excludes those too poor to pay for specialist services and furthermore reflects the failure of advertiser-funded free-to-air television to serve minority interests (Willis & Wollen 1990). Some also argued that the principle of universal coverage, once fundamental to the comprehensive remit, is compromised by the BBC's involvement in subscription services and pursuit of global markets. Public expectations of media services in the age of digital communications, however, have changed dramatically and universality now tends to be defined in terms of on-demand availability across multiple platforms, rather than access, as noted earlier in Chapter One.

In the analogue era prior to the development of digital terrestrial television (DTT), BBC television programming was scheduled according to the ethic of comprehensiveness that optimised diversity of choice in prime-time across its complementary two-channel service. While the BBC's audience share has obviously dropped as the number of competitors has grown, it retains a significant proportion of the audience having successfully resisted pressures that might have relegated it to the market failures model. BBC 1 Programme Controller, Jonathan Powell, defined the concept of programme diversity as:

The broad commitment to provide and to protect mixed and complementary programme schedules. It includes a commitment to certain minority programmes and to covering as far as possible different genres of programme making. (Keane 1991: 117)

Uniting the twin objectives of addressing a mainstream audience and catering for minority interests required establishing a common social domain. This became increasingly difficult as public funding diminished and competition increased. The arrival of digital television and developments in broadband Internet connection are now enabling the BBC to offer more diverse services to different interest groups across a range of platforms – nine national television channels across analogue and digital platforms, plus a rapidly expanding range of online services including catch-up television. However, until digital switchover is completed in 2012, digital services cannot be considered universal. In 2006, in order to expedite universal take-up and thus facilitate digital switchover, the Government diverted a proportion of the BBC licence fee (£603 million) into the Switchover Help Scheme to pay for digital connection for certain groups deemed disadvantaged. While offering greater diversity, the multiplatform delivery of niche services to niche groups in the narrowcast environment has raised concerns about the erosion of the common social domain. As more people connect to the Internet, however, BBC Online's popularity as a web portal is contributing an alternative shared space – a 'digital commons' – a network of educational, cultural and community organisations where the public as 'users' can interact and participate according to their needs (Murdock 2004).

Serving Mainstream and Minority Audiences

Unrivalled access to the British public during its era of monopoly control established the BBC as an 'embassy of national culture' (Smith 1976). With the arrival of commercial competition, the moral tone underlying this status was challenged. In the first years of regulated competition, the BBC's audience share plummeted to a nadir of 28 per cent, but eventually recovered approximately half the national audience following reactive diversification into more popular programme forms (Briggs 1985: 299). Increasing channel capacity since the 1980s has inevitably seen the BBC's audience share decline: from 1981 to 2008, the combined annual share of BBC One and BBC Two declined from 51 to 29.6 per cent (BARB 2009). While it is widely acknowledged that a broadcaster's achievement of public service goals cannot be measured in numerical terms, with surveys undertaken to ascertain public attitudes and support, as previously noted, neither can public service broadcasters afford to ignore audience share, which remains important for continued public funding. In this regard, the BBC has outperformed its main free-to-air rival, the commercial channel ITV 1, which saw its annual audience share shrink from 49 to 18.4 per cent between 1981 and 2008. Like most public broadcasters, the BBC also measures its performance via weekly audience reach, the number of viewers who tune in at anytime during the week, quoting an overall reach of 77.6 per cent for BBC One and 57.4 per cent for BBC Two in 2008/2009 (BBC 2009b: 9). Reach has the virtue of indicating usage and thus relevance without the competitive edge associated with the ratings system, which by reactively driving increased television viewing doesn't really serve the public interest. PSBs nonetheless remain under pressure to perform in terms of ratings since this provides the benchmarks by which market comparisons are made and judged.

In the 1960s, competition for audience and the erosion of social consensus forced the BBC to re-evaluate its role. Under director-general Sir Hugh Greene, the institution adopted a more critical stance in public life, shedding Reithian paternalism for the part of 'honest broker' and endeavouring to 'register the many voices in society' (Kumar 1982: 246). The BBC was subsequently drawn into increasing controversy with criticism from both those wanting traditional values upheld and those who wanted more public participation. In 1969, Mary Whitehouse founded the Clean Up TV campaign to address perceived threats to public morality, while at the same time the Free Communications Group was established to espouse the cause of greater openness in broadcasting (MacDonald 1993: 9).

Realising the need to break with Britain's monocultural past, the Report of the Committee on the Future of Broadcasting chaired by Lord Annan, posed a new task for broadcasting in 1977, that of representing different races and cultures to one another. The then new multi-channel technologies of cable and satellite appeared to offer a solution although, as critics of the time observed, social and cultural divisions in need of representation do not necessarily align with markets.

In 1982, when Channel Four (C4) was established, it was directed to serve tastes and interests not catered for elsewhere, providing a complementary service. The programmes scheduled on C4 subsequently inspired greater diversity at the BBC, proving the value of competition between public broadcasters. Nevertheless, while the BBC acknowledged the cultural rights of Welsh and Gaelic speakers with special services, Britain's immigrant communities have remained largely neglected (Meech 1990: 244). The issue of how to represent and serve the interests of minority groups is highly problematic; inclusion of minority groups in mainstream programming, regional television, and Equal Employment Opportunity (EEO) recruitment policies and minority staffing targets are measures that have helped to diversify the face of national culture on television to a limited extent. In 'representing the UK, its nations, regions and communities', the BBC invariably prioritises the first two larger and historically more significant categories over communities where, in the interests of building social harmony, differences in religious and cultural values arguably deserve higher priority for mainstream representation. A new BBC digital channel broadcasting in Gaelic, ALBA, was launched in 2008 to better serve Gaelic speaking Scottish viewers. Given the disparate needs of the different nations and regions that the BBC is expected to serve, along with the myriad of different ethnic communities that comprise contemporary Britain, delivering diversity is still perhaps the hardest of the BBC's traditional goals (BBC 2009c).

The Licence Fee and its Future

The television license fee has endowed the BBC with a high level of secure income for several decades, enabling it to produce a considerable volume of indigenous programming – 86 per cent of BBC One's schedule in 2008/9 (BBC 2009b: 43). Funding all of the BBC's domestic broadcasting services as well as BBC Online, the licence fee is levied on all owners of television receivers, and is periodically reviewed by parliament every ten years during the renewal of the Royal Charter.

Providing public finance directly from individual listeners and viewers rather than indirectly from government coffers, the licence fee insulates the BBC from the pressures and uncertainties of a government grant. During the 1980s, the Thatcher Government's adoption of neoliberal economics cast doubt on the future of BBC funding. By 1984, the government had signalled its intention to reduce the licence fee, pegging it to the Retail Price Index which ran behind the cost of television production, and subsequent increases were below the requested amount. That same year cable television was introduced into the UK through the Cable and Broadcasting Act (1984), with a Cable Authority rather than the broadcasting regulator, the IBA, established to oversee development (Murdock 1994: 13). Separating the roles of programme production and distribution, this new regulatory regime overrode the principle of assured finance that had insulated television programming from commercial influence through the IBA's monopoly on the sale of airtime. This policy shift was further evident in 1985 when a Committee on Financing the BBC was established under the chairmanship of Professor Alan Peacock – the Peacock Committee.

Established to assess the effects of advertising as an alternative or supplement to the BBC's licence fee, the Peacock Committee's Report in 1986 instead extolled the benefits of subscription services as enabling 'consumer sovereignty'. Having judged advertising as both economically and culturally damaging for the BBC, the Committee advocated subscription as the natural future direction for broadcasting, largely ignoring its potential social and cultural impact. Embracing the virtues of market forces and user-pay mechanisms, the Committee eventually proposed a 'full broadcast market' free from state control, which it likened to publishing, with public service broadcasting envisaged as a 'partial, market-supplementing' model. The Committee recommended that the licence fee be indexed to the annual rate of inflation as the first step towards the full broadcast market. Criticising both the BBC and ITV companies as inefficient and insulated from open competition, the commission recommended both should outsource 40 per cent of their programming from the independent sector – an idea later endorsed by the 1990 Broadcasting Act that applied a quota of 25 per cent (Peacock 1986).

Despite the anticlimactic nature of its central finding, the Peacock Committee had a profound impact on British broadcasting policy, both through the recommendations presented and by its *modus operandi*, which marked a radical departure from past committees of inquiry. Reflecting the pragmatism of the new economics, the public service duopoly, designed to limit the reductionist effects of competitive, commercial broadcasting, was sacrificed in the rush to embrace new technologies and create new market opportunities. Consumer sovereignty displaced public interest as the primary goal of broadcasting. Under stage two of the Peacock Report's recommendations, the BBC was to become entirely subscription-based by the end of the century. Programmes of merit that failed to rate would become the responsibility of a Public Service Broadcasting Council, which would give grants for programme production (O'Malley 1994: 103–8). This was the model that New Zealand was to adopt in 1990 (discussed in Chapter Seven) and one that continued to echo in Britain in 2009 with calls for 'top slicing' the BBC licence fee to preserve public service programming on free-to-air commercial television – ITV and Channel Four – as audience fragmentation and the global financial crisis of 2008–9 eroded advertising revenue. Between 1968 and 2009 the licence fee increased from £10 to £142.50, with each review a fiercely contested decision undertaken following the prolonged consultation and debate of the charter renewal process. In negotiating the licence fee, BBC management must engage with the ideology of the government of the day in what has become a highly politicised process.

In the late 1980s, plans by the Thatcher Government to introduce subscription funding prompted a defensive overhaul of BBC finances in a bid to demonstrate cost efficiency. Initially appointed as deputy director-general to Michael Checkland in 1987, John Birt, who went on to become director-general (1992–2000), oversaw the financial reforms. Birt began with a restructure of BBC News, centralising five separate departments, or 'baronies' as he termed them (Birt 2002: 251), into one directorate; this was followed by a radical overhaul of programme production with the implementation of an internal market. Promoted to staff as 'Producer Choice' and replacing the BBC's long established 'command' economy, the internal market 'separated providers (producers and technicians) from purchasers (commissioning executives)' and was accompanied by a radical 18 per cent cut in staffing. It is calculated to have saved £300 million during 1992–96 (Isofidis 2007: 100). Birt explained his goals:

> Both programme-makers and facilities departments would face the full blast of market pressure. To sell their services and to survive, they would need to achieve competitive levels of efficiency, and to charge market prices. (Birt 2002: 315)

Marking the first contraction in the BBC's history with over ten thousand employees either made redundant or transferred, Birt's reforms transformed institutional culture and outraged many BBC staff, winning notoriety as 'Birtism'. Devised to forestall subscription funding mooted for 1996, the Board of Governors saw improved financial accountability as essential to convince the Thatcher Government that the BBC was serious about being cost efficient; the restructuring, Birt argues in his autobiography, enabled BBC sympathisers in the Thatcher Government to defend retention of the licence fee to free market enthusiasts (Birt 2002: 328; 334). Widely criticised for their impact on staff morale and programming which became more populist, Birt's reforms are nevertheless also defended for having spawned a new culture of entrepreneurialism that equipped the BBC well for survival in the new media landscape (Born 2006: 128).

A similar strategy was adopted in June 2004 by BBC director-general, Mark Thompson, in the run up to the 2006 charter renewal, with the announcement of plans for restructuring and decentralisation, along with a range of cost efficiencies including radical staffing and budget cuts to blunt the arguments of the BBC's critics. Included in the restructuring was the introduction of a Window of Creative Competition (WOCC), which would allow 'independent companies to bid against in-house departments for commissions', with a promised 15 per cent cut in BBC in-house production calculated to increase the amount of independently produced content on the BBC to 40 per cent (Iosifidis 2007: 101).

Revenue from commercial activities has become an established supplement to the licence fee, with the BBC directed to explore alternative sources of income including direct viewer subscription as an eventual replacement to the license fee under the 1990 Broadcasting Act. Launched in the 1980s, BBC Worldwide, then titled BBC Enterprises, was initially justified as subsidising reduced public funding. This involvement in subscriber services broke a long-held egalitarian ideal: that public service broadcasting would provide 'nothing which is exclusive to those who pay more or who are considered in one way or another more worthy of attention'. However, the growth of media oligarchies and widespread acceptance of neoliberal economic philosophy during the 1980s and 1990s eroded the traditional role of national broadcasters in defining the narrative of political and cultural discourse. Thus PSB participation in subscription and commercial services represented both a defence against and a capitulation to free market forces (Murdock 1994: 19).

In 1991, the BBC launched World Service Television News, a 24-hour commercial, international news channel, later re-branded BBC World, and the following year entered a joint venture with Thames Television and the American cable company, Cox, to launch UK Gold, a commercial satellite channel. In the interests of financial transparency, the BBC was restructured under the 1996 Charter, with BBC Home Services (the public service arm) funded under the licence fee, and BBC Worldwide Limited (the commercial arm) directed to seek commercial partners in pursuit of international markets 'as an increasingly helpful adjunct to the licence fee' (BBC 1996: 50). The influx of cheaper imported foreign programming accompanying satellite services in the late 1980s made Britain a net importer rather than exporter of programmes, thus contributing further economic incentives for this directive, internationalising the BBC offered a way to reverse this trend and improve the balance of payments (Sparks 1995). The expansion of commercial ventures within BBC Worldwide placed complex stresses on BBC institutional culture, which Rupert Gavin of BBC Worldwide likened to 'running a brothel in a monastery' (Born 2006: 162). Nevertheless, Worldwide's commercial success has enhanced the value of the BBC in Britain in ways that go above and beyond the revenue returned for programme production, projecting British culture and creative talent to the world, and reflecting international appreciation of BBC production values and news services.

With deregulation and the rise of global media oligarchies, national broadcasters have undergone a process of internationalisation. Drawn into the orbit of transnational media through Worldwide, in 2009 the BBC was estimated as reaching 76 million homes across more than 200 countries around the globe with BBC World News, funded via advertising and subscription, and its 23 channels carrying many BBC programming co-ventures with other commercial providers. With overall sales of £1 billion in 2008–9, income from BBC Worldwide constitutes a major source of revenue for the BBC's public services (BBC 2009d; 2009b: 83).

Worldwide maintains the BBC's corporate profile in Europe and on the international stage, facilitating access to future market opportunities in satellite and digital technologies. Perhaps predictably, the success and prosperity of BBC Worldwide in the twenty-first century has created problems for the BBC as privately owned media struggle with declining advertising revenue and fragmenting market share, and as the industry regulator, Ofcom, endeavours to sustain the public service obligations of Britain's commercial broadcasters. When a merger between Worldwide and C4 (in which the BBC would be a minor partner) was mooted as a solution for C4's funding problems in 2009, BBC director-general Mark Thompson raised the possibility of privatising Worldwide. Another problem for Worldwide and the BBC in general is increased hostility from commercial competitors who resent the secure funding that underlies its success, and cast government intervention as subverting the market. Such hostility was in evidence at the 2009 McTaggart lecture when News Ltd executive James Murdoch lacerated the BBC as 'the Addams family of the media world'. Apparently blind to the problems of vested interest posed by global media conglomerates, Murdoch ended with the extraordinary claim: 'The only reliable, durable, and perpetual guarantor of independence is profit' (Robinson & Brown 2009; Murdoch 2009). As commentator Steve Hewlett later reported in his *Guardian* column, Murdoch's comments signal the beginning of a new war on downscaling the BBC, one that an incoming Conservative government would likely endorse. While envy of secure public funding by commercial competitors suffering the effects of the 2008–9 global recession is understandable, it is questionable whether deconstructing one of Britain's most successful global brands will leave the public or the independent production sector better served. Following Murdoch's attack, the Culture Secretary Ben Bradshaw suggested the BBC had reached the limits of its 'reasonable expansion', and that its licence fee should be cut. In September 2009, the matter of the BBC's scale in the digital era became a subject of study for the BBC Trust (Naughton 2005).

Accountability – from BoG to Trust

The constitutional framework of the BBC is intended to insulate it from the government. Two documents, the Royal Charter and the Licence and Agreement, govern the BBC's operation and structure. The objectives, powers and responsibility of the BBC are defined by the Royal Charter, which is periodically renewed by parliament. It also sets the terms of operation for the BBC Trust (as it did previously for the Board of Governors – BoG). The Licence and Agreement restrains the BBC from expressing editorial opinions on current affairs and empowers the responsible minister to require the broadcast of official announcements and to veto programmes.

Charter renewal, which generally occurs every ten years, involves a comprehensive review prior to the final drafting, subjecting the institution to prolonged public scrutiny and debate about its purpose, performance and funding. During the 2006 Charter review, the communications industry regulator, Ofcom, was also undertaking a review of public service broadcasting, and the Department of Culture, Media and Sport was reviewing the BBC's Internet and digital services. These multiple levels of review and consultation have grown as competition policy has invoked new mechanisms and protocols for ensuring a 'level playing field'. Whilst retaining its own internal systems of accountability regarding charter obligations, the BBC has also come under the purview of Ofcom as a participant in the media marketplace.

In January 2007, the BBC Trust replaced the Board of Governors (BoG) as the key mechanism by which the BBC's independence from Government was maintained. The BoG had administered the Royal Charter in association with the BBC Board of Management, which it appointed (Meech 19990: 233). In theory, the BoG was held to represent the British public, although in practice it had tended to reflect the Establishment being comprised mainly of privately educated men, frequently graduates of Oxford or Cambridge. Nominations for Governors were traditionally directed to the Home Office after 'soundings' from the BBC, until the 1990s when the Report of the Committee on Standards in Public Life, chaired by Lord Nolan, developed a more transparent appointment process. Under the 'Nolan principles' all positions are advertised, then short listed candidates are interviewed by independent assessors and members of the Department of Culture, Media and Sport, with the Secretary of State and the Prime Minister making the final decision (BBC 2006e).

A number of incidents of governmental interference in the 1980s led to a breakdown in the relationship between the BoG and the Board of Management (BoM), a crisis point for BBC management that ultimately resulted in the forced departure of then director-general Alasdair Milne in 1987. Situations where the nation's involvement in war divides public opinion have unsurprisingly proved particularly problematic for public broadcasters. The BBC's reporting on Northern Ireland and the Falklands War were both the source of flashpoints. While the BBC had successfully faced down Government efforts to silence dissent over the Suez Invasion in 1956, its efforts to represent divided opinion on war were less successful during Mrs Thatcher's rule. Reporting the Falklands War in 1982, *Newsnight* presenter Peter Snow noted of a Ministry of Defence report, 'If we believe the British...'. His scepticism invoked public outrage and was decried as 'almost treasonable' by one Tory MP. Refusing to be muzzled, the following week the BBC went on to screen a Panorama programme titled, *Can we avoid war?* (BBC 2009e). In the face of considerable media hostility, the BBC's Managing Director of Radio, Richard Francis, explained the importance of BBC independence:

When the Argentines claimed in the first raid on Port Stanley airport that they had shot down two Sea Harriers and damaged two more, the British Minister of Defence said none had been hit and the world wondered who was right. But when the BBC's correspondent aboard HMS Hermes reported, 'I counted the Harriers go out and I counted them all back,' the world believed. (BBC 2009e)

The affair soured BBC government relations, and reflected fundamental differences of opinion about what role the media should play during wartime.

In 1985 a documentary titled, *The Edge of the Union*, which featured interviews with two Northern Ireland political extremists – IRA member, Martin McGuinness and Loyalist, Gregory Campbell – had already been scheduled and advertised when the BoG, apparently bowing to government pressure, withdrew it without consulting the director-general, Alasdair Milne, who was holiday. In viewing the programme and instructing BBC managers not to screen it, the BoG broke with tradition, placing the interests of Government above those of the public and BBC staff. As a documentary, the interview style used allowed both men to speak unchallenged, and the programme was not subject to the editorial requirements for BBC news that excluded those associated with terrorist organisations. The Home Secretary, Leon Brittan, had issued a public statement saying that broadcast of the programme would not be in the national interest and sent a letter to that effect to the BBC's Chairman, but denied such intervention was an 'act of censorship'. The withdrawal of the documentary provoked a one day strike by the National Union of Journalists, with journalists at ITV and independent radio coming out in support of BBC colleagues. Having viewed the programme, the BoM later decided that it should be shown and agreed on minor changes which Milne communicated to the BoG to resolve the impasse. *At the Edge of the Union* screened two months later (BBC 2009e). The controversy brought government interference in BBC management into public view, casting doubt on the traditional relationship between the BoG and the Board of Management (BoM) at a critical time in the institution's history, in the lead up to a Charter Review and in the aftermath of the Peacock Report. In 1988, the banning of the spoken voices of members of eleven republican and loyalist organisations marked an escalation of Government censorship that Edgerton observes prompted institutionalised self-censorship at the BBC during the Thatcher years (Edgerton 1996: 123).

In October 1986, the Panorama programme, *Maggie's Militant Tendency*, which asserted Conservative party connections to organisations from the far right, prompted two Government politicians to sue the BBC; the affair was settled out of court. In January 1987, under pressure to curb 'left wing bias', the recently appointed Chairman of the Board of Governors, Marmaduke Hussey, sacked the BBC's director-general, Alasdair Milne. BBC accountant Michael Checkland, who replaced Milne, along with his deputy, John Birt, oversaw a return to more stable relationship between the BBC and the Thatcher government. As part of his restructure of news and current affairs into a single directorate, Birt appointed a Controller of Editorial Policy who was directed to draft a cohesive set of editorial guidelines:

They asserted the value of freedom of expression; but they also set out the need to be sensitive to the interests of those who appear in or are directly affected by BBC programmes; and the need to take account of the mood and convictions of the viewers and listeners who receive them. They affirmed the BBC's commitment to accuracy, fairness and impartiality; to straight dealing, to privacy, to the avoidance of stereotyping. They proclaimed the virtue and value of programmes that challenged established ideas and opinions with integrity. (Birt 2002: 277)

At the same time, the staffing and budgets for news and current affairs were increased with the number of overseas bureaux boosted from five to 25, and 80 new specialist reporters recruited to raise the overall quality of BBC news and BBC journalism (Birt 2002: 264; 303).

The BoG's traditional role was to keep the state at arms length, representing the public, BBC management and staff. It was this combination of duties that the Government decided was too conflicting that led to the establishment of the BBC Trust, which has clearer lines of accountability to licence fee payers. Comprising eleven trustees, The Trust sets BBC strategy. Supported by a full-time independent unit, the BBC Trust actively seeks the views of licence fee payers on matters such as BBC iPlayer, Red Button interactive television and impartiality on the BBC, while also undertaking or commissioning research into matters such as the economic impact of the BBC on the market. In addition, the Trust monitors the BBC's performance on its public and commercial services according to a range of agreed protocols, goals and quotas and arbitrates public complaints against the BBC.

Oversight of the BBC's commitment to Fair Trading is another responsibility of the Trust. Maintaining the segregation of different sources of funding, the Fair Trading Guidelines require transparent operational and accounting separation between the BBC's Public Service and Commercial activities. The dual objectives of Fair Trading are now both the protection of public money for public purposes and the protection of the commercial sector from 'unfair' public subsidised competition from the BBC. The latter concern was incorporated in the 2006 Charter through the 'competitive impact factor', which in tandem with the Public Value Test on new services is intended to ensure fair competition across the wider media marketplace (BBC 2009d: 24; 6–8).

Reflecting the idiosyncrasies of competition policy, the Public Value Test (PVT), which 'weighs public value against market impact', is a particularly important role filled by the BBC Trust (BBC 2009f). Under the PVT, which is now required for all new BBC services, the Trust assesses the public value of the 'service', alongside assessment by Ofcom, the industry regulator, of any impact the 'service' might have on market competition (BBC 2009f). While the ultimate decision still resides with the BBC Trust, rights of appeal under the European Commission have seen at least one Trust PVT decision overturned, BBC Jam, an online educational initiative which will be discussed in Chapter Eight. The national communications sector regulator, Ofcom, also has limited jurisdiction over the BBC with regard to statutory quotas, public service programme codes, spectrum management and competition law (Iosfidis 2007: 87).

Reinvention for the Digital Future

Although digital television emerged first in US policy planning in the 1980s from the FCC's Advanced Television Systems Committee, Britain has been a world leader in developing digital terrestrial television (DTT), with the BBC, which was allocated a key role, being largely responsible for the nation's high level of public take-up. Although arguments for digitalization of the electro magnetic spectrum might seem compelling to many – improved picture and sound quality, a fourfold increase in carrying capacity, plus interactivity – nevertheless, digital terrestrial television was not an inevitability and in fact required complex and protracted negotiation. The decision to implement DTT had to be taken collaboratively: first at the international level of spectrum management through the International Telecommunications Union (ITU), and then at the national and regional levels between government departments and a number of industry sectors. In his book, *Switching to digital television: UK public policy and the market,* Michael Starks, who served on key BBC and government planning committees, describes the collaborative effort required as 'a mutual risk reduction scheme' in which the costs/benefits for broadcasters, manufacturers, consumers and government all needed to be reconciled (Starks 2007: 218). The BBC's special role began under John Birt, whose investigations into digital technologies in the late 1980s prompted the critical early decision that the BBC should be available to licence fee payers across all platforms, 'satellite, cable, terrestrial and eventually telecom' (Birt 2002: 454). In his policy paper, *Extending Choice in the Digital Age,* Birt outlined a role for the BBC in the future digital multichannel environment in the run up to the 1996 Charter renewal, 'negotiating an above inflation licence fee settlement for digital channels even before it was clear what they were to be' (Bazalgette 2002). The success of BBC Online, launched in December 1997, also owed much to the decision to keep the site free of advertising (Birt 2002: 471). The BBC's commitment in 1995 to launch digital channels in 1997 was a boon to government policy, providing viewers with a reason to switch to digital. Greg Dyke, who succeeded Birt as director-general in 2000, expanded the BBC's digital initiatives, overseeing the re-launch of the digital channels as dedicated niche services and the launch of the Freeview platform in 2002 following the collapse of ITV Digital.

Rather than simply serving the public, the underlying motives for developing DTT were mixed and reflected the interests of set manufacturers, pay operators and the government. The Blair New Labour Government was keen to move Britain towards an information economy with its associated benefits of 'e-government' and the digital delivery of education and health services, but was also aware of the digital dividend – the money to be made from auctioning excess spectrum to other spectrum users such as mobile phone companies after digital switchover (DSO) – once the analogue television signal was switched off. The public, on the other hand, would have to buy either set-top boxes to convert the digital signal for their analogue sets, or buy integrated digital television receivers. Thus digitalization raised a conundrum for policy makers, how to justify forcing viewers to shift at their own expense to a new technology that held little interest for many of them. While the long-term social and economic benefits of building an information society might eventually prove the enterprise worthwhile, the initial cost to the consumer required a more immediate payback. The fact that digital satellite provided an alternative to digital terrestrial television, one that offered greater interactivity and business synergies and would arguably be cheaper for government, was another issue policy makers had to resolve. Some industry insiders argued for the 'do nothing option' of leaving digitalization to the marketplace (Starks 2007: 18–35). In Britain, this would probably have seen digital television provided only via satellite as a subscription service. While the digitalization of terrestrial television required the cost intensive upgrade of all transmission facilities, it also provided the benefit of the digital dividend seen by many commentators as the key reason behind government commitments to implement digitalization. The constraints of frequency management made turning off the analogue signal essential for the universal provision of digital terrestrial television (DTT), thus there was never any option of continuing the two services, analogue and digital, side by side. It was also necessary to persuade the vast majority of viewers to convert to digital before the date set for DSO to minimise political and commercial damage. Thus planning for digitalization meant planning for DSO and setting a date in order to drive digital up-take by consumers and digital content provision by broadcasters, a process that required a problematic carrot and stick approach, but one in which the BBC was to play a unique role as a public service provider, innovator and market participant. The development of the regulatory framework and timetable for digital television took about a decade. By September 2005, with 60 per cent of UK households already converted to digital, Tessa Jowell confirmed the government's phased switchover timetable detailing the various deadlines between 2008 and 2012 by which each region would be switched over. The timetable was devised to avoid any disruption to viewers' enjoyment of the London based 2012 Olympics, and ultimately required the government provide for 'potentially "vulnerable" consumers who were in financial need and/or practical assistance in order to cope' (Starks 2007: 111; 113).

The BBC was involved across several fronts in the development of DTT: developing the technical standards and the requisite technology – such as a set-top box compatible with all distribution systems – advising government, and collaborating with industry via various planning groups. In early 1995, the BBC ran an experimental digital service to demonstrate the technology, and also mounted a campaign to win the European Parliament to the idea of digital broadcasting as a European venture in which public service broadcasters had a key role to play (Birt 2002: 458).

In August 1995, John Major's Conservative Government released a proposal for launching DTT in the UK, forecasting 18 digital channels. The proposal identified six multiplexes (each representing space for four channels) and guaranteed places for BBC One, BBC Two, Channel 3 (ITV), Channel Four, SC4 (Wales) and Channel Five, signalling public service broadcasting would be maintained and that the analogue signal would eventually be switched off. The BBC secured a multiplex for its public service channels and was also part of a joint venture – UKTV – with Flextech, which secured another multiplex. During this time the BBC was also negotiating shared satellite space with the pay TV operator BSkyB.

For while the BBC was a committed and key driver of DTT, senior managers remained aware of the need for multiplatform delivery in the digital era, in order to avoid the risk of excluding any licence fee payers from receiving BBC services. The digital satellite platform and the rapid take-up of BSkyB potentially represented an enormous threat to the BBC and other terrestrial broadcasters (Starks 2007: 32).

Under the initial allocation of Britain's six digital multiplexes, the first three had gone to the current analogue broadcasters – one to the BBC, the second to ITV with the third to be shared between Channel Four, SC4 and Channel Five. The remaining three multiplexes were granted to British Digital Broadcasting (BDB), a joint venture between two ITV companies, Granada and Carlton, along with BSkyB. Under European Union competition regulation, BSkyB was forced to withdraw from the group because of its pay TV dominance, leaving the fledgling DTT pay service, ONdigital, in open competition with BSkyB's well established and highly successful business. When launched in 1998, BSkyB's digital satellite service carried the BBC's new digital channels – BBC Choice, BBC Knowledge, News 24, an audio feed of Parliament and a digital text service. In a bid to increase take-up, BSkyB began offering a free set-top box to new subscribers in mid-1999. It proved a highly successful strategy for Sky's digital service, in marked contrast to its DTT competitor, ONdigital. By the end of 2000, of the six and half million homes receiving digital television in Britain, five million were subscribing to BSkyB (Starks 2007: 49). As a result of a range of factors, including an excessive payment (£315 million) for the broadcast rights to the Nationwide League's football games, ONdigital, which had been rebranded as ITV Digital, went into administration in early 2002, releasing the three digital multiplexes for reallocation. The pay TV sector initially drove digital television in the UK, contributing to its early success, but with the acquisition of the ITV Digital multiplexes by BBC Worldwide and Crown Castle (now Arquiva) consortium and the October 2002 launch of Freeview, public policy shifted, enabling public service broadcasting to take the lead.

The Blair Government's aspirations for an information society and the accompanying benefits of e-commerce and e-government, along with expectations that digital television could help to bridge the digital divide, informed DTT policy in the late 1990s. The BBC's unique role in the digital era was formally instituted in 2006 through the sixth public purpose of the BBC Trust – 'Delivering to the public the benefit of emerging communications technologies and services' (BBC 2009f). This role was accompanied by an increase in the BBC licence fee to help with the costs of digitalization in 2000 – inflation plus 1.5 per cent (Starks 2007: 66). However, by 2006, with the BBC having officially embraced its new purpose as a driver of digital uptake, a similar rise in the licence fee became a justification for quarantining a proportion of the fee for the Digital Conversion Assistance scheme. The notion of top-slicing the licence fee, as noted earlier, has subsequently been mooted for a range of other purposes, including subsidising the cost of universal broadband in the Digital Britain Report (Carter 2009) as digital television has come to encompass Internet Protocol Television (IPTV).

The initial launch of the BBC's digital channels, BBC Choice and BBC Knowledge, reflected misguided early thinking that envisaged additional digital channels as auxiliaries of BBC One and BBC Two rather than 'internal rivals for audience' (Starks 2007: 45). In 2000, newly appointed director-general, Greg Dyke, announced BBC Television's new line up – seven services across five channels for launch in 2001. In the evening, the new digital services would be BBC Three offering programming for young adults, and BBC Four providing 'culturally and intellectually demanding programming'. In the daytime, these would carry two new children's services; CBeebies for pre-school children and CBBC for primary-aged children. Other digital services include regional versions of BBC One and BBC Two, BBC News24, BBC Parliament, and the more recent additions, BBC HD and BBC Alba, the Gaelic language service. The launch of Freeview in 2002 positioned digital television as a free-to-view service, posing a barrier to any future efforts to make the BBC a subscription service. Targeting the BBC's 'conventional analogue heartland' rather than the households that typified subscription television, the launch of Freeview saw DTT rapidly become the most popular digital platform, allowing the government to finally announce its planned DSO timetable (Starks 2007: 83). By 2009, carrying 50 digital TV channels and 24 radio stations, Freeview was reaching 37.6 per cent of homes compared to the 34.8 per cent taking pay satellite (Ofcom 2009). In 2009, BBC One remained Britain's most watched channel, BBC One and BBC Two led terrestrial prime-time viewing, while amongst the new digital services, BBC Three was the most watched channel amongst 16–34 year olds, Cbeebies was the most watched pre-school channel and CBBC reached more 6–12 year olds than any other children's channel (BBC 2009e).

While DTT generally offers little interactivity, the BBC has promoted various interactive offerings under the brand name BBC-I, to differentiate those services that can be accessed via the red button on the remote control. Red Button interactive programming has included enhanced multi-screen programming for live sports, music events and elections, enabling viewers to move between different stages or locations, but has also included specially developed programming that invites viewers to interact with programme content via live quizzes and on-screen tests. In the interests of universality, Red Button programming has also had to cater for viewers without digital capability, a complication that will disappear after DSO.

Another venture into interactivity, the Creative Archive project – a joint enterprise between the BBC, the British Film Institute (BFI), Channel Four and the Open University – planned to put much of the BBC's back catalogue of programming online for licence fee payers to adapt and use as they please, within the five conditions of the Creative Archive Licence. When the pilot ended in 2006 the project was apparently downscaled, presumably due to the complications of rights management in the digital age. Continuing 'to explore how the scheme can be used' the project is now generating collaborative partnerships between public institutions such as that recently announced in December 2009 between the BBC and the British Library, in order to build a digital archive and develop a uniform regime to facilitate access for researchers and the public (Bunz 2009).

Capitalising on the spread of broadband and parallel development in wireless technology, the BBC has pioneered applications for viewing television online and downloading onto mobile platforms – mobile phones and personal digital assistants (PDAs). The BBC iPlayer, launched in 2007, delivers online 'catch-up TV' and has proven hugely popular, exceeding expectations with 271 million downloads in 2008, prompting concerns that such a level of video downloads would 'bring the Internet to a halt' (Khan 2009). In late 2009, the BBC Trust approved a commercial joint venture, Project Canvas, a set top box that will enable viewers to watch online, on-demand Catch-up-TV from applications such as the iPlayer on their TV sets.

Britain, like other European countries, initially eschewed the charms of high definition television (HDTV) for the multichannel possibilities of standard digital technology and it was content choice rather than quality that drove the uptake of digital television in its first decade. The phenomena of the home cinema as a site for viewing DVDs saw the rise of consumer interest in increased picture and sound quality. Following BSkyB's introduction of HDTV in 2006, the BBC committed to producing all its in-house programming in HD by 2010 (Starks 2007: 179). Launched in 2007 on cable and satellite and in December 2009 on Freeview, the BBC HD channel, which uses the higher quality 1080i line standard, screens nine hours of mixed genre HD content a day, drawing on programming produced for other BBC channel schedules.

BBC online is perhaps the institutions' greatest digital initiative. Launched in 1994, bbc.co.uk offers over two million pages of information about BBC services, supplementary radio and television programme content including blogs and discussions 'fora' of various kinds, and dedicated web content such as the *Video Nation* site, which invites members of the public to upload their own videos. BBC online has become one of the most frequently visited sites in Britain and across Europe with the web information company, Alexa.com, ranking it sixth in the UK, 44th in Europe, and amongst the top 100 sites of thirteen countries around the world in December 2009. BBC Online News was launched under Birt as an advertising free service rather than the commercial BBC Worldwide enterprise originally mooted when the BBC had what he termed a 'false view of the Internet...[as] an extension of the magazine business' (Birt 2002: 303). The establishment of BBC News online helped to consolidate the BBC's lead as a global news service. Under Birt's restructure of BBC News and Current Affairs, the BBC increased its investment in research and overseas bureaux which rose from five to 26 at a time when other broadcasters were downscaling. Birt later claimed: 'Eventually, we would have the most extensive foreign news-gathering capability of any broadcaster in the world, far outweighing CNN or any of the US networks or European broadcasters' (Birt 2002: 264). With newspapers being abandoned by their readers in preference for the diverse offerings available free online, the financial viability of commercial news media is being eroded and with it the traditional benchmarks of serious news journalism. In this environment, the BBC's continued investment in research and investigative and specialist journalism acquires considerable importance. But BBC Online has also brought a new element to the notion of quality in news, enabling user participation through the integration of interactive applications and technologies such as blogs (web-logs), Twitter (an online/mobile text service), social media (personalisable online networks) and 'fora' of various kinds, targeting younger viewers/users through these and other various on-demand services – podcasts, vodcasts and mobile media. Choice in distribution platforms along with the quality and diversity of BBC News content is increasingly necessary to engage a generation disenchanted with commercial media and political spin.

Having survived the political crises and funding challenges of the 1980s and 1990s, the BBC in the digital era is Britain's unparalleled media industry success story, delivering a broad range of popular and cultural programming at home and promoting British talent and culture abroad, while also hosting one of the world's most highly regarded news services. The overall value of the BBC and its commercial subsidiaries to Britain's creative economy in 2008/9 was estimated at £7.6 billion in a 2010 report by the accountancy firm Deloitte commissioned by BBC management, representing the generation of two pounds for every pound of licence fee revenue through investment in jobs and the independent production sector. The report also shows 'funding through the licence fee is a vital source of stability across the whole UK broadcasting industry as the economy slows' (BBC 2010). By 2009, the tables had turned on those global media conglomerates which along with the BBC's commercial multichannel competitor, BSkyB, had once seemed to threaten the BBC's very *raison d'etre*. The 2008–9 global economic recession saw the revenues of commercial and subscription based media plummet with Freeview's digital terrestrial and satellite platforms, launched in 2002 and 2004 respectively, proving hugely popular.

Yet the BBC continues to face the same challenges as public broadcasters elsewhere – free market opposition to public subsidy and government intervention, and advancement of a downsized market failure model as more relevant for the multiplatform era. Such threats prompted the pursuit of increased ratings during the 1980s and 1990s with the BBC pioneering hybrid factual entertainment programming and reality TV. The safe populist approaches of commercial television whereby personalities and stars are the focus around which programmes are 'packaged' have tended to displace the earlier high-risk patronage of original and talented individuals, although scandals over presenter salaries in 2009 may see this trend scaled back. Nevertheless, in the new millennium, the BBC's digital television services, BBC Online and the creative interactive possibilities of user-generated content have brought a democratising participatory look to BBC patronage of the arts with potential for a new wave of creative risk taking, drawing on a broader spectrum of national talent. Regardless of its position of strength – through chartered independence from government, substantial public income from the licence fee, the historical foundation of thirty years of broadcasting monopoly and another thirty of regulated public service duopoly – the BBC must continue to adapt in both structure and purpose to accommodate the changing needs of competition policy and the politics of the day.

In representing Britain's nations, regions and diverse communities, the BBC continues to position itself as a mainstream broadcaster rather than merely redressing the failure of commercial systems. Mainstream status justifies continuance of the licence fee and retention of many aspects of the comprehensive remit: universality of coverage for free to air services; impartial news and current affairs (a particularly costly undertaking); provision of a diverse range of programme forms; and the servicing of diverse minority cultural interests. In the digital age these have been extended, with interactivity and multiple platforms expanding delivery modes and content forms. The BBC's role as an innovator has also been reborn in the new millennium with the Government investing it with responsibility for driving digital take-up and assisting as a venture partner with other media and regional organisations, a role referenced again in the Digital Britain Report (Carter 2009). Government requisition of a proportion of the licence fee for the Switchover Help Service in 2006, and subsequent talk of 'top slicing' for funding public service content elsewhere, along with political concern about the prosperity of BBC Worldwide following criticism from its commercial competitors, suggests reduced independence for the BBC even as the Government repeatedly affirms its commitment to this principle.

The BBC's response, an increasingly corporatist approach, has been facilitated by the existence of Channel Four with its specific remit to provide a complementary service that is both distinctive and innovative. As a public service partner with a potentially threatening, low-budget, commercially funded structure, Channel Four was designed to appease calls for the representation of pluralist cultural needs while accommodating the new enthusiasm for free market systems, and constitutes a compromise of public service ideals and market-liberal thinking.

Chapter 3

Channel Four - 'A Service with a Difference'

Introduction

When it went to air in 1982 Channel Four gave British viewers a very different kind of television service to any they had experienced before. A unique, commercially funded, public service channel, conceived after well over a decade of public debate, it was a compromise resonant of the changing times.

Established as a 'distinctive' complementary service, Channel Four's Charter specified unserved audiences, education and innovation as particular areas for attention. The Channel's interpretation of 'distinctive' integrated public service notions of quality with directives to innovate and experiment opening the airwaves to cultural minorities and community film and video makers. Through intelligent and original programming it eventually found a loyal following. While serving minority interests, Channel Four was also intended to engage the mainstream audience, a role that eventually diminished its early narrowcast intentions and ideals regarding community access. Interpretation of what constitutes a 'distinctive' service has changed over the years, becoming markedly commercial by the end of 1990s and invoking widespread public criticism in the first decade of the new millennium. With new digital television channels coming on stream, competition for viewers and advertising dollars has put the public service remit of Channel Four back on the public agenda. Addressing the future of Four, managing director Andy Duncan's 2008 plan, Next on Four, set out a new public service direction for the channel based on the premise of a new infusion of public funding of some kind. Apart from a suggested merger with the privately owned commercial broadcaster, Channel Five, proposals for Channel Four's future in 2009 – government subsidy by 'top slicing' the BBC's licence fee, and a proposed a tie-up with BBC Worldwide – have been directed at returning the channel to its previous identity as an innovative and distinctive public service.

Channel Four's institutional culture has always been markedly different from that of the BBC, with distinctiveness and complementarity contributing a unique public service ethos based around notions of difference. Since its launch in 1982, Channel Four's interpretation of its audiences has evolved to accommodate changes in corporate management and government policy – although this is less the case with the Welsh language service, SC4, which broadcasts on the Channel Four frequency across Wales. With a simpler and less robust structure than its publicly funded counterpart, the BBC, Channel Four's governance has been less complex, something that is likely to change if the public funding option is implemented. The following discussion explores how Four's original public service mission has developed as public policy and technology changed, and how the Channel is reinventing itself for the digital future.

Interpreting Difference

In 1960, despite being critical of ITV for its trivial content and high profit taking, the Committee of Inquiry into Broadcasting (the Pilkington Committee) endorsed the policy of balancing broadcasting's public and private sectors, proposing allocation of the fourth channel to ITV since the BBC already had two channels. Attempting to pre-empt further public debate on the subject, the independent regulator of the time, the ITA, lodged a formal submission for a new channel, ITV-2, to the Minister of Posts and Telecommunications in 1971, prompting immediate opposition across three fronts: the advertising lobby who resented the ITV companies' restrictive selling practices; broadcasting unions who wanted freer employment opportunities; and the TV 4 Campaign, a loose association of media critics, journalists, TV producers, MPs, trade unionists and others who wanted more public debate on the subject. In an article in the *Guardian* in April 1972, Anthony Smith, a TV 4 Campaigner, introduced the idea of a National Television Foundation (NTF) that would 'publish' programmes. Free of the bureaucratic superstructure and professional elitism of existing broadcasting institutions, the NTF would offer independent producers access to the airwaves and give the previously disenfranchised a voice; avoiding populist scheduling practices, it would address niche audiences with particular interests.

Television attracted criticism from a number of different quarters in the 1960s following the Pilkington Report. The loss of social consensus following post-war immigration affected public attitudes to television (Kumar 1982: 245). The ending of the BBC monopoly and the policies of succeeding directors-general compounded changes to the character of the BBC. In the 1960s, Sir Hugh Greene re-defined the BBC's main task as encouraging 'a healthy scepticism' and loosened controls on impartiality (McDonnell 1991: 50). Programming such as the satirical *That Was the Week That Was* mocked middle class values, angering society's moralists and gave rise to Mary Whitehouse's 'Clean Up TV Campaign'. On the other hand, a widely held perception of the BBC/IBA duopoly as bureaucratic and elitist drew criticism from the public and broadcasting professionals, particularly the independent sector who were excluded from the airwaves.

Embracing a new pluralist vision for Britain, Labour's Committee of Inquiry into the Future of Broadcasting (the Annan Committee) 'broke with imagined unities of national culture', adopting the concept of the NTF in its 1977 report. Rejecting the idea of another competitive commercial channel, the Annan Committee proposed that an Open Broadcasting Authority (OBA) control and operate the fourth channel. The Report adopted Smith's ideas for funding – a mixed regimen of grants, sponsorship and block advertising with a proviso that its distinctive nature would be sustained by a government grant if necessary (Murdock 1994: 9).

Labour's failure to establish the OBA gave the Conservatives a clean slate for allocating the fourth channel when they came to power in May 1979, immediately making known their intention to place the channel under the IBA subject to 'strict safeguards'. Despite rejecting the OBA as too dependent on the state, the Home Secretary William Whitelaw endorsed the broad intentions of the Annan Committee in response to the arguments of the opposition lobby. Complementary scheduling and competition for ratings were out, and 'the largest practicable proportion of the programming was to come from independent producers'. The Broadcasting Bill of 1980, which constituted Channel Four as a subsidiary of the IBA, left most of the fine detail of how the channel would work to the IBA, simply outlining the guiding principles and responsibilities for ensuring that tastes and interests not generally catered for by ITV were met: that educational content filled a suitable proportion of the schedule; that innovation and experimentation were encouraged; and that Channel Four was developed as a distinctive service (Blanchard & Morley 1982: 15).

The channel was to be funded by spot (in-programme) advertising sold by the ITV companies, topped up by a levy on their profits. It was an ingenious mechanism designed to insulate Channel Four's programme purchasing and commissioning arm from commercial pressures. The 1980 Act stipulated that Channel Four was to complement the ITV service, through 'the co-ordinated use of schedules in the best interests of the viewer', which Jeremy Isaacs, the first chief executive, interpreted as entitling Channel Four to draw up its own schedule.

The publishing model that Channel Four pioneered was a radical departure from the existing broadcasting structures of the BBC and ITV where production, editorial control and transmission facility were integrated, resulting in monolithic silos where controlling professional ideologies had a tendency to stifle innovation and experimentation. By removing the production role and limiting editorial control, the publishing model gave the broadcaster responsibility for defamation and copyright, allowing the producer an author's freedom of expression. To maintain this freedom the TV 4 Campaign suggested that 'balance' be provided across the schedule rather than within a single programme, thus giving more scope for a wider range of authorial voices.

The emergence of an independent production sector in Britain in the late 1970s enhanced the validity of the broadcaster/publisher model. Disillusionment with the bureaucratic constraints of both broadcasters had prompted a number of television producers to try their luck as independents. Despite problems in getting their programmes broadcast in Britain, some survived, proving that programme production was not the sole prerogative of the duopoly. In 1979, the British Academy of Film and Television Arts held an event, 'Who are the independents?' that highlighted the creative and entrepreneurial achievements of those outside the BBC/IBA cartel:

Time after time the audience heard how the BBC and ITV refused even to look at independent productions, or (if they deigned to purchase them) offered insultingly low percentages of production costs to buy the UK transmission rights – 10–13 per cent on average, with a maximum of 25 per cent. Christopher Nupen, for instance, described how he had mortgaged his house to make *Itzhak Perlman: Virtuoso Violinist* – one of the finest music films ever produced. The only reliable market for his programmes is Germany: ironically his latest film was ZDF's official entry to BAFTA's International Television Festival – and won the top award. (Lambert 1982: 88)

The commissioning system established under Four's first managing director, Jeremy Isaacs, enhanced the power of individuals to interpret the channel's charter. Opposed to any fixed quota system for independent producers, Isaacs was determined that programmes would be commissioned on the strength of their ideas, not on the basis of who was going to make them. Appointments were made for fixed terms and with a view to encouraging a new critical approach to traditional broadcasting practice; Isaacs and the channel controller, Paul Bonner, deliberately appointed some people without television experience. Of the fourteen commissioning editors, two were to attend to educational programmes and two to fiction, while the remainder were each appointed to specific areas – Actuality, Multicultural programmes, Youth, Independent Grant Aided Sector, One-Off Documentaries, Religion, The Arts, Sport, Light Entertainment and Music. Some of these encompassed other lesser areas. Three separate commissioning editors shared responsibility for documentaries, which were to be diverse in both scale and style, although the possibility of overseas sales was an acknowledged influence on the commissioning of more expensive series. Since single documentaries were the most powerful vehicle for the independent programme maker's voice, diversity of 'tones' was given precedence over diversity of subject matter, and in their commissioning, the editors sought a mix of new and experienced programme makers (Isaacs 1989).

Given the commonly perceived social impact of television, the publishing house analogy was problematic; as gatekeepers of the service, the commissioning editors monitored which voices were heard, thus invariably limiting plural representation. Like other broadcasters, Channel Four was required to be objective, balanced and impartial, and to have regard for society's notions of taste and decency. Interpreting these requirements alongside a remit to be distinctive, innovative and experimental presented commissioning editors with rather more complex challenges than those normally faced by publishers. Editorial policy was subsequently implemented through the script development and commissioning process (Isaacs 1989).

Channel Four addressed a wide spectrum of specialist interest groups from anglers, wine lovers and gardeners, to groups united by a specific social or cultural identity such as ethnic groups, gays, the disabled, the aged and the unemployed; groups hitherto un-served by television. By 1989, the general feeling at Channel Four was that minorities should be dealt with as part of society as a whole rather than pigeon holed. While non-contentious minority groups like the aged and the disabled could be accommodated with informational programmes based on commonality of experience, other groups angry about their exclusion from mainstream culture favoured a polemicist style. The difficulties of serving groups with divided and politically contentious views stretched resources and drew public criticism. Commissioning editors argued that there were too many groups to give coverage to all and that television should not become 'small groups talking to small groups'. It was, however, a common staff regret that the channel had lost touch with its 'access' beginnings (Docherty et al. 1988: 58–60).

Observers noted there was no rainbow coalition amongst minority groups (Docherty et al. 1988: 58). The fact that most of the population will at some time be part of a minority doesn't make defining fair representation easier. Is it to be on the basis of size or of some measure of marginalisation? Should the programming servicing each minority be exclusively for it, or rather be about it? Isaacs' approach to this dilemma was evident in his policy on women. While obviously not a minority, women have frequently been marginalised in the media as a special interest group, an anomaly Isaacs sought to redress by putting women in positions of authority within the channel. There was to be no commissioning editor for women's programmes. Women's viewpoint it was hoped would emerge through the commissioning process, through their broad representation across the channel (Isaacs 1989). Two of the three senior editors were women (Education and Actuality), and women managed the departments of Presentation, Marketing, Personnel and Publishing.

There was no equivalent employment policy for racial minorities who were initially catered for via special interest programmes addressing problems common to ethnic groups in Britain and covering cultural and political issues from their home countries. Since it was deemed impracticable to do this for every ethnic group, only the larger ethnic communities were catered for and all programmes were broadcast in English. A West Indian and the only black staff member at Channel Four, Sue Woodford was the commissioning editor for Multicultural Programmes. She commissioned *Black on Black* and *Eastern Eye* for Afro-Carribeans and Asians respectively. Produced with an all ethnic crew, *Black on Black* was a current affairs magazine programme covering issues of concern to the West Indian, Indian and Pakistani communities in Britain. *Eastern Eye* fulfilled a similar role for the various sectors of the Asian community.

Catering for particular racial groups was decried as racist by some (Isaacs 1989: 132), and when Farrukh Dhondy took over Sue Woodford's role, he replaced both programmes with *The Bandung File*, a current affairs programme covering both the Caribbean and the Asian sub-continent, scheduled in prime-time and targeted to a wider, more general audience. Like many Channel Four commissioning editors, Dhondy opposed the notion of minority audiences and, wanting to see blacks integrated into the whole, favoured the development of an independent black sector with access to commissions like other independent producers (Docherty et al. 1988: 58).

In the 1980s and much of the 1990s, as a free-to-air public television channel serving 'diverse tastes and interests' not otherwise catered for but with an entitlement to target the wider viewing public, Channel Four catered 'for all of the people some of the time', expanding opportunities for public exploration of shared interests, building common junctions across different groups. Contributing further diversity in programme content, form and style, the

Independent Film Makers Association (IFA) had initially proposed a separate foundation be established to provide programmes of cultural and social value. The IFA also advocated the establishment of workshops to foster experimentation, and wanted a relaxation of the established conventions of television production – rapid pace, instant recognisability and traditional industry standards of image quality (Blanchard & Morley 1982: 17). Rejecting the IFA's independent foundation, Isaacs instead established regional workshops funded on a bursary basis under a commissioning editor for the Grant Aided Sector. As the first to fill this role, Alan Fountain drew on work from the film and video workshops operating around the country between 1981 and 1983. Channel Four invested £675,000 in this sector, receiving in return the right to purchase television rights to any resulting work. Such programmes generally attracted only small audiences but placed Channel Four at the cutting edge of experimental film making, thus genuinely honouring the innovative and experimental clause of the remit. In the programme slots, *The Eleventh Hour* and *People to People*, Channel Four screened experimental drama and documentary respectively, originating from both British and international sources (Isaacs 1989: 174). Pushing the boundaries of television, Four's early access productions still appeared innovative fourteen years later:

> The channel's most experimental initiative – a legacy of 1970s radicalism – was the cultivation of a 'Workshop' production sector that trained people from under-represented groups…in the mid-1980s it was possible to speak of an avant-garde space of uneven quality in British television, at times uniting aesthetic and political invention, at others purely polemical. (Born 2003: 778)

One of Isaac's initial prime objectives for Channel Four was to lend support to the feature film industry through the establishment of Film on Four, later re-badged Film4. This investment strategy proved a shot in the arm for the failing British feature film industry with 130 feature length films completed by the end of 1989. Historically, the relationship between the two industries had been financially advantageous to television but disadvantageous to viewers since the first television broadcast was delayed for three years to protect the interests of film distributors and exhibitors. Italian and German television were the pioneers here, with Italy's RAI investing in the films of Fellini, Bertolucci and the Taviani Brothers, and Germany's ZDF similarly supporting the films of Herzog, Wenders and Fassbinder. Committing an initial investment of £300,000 each to 20 films per year (which grew to £1 million in later years) Channel Four shared production costs in return for television rights (Rothschilds 2008: 4). The arrangement acknowledged that cinema exhibition would precede the television broadcast, which was generally seen as being in the channel's interests, invariably drawing a larger audience on the back of the cinema marketing campaign. The opportunity created by Film on Four saw considerable growth in British film production. Films that attracted Channel Four investment were those that broke new ground and were less likely to attract finance through mainstream channels, such as *Distant Voices: Still Lives* directed by Terrence Davies, *The Draughtsman's Contract* directed by Peter Greenaway and

My Beautiful Laundrette directed by Stephen Frears. Film investment was not pursued from a profit motive but as part of the channel's evolving philosophy as a distinctive, alternative service. However, many of Four's films like those mentioned went on to achieve critical acclaim and international release, proving the value of the channel's considered endorsement of creative risk-taking.

From the beginning, innovative practices were employed in programme purchasing as well as programme production. Networking independent film distribution outlets and avoiding the more expensive mainstream distributors, the channel's two film purchasers organised seasons of 'classic' films and the work of European and Hollywood auteurs. Popular culture was accommodated with the biweekly indigenous drama, *Brookside*, which was shot in a Merseyside housing estate and used the TV soap format to raise issues of social justice, employing low budget innovative production techniques. Breaking with past formats, the commissioning editor for Youth programming Mike Bolland, involved youth at the production level as researchers. Youth TV, an independent youth lobby group came up with the ideas for *Images of Youth* and *A Sketch for Someone*, both of which broke new ground in youth programming. Bolland also pioneered some of that generation's most original comedy with *The Comic Strip Presents*. The first commissioning editor for the arts, Michael Kustow, set out to 'affect, not just reflect' the arts and the two hour performance slot on Sunday night was committed to this sentiment. Productions included the Royal Shakespeare Company's *Nicholas Nickleby*, Peter Brook's *Tragedy of Carmen* and *The Mahabharata*, a dramatisation of the Hindu book of scriptures. While never successful in strict financial terms, FilmFour's contribution to the renaissance of the British film industry has been widely recognised, prompting the BBC to imitate the concept. Launching its own film investment arm in the 1990s, the BBC was able to offer much bigger budgets, subsequently drawing in overseas financiers (Foster c1995: 2).

When Channel Four took over responsibility for selling its own advertising in 1993 additional funds were directed to Film on Four. The 1990s proved particularly profitable times and in 1997, under pressure from government to invest more in film, chief executive, Michael Jackson initiated a new commercial British 'Studio' with support from the Arts Council. Jackson took Four's film venture in a new direction, re-branding it Film4 and launching a digital subscription channel of the same name. Eschewing low budget innovation, FilmFour pursued big budget populism and Hollywood collaboration (Rothschilds 2008: 396). The greatly enhanced £30 million budget failed to return the bigger profits anticipated, and the venture was declared a financial failure five years later. FilmFour was re-established in-house with a reduced £10 million budget, announcing a return to its earlier creative risk taking, a claim vindicated to large extent by the critical success of films such as *The Last King of Scotland* (Kevin McDonald 2006), *This is England* (Shane Meadows 2007), *Brick Lane* (Sarah Gavron 2007), *In Bruges* (Martin McDonagh 2008) and *Slumdog Millionaire* (Danny Boyle 2008). In 2008, Andy Duncan was able to claim that Four had won 'five Oscars in the last four years' (Duncan 2008). The Film4 channel was re-launched in July 2006 as a free to air service on Freeview, the UK's digital terrestrial platform.

Sport provided an opportunity to draw a larger audience even when fulfilling its remit to be different; Channel Four broadcasts of American football brought the relatively unknown sport into popular favour, and sumo wrestling, cycling and baseball were other notable successes. Other innovations included providing more informative commentary to draw in new audiences, and targeting different age groups by broadcasting secondary school and masters events (Isaacs 1989). Some viewers found Channel Four too radical in is early years, disconcerted by the representation of gay viewpoints. For others, however, it was not radical enough; serving the interests of disaffected minorities was inevitably bound to offend some viewers, while the decision to contract out news and current affairs to the ITV companies' news gathering organisation, ITN (Independent Television News), angered left wing critics for failing to represent a genuinely alternative viewpoint.

From the beginning, Channel Four challenged the conventional notion of balance, arguing for the right to present balance across the schedule rather than within each programme. Noting that 'more intelligent regulators' had begun to appreciate the need for changes to existing practice on the issue, John Ellis quotes David Glencross, who was Director of Television at the IBA in 1983:

> What impartiality means, or should mean above all, is fairness, an absence of editorial line. Impartiality…does not insist on equal time, nor on some precise mathematical balance, though there are times when impartiality is best achieved through equality. (Qtd. in Ellis 2008: 335)

Four's new interpretation outraged the BBC for its breach of the 'formal rules of balance and impartiality', which were established markers of professionalism (Ellis 2008: 337).

Balance across the schedule raised another dilemma for the commissioning editors committed to supporting quality and innovation; if no good programmes expressing the other viewpoint were available, how was balance to be achieved? At what price to the remit must balance be accommodated? In the 1980s, the channel was criticised by both the media and the IBA for its leftist leanings, criticisms that perhaps misunderstood some of Four's innovations. Describing one early programme, *The Friday Alternative* (1982–83), which offered an alternative to ITN news, Ellis argues some of the team were more 'radical' than 'leftish', espousing the values 'of the critical journalist rather than the political vanguard' and having a 'distinctly populist tendency' through the involvement of 'viewers' groups' from across the country (Ellis 2008: 340). Initially many Channel Four staff thought that given the right wing or consensualist bias of existing television, the channel's complementary remit validated a left wing bias. Looking back, Isaacs found only one politically divergent voice among commissioned programme makers, that of Diverse Productions producer, David Graham, who had represented the ideas of the new right. His programme, *Diverse Reports*, had also broken new ground in giving producers of differing political persuasions and viewpoints an opportunity to make opinionated television, not through simple polemic, but by presenting their viewpoint through argument and counter-argument. Through this 'thesis led' approach, the channel's policy on balance found a compromise between its early ambitions of providing an open forum for all voices and the traditional neutral stance associated with the 'professional' product (Docherty et al. 1988: 43).

The channel's remit to represent 'alternative' viewpoints meant that Four often overstepped conventional social boundaries regarding decency, while the FilmFour collaboration with the film industry also meant accommodating a more relaxed, different standard of censorship. Catering for tastes and interests not otherwise served necessarily implicated the channel in testing audience tolerance, a process that occasionally evoked public outcry, as with Derek Jarman's film on homosexuality, *Sebastiane*. Four arrived at a compromise, both protecting the vulnerable and giving viewers the right to censor their own viewing by the superimposition of a red triangle, noting Special Discretion Required, on programmes with explicit sexual content or subject matter likely to offend some viewers.

But while Channel Four won the battle over broadcasting sexually explicit homoerotic content, it was arguably less stalwart in defending politically contentious programming from censorship (Jivani 1990: 27). In 1985 the IBA banned a *20/20 Vision* program, *MI5's Official Secrets*, which included revelations from a former MI5 Officer, Cathy Massler, that organisations like the National Council for Civil Liberties and Campaign For Nuclear Disarmament (CND) were classified as subversive by the agency. The programme also alleged that the agency breached its own operational rules on political bias, and that 'in March 1983 the Secretary of State for Defence established the DS19 unit to counter the growing effectiveness and popularity of the Campaign for Nuclear Disarmament' (Hansard February 1985). Although prompting questions in the House of Commons, Isaacs lost the battle to screen the programme, reflecting that the incident illustrated a conflict over accountability – of the IBA's to parliament and Channel Four's to the public (Isaacs 1989: 140–3). Regretting the channel's avoidance of political controversy, one staff member, Ranelagh, noted, 'we could have interpreted the requirements to validate hard hitting investigations of matters that (would) vitally affect our future as a nation' (Docherty et al. 1988: 68). Despite innovations such as its stand on balance and the introduction of an hour long evening news bulletin, the channel which took its news from ITV's news service, ITN, was accused of hanging on to 'a notion of news and current affairs which reproduces directly the characteristics it should have contested most vigorously: professionalism, insularity, metropolitanism and the tyranny of established news values' (Goulden et al. 1982: 80).

In Educational programming, the first commissioning editor, Naomi McIntosh, a former Open University professor, adopted a broader, more engaging and informal approach in her role, seeking to draw 'the 75 per cent of the population who think that education is not for them' (Lambert 1982: 143). Adults and adolescents rather than children were the main target audience, and Four initially avoided subject areas already covered by BBC Two, covering the fields of active leisure, access to culture and the arts, health, consumer protection, visual awareness and new technology. This changed in later years with Channel Four Learning, launched in 1993, moving into primary and secondary school broadcasting, and later into the provision of multiplatform content, which will be discussed in the final section of this chapter on Four's digital reinvention.

Insulated from audience ratings until 1990, the channel was well placed to be both risk taker and innovator. As first chief executive, Jeremy Isaacs played a formative role in defining Four's complementary service. The celebration of difference was apparently more radical than many in government had intended with Conservative MP, Norman Tebbitt, intimating to Isaacs that the different interests and tastes the channel was supposed to serve were 'Golf and sailing and fishing. Hobbies, that's what we intended' (Murdock 1994: 11). Discussing the political climate at the time of Four's conception, Ellis observes that the impetus came from a 'liberal/left consensus' driven by those wanting more space for television advertising and others wanting more opportunities for programme makers; the resultant compromise was 'an adventurous channel that financed itself from advertising' (Ellis 2008: 332). Certainly the low overheads of the publishing model had strong appeal to a government committed to neoliberal economics. With independent production budgets well below those of other broadcasters and with a high proportion of foreign programming, Channel Four constituted an implicit threat to the publicly funded BBC and the relationship between the two broadcasters remains a conflicted one in which complementarity and competition are intricately intertwined.

From Minority to Mainstream

Providing a service for all of the people some of the time, addressing minority tastes and interests instead of a broad general audience was a radical break with past broadcasting practice, but made it difficult for Channel Four to prove itself a legitimate enterprise in the channel's first decade. The right wing press derided controversial minority programming and dubbed the service 'Channel Snore' and 'Channel Bore' (Jivani 1990: 22). Ratings were low in the first year yet changes to commissioning and scheduling saw the audience grow. A year later, the Daily Mail, approving programme changes, applauded improved production values:

> Its appeal has greatly broadened...To be sure it still caters for minority tastes and so it should. But it doesn't matter if the interest is a minority one, so long as the programme is well done. (*Daily Mail*, 22 October 1984)

A decade on Channel Four was thriving commercially, maintaining around 10 per cent of the total viewing audience (having acquired responsibility for selling its own advertising under the 1990 Broadcasting Act), with a weekly homes penetration of more than 80 per cent (Channel 4 1984: 36). With the advent of digital television and increased multichannel competition for audience and now itself a multi-channel provider, Channel Four has maintained its position reporting a 'portfolio share at around 12% for the third successive year' in 2008 (Channel 4 2009: 5).

The Annan Committee's intentions for Four to be 'a force for plurality in a deeper sense' problematized how minorities should be defined and who should be represented (Annan 1977: 15–18). Those advocating niche subscription services regarded user-pays as the obvious solution to disparate consumer interests – an approach that contributed little to addressing social divisions. On the other hand, representing minorities only in the mainstream could be viewed as a rejection of the remit; some ethnic groups resented the axing of specialist ethnic programmes *Black on Black* and *Eastern Eye*. Many also rejected the principle of proportionality as a guide for representation, arguing for representation on the basis of need as signified by under-representation on other channels. The success of *The Bandung File*, however, did inspire the BBC to launch magazine programmes targeted to the Asian and Afro-Caribbean communities in similar prime-time slots; a development anticipated by the channel's 'intellectual parent', Anthony Smith, who had previously observed, 'the reform of the BBC is the real objective for the institution of Channel Four' (Docherty et al. 1988: 176).

Channel Four's multicultural department was axed under Mark Thompson in 2002 when it became evident that Black and Asian audiences were more attracted to the content on cable and satellite platforms (Guardian 2007). This trend had already prompted the establishment of the Cultural Diversity Network (CDN) in 2000, aimed at raising awareness of the importance of ethnic representation across the British broadcasting sector. Channel Four has since pursued a mainstream agenda endeavouring to represent ethnic groups across the schedule via reality programming such as *Big Brother*, a strategy that arguably helps reduce intolerance by eroding the strangeness of the 'other', but which still fails to address the need for multicultural programming to facilitate greater cross-cultural understanding or the nurturing of ethnic production talent, a requirement for societal equality. The CDN introduced a pledge and a mentoring programme to address these issues. Four's re-evaluation of its approach to representing multiculturalism is discussed in more detail in the final section on digital reinvention.

A national, terrestrial broadcaster, Channel Four is accessible throughout the UK but not in Wales where the fourth channel took on a different look from the start. Prolonged agitation by Welsh nationalists for a Welsh language channel culminated in September 1980 with Gwynfor Evans, President of the Welsh Nationalist party, threatening to starve himself to death unless the government allocated the fourth channel accordingly. The official attitude had been that audience numbers for such a service could not justify the cost, but fear of public anger should Evans die prompted a government rethink. Sianel 4 Cymru (S4C) is governed by an independent Welsh Fourth Channel Authority, operating within the framework of the IBA. When Welsh programmes are not being shown, S4C selects material from Channel Four UK and from Harlech Television, the ITV company of the region, as well as from independent producers and the BBC.

When Channel Four began operating as an independent corporation after 1993, it changed direction targeting a more mainstream audience, scheduling more US programming and soaps in peak viewing time to attract bigger audiences in the ABC1 and youth demographics popular with advertisers. While no longer pushing the boundaries of television as it had in the 1980s, Channel Four still made a special contribution to the overall mix of free-to-air television in Britain by providing competition for the BBC:

> Overall the broadcasting ecology evinced a doubling of the fertile competition characteristic of the 1960s and 1970s: now not only BBC1 and ITV, but BBC2 and C4, were engaged in mimetic competition. (Born 2003: 779)

Since the development of digital platforms in the late 1990s, Channel Four has been able spread its remit for serving difference across a portfolio of digital terrestrial and online channels, retaining a more mainstream identity for its main channel.

The Public-Commercial Funding Conundrum

Under the 1980 Broadcasting Act by which Four was established, the ITV companies sold advertising time on the channel on a regional basis. Four was financed by a levy on those companies that was proportional to ITV's total revenue. In this way programme purchasing was insulated from funding and direct commercial influence. In the channel's first year Isaacs successfully pushed the proposed operating budget from £80 million to £104 million, but financial forecasts for the future looked uncertain. IBA projections estimated an increase of only 10 per cent for Four's advertising revenue, which would have left ITV subsidising the channel by £15–35 million annually. Since this would reduce profit margins, affecting the government's annual levy on the ITV companies, concerns were expressed about the cost to the nation. A government investigation, subsequently estimated that the channel would be paying for itself within four years (Lambert 1982: 109).

With a guaranteed minimum income and insulated from direct commercial pressure, Channel Four added another dimension to the BBC/IBA public service duopoly, incorporating the principle of assured finance with a complementary remit. In its first year, the channel commissioned an unexpectedly large amount of independent production, 416 projects, which suggested a greater preparedness on the part of independents to adapt to the relatively modest budgets being allocated – an average of £30,000 per programme hour. The programming consisted of 30 per cent produced by independents, 40 per cent from ITV/ITN, and the remaining 30 per cent from other sources. The ITV companies had never calculated their costs on a programme by programme basis before and the exercise proved a shock. Resisting the low budgetary levels of the independents, they endeavoured to negotiate a 'single terms of trade' contract until Thames Television, which had lost some of its broadcast time in the recent franchise allocation, accepted a price far below the deal being sought. This eventuated in separate agreements with all ITV companies as each eventually realised that the channel's success was in their own financial interests (Lambert 1982: 130–2).

As a publisher broadcaster, Channel Four eliminated the staffing and equipment overheads of a production facility. As a consequence, its cost structure is lower than that of the BBC or ITV. Sylvia Harvey notes that in 1986 Channel Four's 1987 operating costs were an average £32,866 per hour, while the ITV's were £161,817 and the BBC's were £60,365 (Harvey 1989: 68). The Channel achieved efficiencies through subcontracting independents, a high level of repeat screenings and imported programming. Yet despite these economies in the Eighties, Lambert argues that by virtue of its innovative style and the good management and judgement of its commissioning editors, Four did not project a low budget image to its audience (Lambert 1982: 67–8). This point is also made by Ellis, who having commented on innovations on *Friday Alternative* that dispensed with the need for a presenter, proceeds to outline the cost pressures on those commissioned to make programmes for Four:

> The standard contract for Channel Four was a cost-plus arrangement, in which the actual costs of production were minutely inspected by Channel 4 production accountants and a standard percentage 'fee' was calculated on the basis of the agreed total. (Ellis 2008: 341)

In the 1980s, the arrival of cable and satellite technologies providing access to a multiplicity of channels raised questions about the future need for investment in public service television. The Peacock Committee Report of 1986 which, as noted in the previous chapter, had advocated pay-TV as the best means of serving the multifarious needs of pluralist society had also recommended that Channel Four sell its own advertising air-time (later adopted in the 1990 Broadcasting Act). Heralding the end of the ITV companies' monopoly and the principle of assured finance that had underpinned the duopoly system, the change ultimately proved a bonus for advertisers opening the way for competitive bidding with opportunities to influence programme scheduling. In 1988, a government White Paper, 'Broadcasting in the 90s: Competition, Choice and Quality', adopted many of the Peacock Report's recommendations. While Channel Four's remit was left intact, the White Paper stressed a need for greater competition between those selling television air time, noting 'a pressing demand from those whose expenditure on advertising has paid for the independent television system' (HMSO 1988: 1). This market oriented perspective was a reversal of the earlier view that repudiated the advertising lobby's arguments in 1972, arguing for protection from lowest common denominator programming.

The 1990 Act made Channel Four an independent non-profit corporation responsible for selling its own airtime. However, in the event of Four's advertising revenue falling below a minimum level (14 per cent of the combined revenue of ITV, Channel Four and SC4), Four was guaranteed a minimum income, with ITV required to pay up to 2 per cent of its qualifying revenue – after Four's statutory reserves had been depleted. In return for this safety net Channel Four was required to pay half of any surplus revenue to the ITV companies. By 1994, having paid £95.5 million since 1990 to the ITV companies, the Channel Four Board was agitating for the removal of the ITV safety net (Channel Four 1994: 6–7; 44). As a result the levy was gradually reduced and 'between 1993 and 2000 C4's revenues nearly doubled (from £330 million to £650 million)' (Born 2003: 778).

Although much of Four's original remit was retained in the 1990 Broadcasting Act and again in the 2003 Communications Act, survival as a distinctive complementary public service broadcaster was increasingly subject to financial pressures aggravated by audience fragmentation. During the 1990s, the application of conventional technical standards constrained experimentation, bringing a more commercial look, beginning under Michael Grade's management (1988–97) and increasing under his successor, Michael Jackson (1997–2002). Later chief executives Mark Thompson (2002–2004) and Andy Duncan (2004–2009) signalled intentions to revitalise Four's public service identity, but faced a declining income base that inevitably saw the channel increasingly dependent on populist lifestyle programming, most notably the reality show *Big Brother*, secured by Jackson in 2000.

Accountability

Accountable through neither the constraints of the licence fee renewal process nor the pressure of shareholder expectations, Channel Four has greater independence than Britain's other free-to-air broadcasters. This has allowed the individual personalities of successive chief executives to have considerable sway. In 2009, Four's role as an innovator, developed during its first decade, re-emerged in future readings of its role with Lord Carter's *Digital Britain* report identifying 'difference' as key, and again nominating a special role for Channel Four alongside the BBC (Carter 2009: 146).

Channel Four operated as a subsidiary company of the IBA until it became a publicly owned statutory corporation under the 1990 Broadcasting Act, with the ITC replacing the IBA as regulator in 1993 until the 2003 Communications Act instituted Ofcom as Britain's single communications regulator. Ofcom is now responsible for: appointing the fourteen members of the Channel Four board following consultation with the chairman and the approval of the Secretary of State for Culture, Media and Sport; setting the terms of the licence and programmes codes; and monitoring complaints with power to revoke a licence for breaches of compliance. Appointed for a three year term, board members have joint responsibility for ensuring adherence to the licence and compliance with board policies. The eight non-executive members, who have equal voting rights, are intended to bring strong, independent judgement, knowledge, and experience to the board's decisions. The board delegates formulation and operation of detailed policy to the chief executive (appointed by the board) and the five other executive members (nominated by the chief executive and chairman). While initially concerned with oversight of the public service remit, following the 2003 Communications Act the board's function turned more to risk management which involved identifying risks and formulating actions to mitigate them (Channel Four 2006: 7–11).

Many had initially expected Channel Four to address a specific inadequacy of pre-existing broadcasting as identified by the 1972 Select Committee on Nationalised Industries, relating to the need for greater public participation and accountability (Lambert 1982: 55). The 1980 Act, however, stipulated only that the fourth channel should have a 'distinctive character of its own', leaving the detailed interpretation of this to the IBA, which was primarily concerned with the channel's commercial viability. As a publisher broadcaster, it could be argued that the high proportion of programming Channel Four commissioned from the independent sector enabled greater public participation. The number of separate companies commissioned as programme producers by Channel Four grew from 281 in 1984 to 539 in 1994, suggesting fears that a select few companies would gain dominance were ill founded (Channel Four 1994: 23). However, there is also evidence that Four's contestable funding system in driving budgets down eventually favoured bigger companies able to leverage economies of scale (Harvey 1994: 125–6). By 2008, Channel Four was commissioning from 300 companies, a quantity that still outranked other British broadcasters (Duncan 2007).

Despite developments in user-friendly technology, impediments to public participation in television continued. The more stringent application of professional technical standards that accompanied changes in the 1990s generally favoured professional independent producers over novices or community groups. With the advent of the Internet and websites like FourDocs, Channel Four's online site for aspiring documentary makers, along with the possibilities offered by user generated content and social networking sites, arguments about professionalism excluding access may seem quaintly archaic. Nevertheless, with the complexity of rights management in the digital era and increasing media conglomeration, the possibility of commercial values excluding small-scale creative content producers from where mainstream audiences gather remains real.

Channel Four's initial response in the 1980s was to initiate public participation through a number of programme forms; *Comment*, and the three minute *Viewpoint* slot following the evening news, gave individuals an opportunity to voice their opinions on topical issues; *Right of Reply* offered viewers the right to voice their complaints in the presence of programme producers, with the presenter acting as their advocate and the provision of video boxes around the country enabling the involvement of regional viewers; along with programmes produced through the grant-aided sector which had close community ties. Innovations in style also led to less editorialised documentaries and closer working relationships with subjects, giving the latter more say in the portrayal of their stories (Harvey 1989: 73). With Four now firmly focused on the youth audience and new digital developments offering a level of interactivity unimaginable in the 1980s, the Channel has been able to reinvent its commitment to public access, taking it in a number of divergent directions via multiplatform content.

Reinvention for the Digital Future

Under Michael Jackson, Four entered a highly commercial phase, applying strategic market analysis to identify the business opportunities of the digital era and launch Four as a 'cross platform media company' (Born 2003: 779). A former BBC controller under John Birt, Jackson pursued an aggressive commercial direction, conflating Four's commercial and public service roles in an endeavour to future proof corporate finances in the increasingly competitive digital media marketplace. Jackson's strategies included: two subscription channels – Film4 (as discussed earlier) and E4, a youth entertainment channel – launched in late 1998 and early 2001 respectively; a share in the horse racing channel, *At the Races*, a joint venture with BSkyB and Arena Leisure (later sold to Sky); another co-venture with the Sky in April 2001 which saw four channels launched on Sky's digital platform under the FilmFour brand; and 4 Ventures Ltd, an umbrella company established in February 2001, differentiating Four's commercial enterprises from the channel's public service operations (Born 2003: 780–1). By late 2001 however, an economic downturn had hit television advertising, prompting the collapse of ITV digital and a general decline in Channel Four's prosperity.

The next chief executive, Mark Thompson, served only two years as Four's chief executive before leaving to become BBC director-general in 2004; his successor, Andy Duncan, went on to make significant changes to the Channel's commercial direction. Having been the first chairman of Freeview, Britain's highly successful free-to-air digital terrestrial television (DTT) platform, Duncan was associated with its rapid success and deemed well equipped to re-establish Four in the digital environment. Under his management, Four launched a portfolio of new channels. In 2005, E4 was reinvented as a free-to-air digital channel alongside the launch of another new digital channel, More4, targeting an older demographic, followed by the re-launch of FilmFour as Film4 on the Freeview platform alongside the new 4oD time shifting channel in 2006. It became evident by then that subscription channels were not always in Four's best interests and that relative commercial success also posed a threat, with many commentators deriding Four's financial dependence on its popular reality show *Big Brother* as being in conflict with its remit. While seeking to retrieve Four's former image as an innovative public broadcaster, Duncan continued to launch more digital services in 2007 with C4+1, which offered repeats of various programs on a one hour delay, and C4 HD, offering main channel programming in high definition when available. Less consistent were a venture into radio – 4 Radio, subsequently divested in 2009 – that attempted to leverage Four's popularity with the youth audience, and a joint venture shared with Bauer Consumer Media Ltd in Box Television, a subscription music channel that was re-branded 4Music in 2008 (Channel 4 2008: 84).

The launch of the British version of *Big Brother* in 2000, one of Britain's first ventures into cross platform programming, proved Four's greatest financial boon but also attracted considerable criticism. E4 hosted extensive live coverage of the show in addition to the edited programme that screened on the main channel in prime-time, boosting the show's audience and the revenue earned, eventually returning up to 10 per cent of the Channel's revenue at the height of its popularity (Ellis 2008: 342). The controversy that arose during the fifth series of *Celebrity Big Brother* in 2007, when Bollywood star, Shilpa Shetty, who later emerged as the series' winner, was racially taunted on air by other contestants, ended badly for Four.

The racist insults resulted in 44,500 public complaints and an investigation by Ofcom, which found the broadcaster had breached the broadcasting code on four occasions by failing to properly contextualise the comments, which it found could have been done through the off-screen voice of Big Brother questioning the participants concerned. Ofcom's adjudication of the incident also reflected the dangers inherent in the independent production process, identifying that the production company had failed to alert the broadcaster to warnings evident in comments in earlier footage that had not been broadcast (Ofcom 2007). In 2009, Andy Duncan announced *Big Brother* would end with series 11 in 2010, noting new initiatives in creative drama and youth programming were planned to replace it. By the time of this announcement, income from *Big Brother* had declined as a result of a hefty increase in the franchise fee charged by Endemol in 2006 along with a drop off in audience in response to the onscreen racism of 2007 (Sweney & Holmwood 2009).

The announcement that Four was dropping *Big Brother* also came after Duncan had spent a year lobbying for public funding for Four. Having previously announced an impending deficit of £150 million in advertising revenue by 2010, Four's chief executive was seeking to remedy the problem via public subsidy through either top-slicing the BBC's licence fee, a strategy previously actioned by the Blair government to assist economically disadvantaged viewers' upgrade to digital, or a merger between Channel Four and BBC Worldwide. Although no doubt concerned that another commercial UK broadcaster would pick it up and profit from the show, the channel's management was well aware that highly remunerative reality television such as *Big Brother* was an uncomfortable fit with Four's pleas for public funding and promises to return to creative risk taking. In 2008, Duncan had presented the argument that the effect of digital switchover amounted to a funding gap of £100 million, the value of the analogue spectrum allocated free to Channel Four as a public service broadcaster, an 'implicit subsidy' worth '15–20% of turnover' at its height. Duncan's argument continued:

> Channel Four will therefore require a revised funding model to deliver its public role in the future. We remain open to the best model of support for the organisation – whether another form of indirect support, to replace the value of gifted analogue spectrum, or some kind of direct public subsidy. We are however clear on the criteria that should be used to assess the various options i.e. to ensure they are efficient and flexible, accountable and transparent, and to protect Channel 4's editorial independence and ability to deliver its public purposes. (Duncan 2007)

Under the 2003 Communications Act (schedule 9), the public service remit of Channel Four is stated as: 'the provision of a broad range of high quality and diverse programming' which in particular demonstrates innovation 'in the form and content of programmes'; appeals to a 'culturally diverse' society; makes a significant contribution to programmes of an 'educational nature' and 'educative value'; and that exhibit a 'distinctive character' (Channel Four 2006). The site of ITV's Schools Programming on Four in the 1980s, Channel Four Schools was launched in 1993 and re-branded 4 Learning in 2000. Educational content is an area that has leant itself to reinvention in the digital era, with multiplatform projects offering ways of optimising viewer/user engagement along with production and distribution costs and opportunities for cross promotion; for these reasons it is also a potentially lucrative field for commercial media. Moving its £5 million educational programming budget for 14–19 year olds away from linear television programming to the online environment, Four has opted for interactivity and multiplatform projects where game structures, social networking, user generated content and blogs can be adapted to educational purposes. Four's submission to the BBC Trust's Review of BBC services for younger viewers, following the complaints about the BBC's digital education site, reflects its conflicted status as a complementary commercial public broadcaster competing with the BBC in the digital era. Making well argued claims for its 'strong connection with younger audiences' in its projection of an 'authentic, non-judgmental attitude', and for its pioneering role in multiplatform programming, Four's submission contends that the BBC should not compete with Four for this age group and should instead target areas of market failure. Yet complementing and providing competition for the BBC is a key *raison d'être* for Four.

Under Duncan, the channel launched an 'innovation pilot fund, 4iP', aimed at stimulating the development of new digital media such as video games dealing with topics across 'the arts, democracy and sport' (Channel Four 2008). Certainly Four's expertise in commissioning multiplatform programming for teens is evident in projects such as *Battlefront*. The basis of a Channel Four television series on youth related issues such as cyber bullying, the *Battlefront* website invites individuals to share their stories through video uploads or comments, providing a flexible and engaging social forum in which youth can choose their own level of participation. Innovative arts content developed through Four includes the digital animation site, 4mation, a co-venture with Aardman Animation, a portal site for would be animators to reach an audience and network with other animators. Four's role in educational content production was again raised by government in late 2009 with the Digital Economy Bill recommending that Channel Four 'must participate in the making of relevant media content that appeals to the tastes and interests of older children and young adults' (PACT 2009).

Of course much of Four's documentary output could also be deemed educational and has included some landmark television. In 2008, a programming strand, *The Big Food Fight*, marked a campaign to challenge Britons to think about what they eat. The series included cooking commentary from Channel Four presenters such as Jamie Oliver, along with insights into farming practices and nutrition, ultimately culminating in *Gordon Ramsay: Cookalong Live*, in which 500,000 viewers participated, resulting in supermarkets selling out of key ingredients. The series also had some notable impact on British eating habits with a 50 per cent increase reported in the sale of organic chicken (Channel Four 2008). The three part documentary series, *Embarrassing Bodies* and *The Sex Education Project*, similarly offered a social payoff with its website providing additional educational video content and forums for viewer participation. Such public information campaigns are able to reap the benefits of both television and online platforms, maximising audience and word of mouth publicity via television's mainstream reach, and offering opportunities for individuals to personalise and expand on that information through participation online.

As a publisher broadcaster commissioning the bulk of its local television and multimedia content from Britain's independent production sector, Four has filled an important role in nurturing British production talent and continues to do so in the digital era. In 2008, Pricewaterhouse Coopers estimated that Channel Four's activities contributed £2 billion annually to the UK's creative economy, supporting 22,000 jobs (Channel Four 2008). Channel Four has been at the forefront in according producers digital and secondary rights, overriding the code of practice implemented under the 2003 Communications Act to renegotiate the terms of trade agreement with the independent production sector's membership body, PACT. Four reserved any claim to a share of secondary rights to those programmes for which it had contributed special input. In 2009, Four's relatively generous terms of trade drew a salvo from the Conservative party's shadow culture secretary, Jeremy Hunt, who said Four should make its own programmes rather than outsource them so that it could 'make more money from exploiting hit programmes' (Sweney 2009). Hunt's comment raised a possible new conflict for the channel between its role in nurturing the independent sector and its need to maximise sales from commissioned programming and creative content as advertising revenues decline.

A much awarded broadcaster for both its services and programmes, Channel Four's creative pulse continues to beat in its digital initiatives. In 2005, Four produced a website, Four Docs, for aspiring young documentary makers. Now a collaboration with the Britdocs Foundation which arose in Four's documentary department and brokers philanthropic funding, Four Docs provides a platform for screening short documentaries and micro-docs as well as providing a generously stocked resource including: a blog listing news, events and reviews; a history of the documentary genre; an archive of classic documentaries, along with downloadable guidelines covering technical, legal and funding issues as well as advice on how to exhibit and distribute your documentary. Another of Channel Four's many micro-sites, *Disarming Britain,* a collaboration with the social networking site, Bebo, brought a new digital interpretation to Channel Four's tradition of stranded programming by which a theme is employed to tie multi-genre content together for block scheduling. As a multiplatform project coinciding with Britain's Street Weapons Commission chaired by Cherie Booth, *Disarming Britain* explored the increased use of street violence and weapons amongst youth. The project connected a television drama, a documentary, a television debate, a game, and user generated content (UGC) in the form of short web videos and blogs, along with a partnership site on the social networking site, Bebo. Nearly six million watched or used some part of the television series while the website drew 10,000 visitors a day and the YouTube clip got 60,000 plays (Channel Four 2009: 43). Representing a more focused form of multiplatform content, the Castleford Project entailed a reality television series, *The Big Town Plan*, which took five years in the making. Comprising four one hour programmes, the series, which was the brainchild of television presenter and architect, Kevin McLeod, set out to engage community participation in town planning in the small economically depressed town of Castleford in west Yorkshire. Along the way, Channel Four's initial £100,000 investment was used to leverage another £14 million in support from 18 various partnership organisations ranging from national agencies to more local groups, eventually attracting a further £200 million in commercial and residential investment (Channel Four 2009: 71). Focusing on four separate developments in the town, the series tracked the town's regeneration as design consultants teamed up with the citizens of Castleford to help them plan their town's future. The website provides a record of each stage of the project between 2003 and 2008, and an opportunity for viewers and the town residents to exchange views on the changes made.

As a distinctive complementary service, Channel Four initially 'extended the range of political ideas and cultural forms available through television' (Harvey 1989: 61). It has also proved the viability of the publishing model, breaking with the bureaucratic constraints and professional elitism that characterised the BBC/IBA duopoly, providing opportunities for wider representation. In the 1980s, Channel Four's difference to other broadcasters was visible in endeavours to bridge minority and general audiences by mainstreaming special interests in innovative programme forms. While this extended viewers' diversity of choice, representation of diverse voices was more problematic. The need to sustain a reasonable audience share and the editorial function of the commissioning system were at odds with narrowcasting and opinionated programming.

Catering for diverse tastes and interests often involves annoying or offending some viewers while pleasing others and thus necessarily attracts controversy. While Channel Four has pushed the boundaries of public tolerance, redefining 'good taste and decency', it appears to have become less radical in defending the interests of ethnic minorities since the 1990 Act. In 2002, Four's department for multicultural programmes was abolished. The closure marked a watershed in the way that Four represented cultural diversity and is seen by some as driven by commercial interests, bowing to a more conventional agenda and signalling a retreat from its original proactive anti-racism stance:

> Once a pioneer in introducing the idea of anti-racism into the liberal project, the channel now assumed a more customary position, using the language of integration. Of course, in many ways, specialist minority programming did work against public services broadcasting principles of universality. This approach is always in tension with, on the one hand, the 'struggle for recognition' and, on the other, the critique from neo-liberalism that it represents a drag on the market. It is open to the idea that there is no payoff from an apparent engagement of political debate into structural questions of redistribution in the economic sphere. It also calls into question the idea that 'difference' can be the basis for effective political agency. (Malik 2008: 347)

Instead of a separate department for representing minority ethnic cultures, the issue of minority representation was delegated to an editorial manager for diversity whose role was to persuade independent producers and commissioning editors to reflect diversity in the channel's programming. The strategy was ultimately deemed flawed, with one producer observing, 'it's very hard to change the culture around commissioning', and was eventually replaced by a multicultural commissioning editor position. In early 2009, Channel Four announced the appointment of Oona King, a former Labour MP and prime ministerial advisor, as its new head of diversity (an appointment some inferred as intended to win political favour for the channel's efforts to secure public funding). Four also announced that it had allocated 'primetime slots supported by ring-fenced budgets to produce programming' to develop 'multicultural ideas and talent' and reflect 'social diversity'. The renewed investment in programming for cultural minorities followed concerns regarding the 'perpetuation of a parallel lives scenario' associated with fears that a generation is growing up with 'little attachment to mainstream culture' (Hundal 2009).

In the late 1990s under Four's more commercial agenda, the channel's 'difference' was often defined through controversy. Replacing innovation and experimentation, this commercial trend, which drew bigger audiences, accelerated in the digital era. In 2007, the need for balance provided justification for investment in *The Great Global Warming Swindle*, a documentary by Martin Durkin representing the views of climate change sceptics which controversially misrepresented the opinions of a number of scientists who appeared on it. Channel Four's website claimed the film was 'an important part of the wider debate on the causes of climate change' (Channel Four 2007). Media commentators, however, were unconvinced with George Monbiot of the *Guardian* noting: 'The science might be bunkum, the research discredited. But all that counts for Channel 4 is generating controversy' (Monbiot 2007). The accusation followed years of public criticism of Four over its pursuit of ratings with the populist reality hit *Big Brother*.

In June 2007, Andy Duncan announced that 'Channel 4 had embarked on a major review of its role and purposes as a public service broadcaster for the digital age' (Channel Four 2009). Reasserting Four as an innovative public service broadcaster in his subsequent report, *Next on Four*, Duncan set out new initiatives: the new pilot fund, 4IP, to support public service content in digital media; and the encouragement of new talent and new voices; along with initiatives to assist smaller start-up companies and regional producers. The report, intended to inform decisions by Ofcom on Channel Four's remit and funding in its Second Public Service Broadcasting Review, went on to note anachronisms in the channel's existing legislative requirements, which defined Four 'purely in terms of the core channel' and omitted its contribution to the creative economy.

By mid 2009, two important policy documents, both Ofcom's Second Public Service Broadcasting Review (2008) and the Digital Britain Report by Lord Carter (2009), had considered the issue of public funding for Four noting the options already discussed: a merger with the commercial broadcaster Five, a suggestion strongly opposed by ITV; a merger with BBC Worldwide, strongly opposed by the BBC; and top-slicing the BBC, also opposed by BBC management. While endorsing the benefits of retaining the channel as a public service broadcaster with a special updated remit 'championing and promoting creativity and new talent across all digital media', and acknowledging Four's funding problem

through the endorsement of a proposed merged with BBC Worldwide, the Digital Britain Report nevertheless left the matter open for further negotiation and debate, noting the potential problems such a merger might pose for competition policy (Carter 2009: 146–8). In September 2009, having failed to seal any agreement between Four and BBC Worldwide, Andy Duncan resigned as Four's chief executive. In January 2010, chief executive of multichannel UKTV, David Abraham, was confirmed as Duncan's replacement. The possibility of public funding for Four remained a subject of surmise at the time of writing, with the proposal of a merger with Channel Five also being mooted as in the interests of Five's German owner RTL given the downturn in advertising revenue, and as a likely outcome by some at the Royal Television Society's Cambridge Convention in September 2009 (Robinson & Brown 2009b). While either proposal would involve big changes for Four, a merger with Five would have substantial impact on its public service status and functions.

The remit and the structure by which Channel Four was constituted was a compromise between two opposing lobbies, those advocating an ITV-2 with complementary scheduling to ITV-1, and the TV 4 campaign which wanted freer access to public communication. Channel Four has been viewed as trialling the demise of public service broadcasting by testing the viability of a low budget, commercially funded system. Four's publishing model is often presented as a solution to the BBC's high overheads and led to the establishment of the 25 per cent independent production quota. Some have argued 'that the only way to preserve the tradition of public service broadcasting in an age of increasing competition is to encourage the development of public service values in the independent sector' (Docherty et al. 1988: 175). Certainly the relatively high standard of British commercial television has commonly been attributed to government regulation and institutional cross-pollination of public service values. However, with the growth of the independent sector and the spread of multichannel media that institutional culture is fading. The publishing model has driven the casualisation of the television production workforce with increasing numbers of producers competing for finite resources. Instilling public service attitudes to innovation, quality and diversity in this divided, competitive environment seemed like an uphill battle in 1990, but has been increasingly embraced since 2006 by key Channel Four commissioning staff keen to reinvent Four as a multiplatform media 'service with a difference' for the digital age. Given the historical narrative around public service funding – which cast the publisher model and then subscription as solutions to the licence fee – there is some irony that Four's future may now depend on either top slicing the licence fee or merging the broadcaster with the BBC's commercial arm, BBC Worldwide.

The combination of commercial funding and a public service mission places distinct limits on the full representation of dissenting viewpoints, carrying the obligation to accommodate advertisers' needs to target specific demographic groups, which infiltrates and colours all, as John Keane observes: 'advertising is a scavenger that feeds upon others to make itself a universal language' (Keane 1991: 88). As a complementary service, Channel Four has never carried the same expectations from the public as the BBC and thus cannot be measured on equal terms with the BBC's comprehensive remit. Despite the shortcomings of its constitutional form, however, Channel Four's remit and commissioning system have opened up new ways of engaging special and general audiences, developing greater commonality of experience through extending the narrative and aesthetic scope of the television medium. If the plea for public subsidy in return for a renewed commitment to a public service direction eventuates, the Channel Four brand will obviously help to keep Britain at the forefront of public service media provision – as a free-to-air cross platform media company delivering diverse, innovative, multicultural content, and as an international brand associated with creative risk-taking in film, comedy and documentary production – bringing valuable complementarity and competition for the BBC. One important area where there might have seemed to be ample scope, in education, has already proved problematic with the BBC Trust's withdrawal of BBC Jam following complaints from commercial competitors of unfair competition, as related in the pervious chapter. While the rising interest in digital educational content from the commercial sector might suggest that children are being well served by the new media, this is not the case in television. In 2009, the UK trade body, PACT, estimated that 'less than 1 per cent of children's programmes broadcast in the UK are made in the UK' (PACT 2009). In early 2010, the report of a House of Lords communications committee chaired by Lord Fowler confirmed the trend, with an estimate that spending on children's programming had fallen by 48 per cent since 2003 and recommending government assistance through tax incentives (Wray 2010). Four's strong connection with the youth audience built through its mix of comedy, music and reality programming, and unique relationship with the independent production sector gives it an obvious edge in reversing this trend. Whether or not Channel Four gets to contribute to this reversal will depend on political will and how its current funding crisis is resolved. What remains beyond doubt is that there is still a role for a public television broadcaster delivering a service with a difference.

Chapter 4

The ABC – 'The National Broadcaster'

Introduction

Austrialia's first public service broadcaster, the Australian Broadcasting Corporation (ABC), is frequently referred to as the national broadcaster in reference to its instrumentalist origins. Initially the Australian Broadcasting Commission, it was established as a radio broadcaster in 1932 following the government's decision to nationalise the existing 'A' class radio stations, leaving the lesser 'B' class stations to the private sector. Although modelled on the BBC in terms of its purpose and goals, the Australian Broadcasting Commission Act established public broadcasting within a dual system, leaving scope for the development of the commercial radio sector rather than copying Britain's state monopoly. As a public corporation the ABC's role was to deliver radio services across the nation, something existing operators had failed to provide (Inglis 2006a: 15–17).

A similar approach was applied to television which arrived relatively late in Australia due the Liberal Prime Minister Robert Menzies' reluctance to engage with its challenges. On winning the 1949 election, Menzies dumped the outgoing Labor Government's plans for a non-commercial national ABC television service like the BBC's monopoly model. Opting instead for the dual system implemented in the Television Act of 1953, Menzies legitimised his choice by establishing a Royal Commission, even though the key decision was already made and legislation drafted. In line with the recommendations of the Royal Commission, the ABC was allocated responsibility for delivering a national television service which, given Australia's geography and uneven spread of population, was not a viable commercial venture. This responsibility, however, bought no special privileges with ABC television launched in 1956 alongside two commercial competitors in Sydney and in Melbourne, just in time to host Melbourne's Olympic Games. Firms with existing newspaper interests subsequently acquired all the commercial television licences (Inglis 2006a: 193–5). Originally the Australian Broadcasting Commission, the ABC was re-instituted as a corporation in 1983, in accordance with the recommendations of the 1981 Committee of Review of the Australian Broadcasting Commission chaired by Alex Dix (the Dix Committee).

Identifying elements of the ABC's uniqueness, cultural relevance and future viability, this chapter explores Australia's national broadcaster from four perspectives: cultural ethos; the evolving relationship with audiences; the struggle for funding; and mechanisms for ensuring accountability.

Non-commercial, Mainstream and Minority

Under the ABC Act of 1983, the non-commercial status of ABC television is guaranteed by a prohibition on the sale of airtime for advertising. The ABC Charter, section 6 of the Act (1983), requires that the broadcaster (as one side of the dual broadcasting system) must remain non-commercial and deliver 'specialized' programming, but must also remain a mainstream player alongside its commercial competitors – providing programming of 'wide appeal' – directing the broadcaster to perform a difficult double act. Within Australia, the Corporation's functions include the provision of 'innovative and comprehensive broadcasting services of a high standard', of programming that contributes 'to a sense of national identity', that is informing and entertaining and reflective of 'the cultural diversity of the Australian community', along with 'programs of an educational nature'. The ABC is also directed to broadcast particular types of programmes to countries outside Australia: 'news, current affairs, entertainment and cultural enrichment', intended to facilitate 'awareness of Australia and an international understanding of Australian attitudes on world affairs', and to service the information needs of Australians travelling abroad. Additionally, a separate coda directs the ABC to nurture 'musical, dramatic and other performing arts' within Australia. With reference to these various functions the ABC is also directed to: consider the services of the commercial competitors; endeavour to balance programming of wide and specialized appeal; take account of Australia's multicultural character; and consider the separate responsibilities of the states in delivery of educational programming (ABC 2008).

The ABC's role thus involves a national service that reflects Australian culture and identity, targeting the mainstream while also being complementary, innovative and diverse, and servicing the needs of minority, special interest audiences. Although given no special consideration in the charter, indigenous Australians receive special mention in the ABC's guidelines on Editorial Policies, which notes a 'responsibility to reflect, to the wider community, issues and developments affecting indigenous Australians', and that 'significant cultural practices of indigenous Australians should be observed in content and reporting' (ABC 2008d: 66). While ABC radio, which includes multiple rural, city and national services can arguably do all of this, it has been a much harder act for ABC television.

The requirement for balance between 'wide appeal' and 'specialized' minority interest programming always posed a considerable challenge, particularly given it had to be achieved while also taking account of what commercial competitors are doing – a directive that simultaneously invites both a market failure and market competitive approach. Over the years, expectations of the ABC have undergone several significant shifts. In 1962, the Senate Committee on the Encouragement of Australian Productions on Television (the Vincent Committee) defined the ABC as 'primarily complementary to the commercial stations', and specified the national broadcaster's importance in setting quality benchmarks in taste and in broadcasting. But by 1970 new emphasis was being given to ABC television's role in 'catering to both minority and majority audiences', on the basis that since the service was funded by all of the public, it should cater for all. Moran argues that this 'mix and balance' approach to minority/majority programming came to characterise ABC organisational culture, informing claims of balance between imported and local programming and of providing counter balance to commercial television. Conveniently flexible, 'mix and balance' justified almost any ABC institutional judgement by invoking either the audience or 'notions of professionalism and cultural vanguardism' according to political preferences (Moran 1992: 120–2), thereby offering a pragmatic solution to the double-headed remit.

While the ABC prospered under Gough Whitlam's Labor Government, which invested liberally in Australian arts and culture, funding cuts and other problems under the following Liberal-Country Party Government of Malcolm Fraser (1975–1983) were eventually aired before the 1981 Committee of Review of the Australian Broadcasting Commission chaired by Alex Dix (Davis 1988: 2). Focussing on internal shortcomings, the Dix Report's primary recommendation was that the ABC be restructured as a corporation. The 1980s proved equally turbulent, with the ABC unable to redress declining audience numbers. In 1986, following 'parliamentary accusations of poor financial management' and a public outcry by ABC staff over management intervention in a *Four Corners* programme on New Guinea, the ABC chairman, Ken Myer, resigned followed by the managing director, Geoffrey Whitehead. David Hill, the newly appointed chairman, immediately assumed the management role vacated by Whitehead without the formalities of a selection process (Whitehead 1988: 187).

ABC television's independence is best represented by its flagship news and current affairs service, which along with its role as national broadcaster has attracted a high level of public trust (Newspoll 2007). News remains ABC television's most consistently high rating programme, arguably due to its independence and freedom from commercial interests. Nevertheless the history of ABC television current affairs includes incidents of political interference and of management self-censorship, or 'pre-emptive buckle' as such practices have become known amongst ABC staff.

As chairman of the Commission when the new medium was launched, Sir Richard Boyer (1945-61), sought to secure 'a position of special independence of judgement and action' for ABC television arguing for discretion over 'political or controversial matters'. It was something he subsequently died fighting for when Menzies blocked production of an Intertel documentary – *Living with a Giant*, a Canadian perspective on US /Canadian relations – on the grounds that it dealt with a 'matter of international delicacy' (Inglis 2006a: 248). The new chairman, Dr James Darling (1961–1967), subsequently agreed to programme vetting by the Department of External Affairs. Another low point occurred in 1963 when the Post Master General (PMG) asserted his right under the Broadcasting and Television Act to stop a programme going to air. The programme, a BBC interview with the former Prime Minister of France, Georges Bidault, marked the first time the Act had been used in that way. The action was widely criticised in the press and the veto was not invoked again (Inglis 2006a: 248–395; 2006b: 7).

The ABC has played a leading role in television current affairs, primarily through *Four Corners*, a show based on the BBC's *Panorama*, launched in 1961 and still running in 2010. Originally a magazine format, *Four Corners* evolved into exploring single topics in depth, covering both national and international issues, fulfilling a unique role on Australian television and winning record audiences – regularly 'up to one tenth of the population'. Those working for the programme have often had to fight for its independence; in the early 1960s, government restrictions prevented crews from covering stories in New Guinea, Indonesia and China. The programme was also handicapped by the requirement for management permission to approach a federal politician for comment. However, during the Vietnamese War, despite Australia's participation, managing director Talbot Duckmanton, supported by the ABC Commission, maintained balanced news reporting on the ABC on the understanding that 'extravagant, unrestrained or inflammatory language' would be avoided. The policy came into being in 1966 following an ABC broadcast of an interview with Ho Chi Minh, which the federal Cabinet deplored (Inglis 2006a: 217–8; 264).

Throughout the 1960s there were other incidents of 'pre-emptive buckle': a government minister sought and was given a right of reply; a *Four Corners'* reporter was taken off the programme because of complaints from the Return Servicemen's League (RSL); the ABC's assistant general manager, Clement Semmler, endorsed parliamentary criticism of a story that opposed capital punishment; and the ABC failed to back the journalist, Rohan Rivett, when he refused to name his source in court. A further controversy reflecting the precariousness of ABC independence occurred in 1983 when an interview with James Nyaro, a rebel leader with the Free Papua movement, was cut from 'Borderline', a *Four Corners* story set in Papua New Guinea (PNG). Fearing Indonesian disfavour since Nyaro opposed Indonesia's acquisition of Irian Jaya (previously known as Dutch New Guinea), the PNG government appealed to the Australian government to intervene. While the Minister, Bill Hayden, considered it inappropriate to interfere, the Department of Foreign Affairs sent a 'message of concern' direct to the broadcaster. With the PNG government threatening to 'review' the position of the ABC's resident correspondent, the interview was judged as not integral to the story and subsequently cut. ABC staff, claiming political interference, protested, prompting the ABC board to over-rule the acting managing director, Stuart Revill, which in turn prompted the managing director, Geoffrey Whitehead (1984–6), his deputy, Stuart Revill, and the chairman, Ken Myer, to all threaten to resign until a clarification of roles resolved the situation (Inglis 2006a: 221–2; 2006b: 59–61). The incident reflected the different concerns and priorities of ABC staff and management.

Another key programme in the history of ABC current affairs was *This Day Tonight* (*TDT*). Based on the BBC's *Tonight* show and fronted by a popular host, Bill Peach, *TDT* ran from 1967 until 1978 and brought an irreverent approach to the news, provoking politicians, creating controversy and winning viewers (Turner 2005: 28–48). Having pioneered a courageous, inquiring and popular form of television current affairs, *TDT's* success, as ABC historian Ken Inglis observes, was to prove elusive:

With it died the hope that the ABC could win audiences as large as any commercial competitor's by expressing its own best qualities: intelligence, honesty, guts and good humour. (Inglis 2006a: 424)

In the 1980s, with the newly appointed British journalist, Jonathon Holmes, as its executive producer, the hour long *Four Corners* reasserted the ABC's independence and leadership in television current affairs with a series of ground breaking exposés. *The Big League* (1983) uncovered a conspiracy involving football and politics and corruption in the NSW justice system, implicating the long serving NSW Premier, Neville Wran, and eventually prompting a Royal Commission. The NSW chief justice, Murray Farquhar, was subsequently convicted of conspiring to pervert the course of justice and sentenced to four years gaol (Inglis 2006b: 27). Exposés in later years included: *The Moonlight State* (1987), which exposed corruption inside the Queensland police force, again prompting a Royal Commission resulting in the gaoling of the Police Commissioner; and *Bondy's Bounty* (1989), which exposed the off-shore shelf companies used for tax evasion by the Australian entrepreneur, Alan Bond. Such scrutiny was not always welcomed by government and *The Big League* was viewed as anti-Labor by many in the Hawke Labor Government. Prior to the 1984–5 budget, when ABC funding cuts were expected, Geoffrey Whitehead received a list of incidents that Prime Minister Bob Hawke considered evidence of ABC bias against the Labor Government. When *The Age* reported the 'censorship hotline' between government and the ABC, the Minister, Michael Duffy, keen to maintain ABC autonomy, demanded of his party that the broadcaster's statutory obligation to be independent from government be either honoured or changed (Inglis 2006b: 182; 99).

The directive to reflect national culture involved the costly and risky business of local drama production, in addition to documentary and other cheaper magazine forms. Serving a predominantly English-speaking nation, Australian broadcasters have had access to a vast range of British and North American programming at relatively affordable prices. That this has been a disincentive for commercial broadcasters to invest in the business of local production is well known, with legislation – the Australian Content Standard – imposing a quota of 55 per cent of local content in prime-time commercial television schedules. Although the ABC is not subject to the quota, there has been an expectation for at least half the ABC television schedule to be local content and for local drama to be a prominent part of that. In 1986, managing director David Hill (1986–94) set a target of doubling local drama production to 100 hours by 1989; this was subsequently achieved by Sandra Levy, head of television drama at the time. Inevitably budget dependent, finance available for drama production waned under the Keating Labor Government and the Howard Coalition Government, prompting concerns about its decline and the trend towards co-productions, with the needs of co-financiers diluting indigenous content. The four part mini-series, *Come in Spinner* (1989), based on the novel by Florence James and Dymphna Cusack about the lives of three women living in Sydney during World War Two, was the 'last major drama project' fully financed by the ABC. Drama production commissioning at the ABC under Sandra Levy, Penny Chapman and later Sue Masters contributed some highly popular and successful programming: *Mother and Son* (1984–94) written by Geoffrey Atherden and starring Ruth Cracknell and Gary Macdonald, was a bitter-sweet comedy about old age and caring for someone with Alzheimer's disease; *Brides of Christ* (1991) written by John

Alsop and directed by Ken Cameron reflected 1960s Australia through a group of nuns running a boarding school; *The Leaving of Liverpool* written by John Alsop and Sue Smith and directed by Michael Jenkins related the story of English children sent as migrants to Australia. Other longer running series included *GP* (1988–96), which explored various social issues through the lives of doctors in a Sydney medical practice and *Phoenix* (1992–3), a gritty Melbourne-based crime series that drew on real investigations. While the volume has waxed and waned, ABC television dramas have been among the nation's most awarded and provided a training ground for writers, directors and actors across the film and television sector; as Inglis observes, such efforts were also generally achieved by 'doing more with less' (Inglis 2006b: 188–90; 259). From a high of 100 hours of Australian-made drama, the ABC's performance had slipped to just 17 hours by 2008 (Meade 2009).

The call for the ABC to reflect multiculturalism arrived relatively late, articulated only after the Dix Report's introduction of a charter invoking diversity, innovation and national identity (Inglis 2006b: 7). With the establishment of SBS as a multicultural television narrowcast service by the Fraser government in 1980, the ABC's sense of obligation to deliver wide and minority appeal was inevitably eased. The broadcaster's on-screen representation tends to reflect the Anglo-Australian background that typifies the bulk of ABC viewers, with few non-Anglo presenters. In 1992, a survey of ABC drama found ethnic minority representation 'woefully absent'; between 1975 and 1990, only eleven out of 233 productions included multicultural subjects (Inglis 2006b: 251). In 1993, the ABC was also criticised by its National Advisory Council for the 'quantity, scheduling and content of programmes involving Aborigines' and for the late scheduling of *Blackout* at 10.30 pm (Inglis 2006b: 252). Established in 1987, the Indigenous Programs Unit began producing television documentaries then magazine series, with *Blackout* commencing in 1989 followed by *Kam Yam, Songlines* and *Message Stick*. By 2009, *Message Stick* was screening three times per week across ABC1 and ABC2. In 2003, in a bid to better communicate the needs of indigenous Australians, the ABC's indigenous staff established a formal indigenous advisory committee, the Bonner Committee – named after the ABC's only Aboriginal board member, Senator Neville Bonner – to advise on indigenous issues (ABC 2008b). With Aboriginal people generally represented as disadvantaged on prime-time television, the indigenous cultural programming on the ABC has a critical part to play in building cultural bridges.

The representation of cultural diversity noted in the charter also infers other special interests, which along with promoting the arts and educating and informing have been a key marker of the ABC's difference from other commercial television broadcasters. Specialist programming reflects another side to delivering diversity, and although content areas such as science and the arts may not have been especially well served, they have nonetheless been far better served than on Australia's privately owned free-to-air commercial television channels. ABC television's science programming began in 1961 with *University of the Air*, but soon took an original direction in 1963 with Professor Julius Sumner Miller demonstrating scientific principles in *Why is it So,* enlivening classroom experiments with enthusiasm and a quirky dramatic flair. In 1981, *Towards 2000* brought a more populist look to science with an attractive team of globe trotting reporters exploring the future implications of new developments in science and technology. From 1985–2001, the ABC returned to representing the more serious side of science with *Quantum,* which screened in mid-week prime-time until it was axed in the brief but turbulent period during which Jonathan Shier (2000–1) served as managing director. The cancellation of *Quantum* invoked the wrath of ABC staff who saw it as threatening the future of in-house production, and who along with a number of eminent Australian scientists added their voices to 'Save the ABC' rallies held across the nation in April 2001. Following a short-lived experiment in the outsourcing of science programming with *Aftershock,* in-house science production was reinstated. A new team of scientist/reporters investigate contemporary scientific developments on *Catalyst,* which has retained the mid-week, prime-time-slot (ABC 2009).

The arts have fared rather less well than other specialist areas partly because of definitional vagueness about what actually constitutes 'art', with high culture sometimes eclipsed by popular culture content, and also because of the need for commentary and review, as well as the exhibition/performance of new and original works. Nevertheless, a 2004 report for the Community and Public Service Union on ABC arts programming found a 'proud tradition' in arts programming had been 'central to the way ABC television saw its public service remit', with arts magazine programmes included in prime-time schedules since the 1980s. *Express* (1997–9) and *The Arts Show* (1999–2001) were highlights of the ABC's prime-time arts programming. Screened in mid week, late evening timeslots, they won far better audiences for the arts than weekend afternoon timeslots (Jacka 2004).

In response to low ratings and a belief that the arts were commonly viewed as elitist, ABC arts programming policy changed in 2000. A new strategy, 'arts by stealth', saw arts content 'smuggled' into the schedule via other programme strands, largely documentary slots. Although this policy arguably promoted the arts to the mainstream audience, it left arts communities underserved, providing no prime-time commentary or review of contemporary developments in the arts. In her 2004 report on ABC arts programming, Liz Jacka asserts that prioritising ratings means 'making scheduling decisions on the basis of the methodology of dollars per audience member', thereby neglecting the broader cultural and social role that an ABC television arts strategy could potentially fulfil (Jacka 2004: 1–30).

Between 2004–9 ABC arts programming had some prime-time rating successes among them *Operatunity OZ,* which borrowed the Channel Four format, blending a low culture, reality-TV, game-show format with the high culture art form, opera. Following several short-lived experiments with arts panel shows, a new strategy emerged with a prime-time documentary strand, *Artscape,* launched in 2008, mixing local and imported documentaries along with a series of cross platform collaborations with other government arts agencies, offering a new take on 'wide and specialised appeal'. Screening on the main television channel, ABC1, *Artspace* alternated popular, high culture and indigenous subjects while more diverse coverage of the arts was delivered on ABC Online – new works of various kinds, artist profiles and reviews, along with opportunities for user interactivity and feedback. A strategy for the broadband future, delivering both popular and serious content, it also fitted the ABC's straitened finances. In 2007, another prime-time arts documentary series, *Painting Australia: Three Artists, Two days, One landscape*, integrated scenery and a master class while representing the work of several local artists, and another innovation, the *First Tuesday Book Club*, conceived a popular book discussion format for the small screen, having run continuously for over two years at time of writing. By October 2009, changes to ABC arts programming were on the agenda again with media reports of television arts coverage being reduced and 'shunted online'. While the online platform offers a cost efficient means of delivering minority-interest, public service goals such as promoting the arts, complaints from arts lovers seem likely to continue until broadband connection is more accessible (Quinn 2009).

While educational programming and children's television were often conflated at the ABC, adults continuing education tended to be neglected. One early venture produced in collaboration with the Australian Vice Chancellors Committee titled *University of the Air* (1961–1966), although it offered no degree or diploma, revealed the challenges of making educational television engaging. On the other hand, school broadcasts found a more ready, captive audience with *Behind the News (BTN)*, which began in 1968, serving upper primary and lower secondary classes and proved very successful. When the cash strapped ABC dropped BTN in 2003, there was a media outcry and teachers and students protested, winning the programme's reinstatement in 2004 (Inglis 2006b: 210–349; 553–4).

Television for pre-school children, traditionally a strong justification for public funding given the general neglect of commercial providers, is where the ABC really hit its mark although not without controversy. The locally produced *Play School,* which began in 1966, later spawned the super-stars, *Bananas in Pyjamas,* who went on to have their own show in 1992 – now syndicated around the world and ABC Commercial's biggest money earner. Another early pre-school hit, *Mr Squiggle,* featuring a puppet with a pencil nose who 'made pictures out of squiggly lines sent in by little viewers', became Australia's longest running children's television series, screening for forty years from 1959–99 (Inglis 2006a: 211; 260–1). The ABC also played a key role in the worldwide success of the pre-schoolers' rock band, *The Wiggles*, distributing their original CD and backing their TV series. Broadcasting a considerably greater volume of children's programming than any other free-to-air television station, ABC television adopted the brand, *ABC for Kids*, later truncated to *ABC Kids*.

A Changing Relationship with Audiences

The ABC's obligation to deliver a national service underlines the technical difficulties and expense involved in delivering broadcasting across Australia's island continent. Servicing the 'bush' is fundamental to the role of the ABC because much of rural and regional Australia will never be a viable market for commercial providers. Thus a universally accessible broadcasting infrastructure enabling national audience reach was a primary aspiration for the first decade. ABC management eventually found that while quality and diversity differentiated the ABC, audience size definitely did matter, even though it perhaps shouldn't. As one of four (and later five) free-to-air television broadcasters in Australia's dual system, the ABC would never perform as well as the BBC on which it was modelled, yet it was troubling that even the aspiration of 20 per cent of the audience remained illusive.

In 1964, concerned about the small number of viewers watching the national broadcaster, newly appointed general manager, Talbot Duckmanton, initiated a campaign to renew the ABC audience, and began watching ratings in the same way as the commercial channels (Inglis 2006a: 258). The new policy to 'target audiences' was carefully differentiated from commercial broadcasting policy:

> The Commission emphasises that it is not advocating that the ABC try to obtain a mass audience at all times, but that it should obtain the maximum possible audience for the types of programmes it presents. (Inglis 2006a: 258)

Radio and television were disintegrated and efforts made to increase on-screen pace: programme promotions replaced the musical interludes of seagulls flying or kittens playing that characterised early ABC television, and on-screen presenters or 'hostesses' were also removed and announcers with Australian accents recruited (Inglis 2006a: 258). Identifying Australian content as a key to building audience, Duckmanton achieved a 30 per cent increase in local drama, pushing it from 100 hours to 130. In 1966, a drama department, a science unit and a special projects unit to make programmes about the arts, humanities and adult education were all established. By 1968–9, the ABC schedule was 52 per cent Australian. Current affairs programming played a key role in building the ABC's national audience at this time with *Four Corners* host Michael Charlton voted *TV Week's* most popular personality in 1962, although it was *This Day Tonight* (*TDT*), hosted by Bill Peach, that gave the ABC its biggest audience boost (Inglis 2006a: 259; 299; 217; 266–7).

In 1973, McKinsey consultants advised the ABC to concentrate on audience 'reach' over audience 'ratings'. Rather that the proportion of people tuned in at any particular moment, reach measured how many people had tuned in during the course of a week. In 1983, ABC television recorded a reach of 65 per cent. However, with the ABC's prime-time audience share around only 11 per cent in 1984, Whitehead secured board endorsement of a ratings target of 20 per cent in prime-time. While the objective was to attract viewers beyond the ABC's traditional audience – younger viewers from different socio-economic backgrounds – the goal created obvious tension with the charter's directive to balance mainstream and minority appeal. Although audience ratings under-reported ABC performance in several areas, level of viewer appreciation, measure of rural audiences, school audiences and later or repeated viewing via videocassette recorders (VCRs), it nevertheless became accepted that some engagement with the ratings system was necessary; the difficulty lay in getting the balance right (Inglis 2006b: 67–9).

Whitehead also set a target of 65 per cent for Australian-made content; this was problematic and challenged the ratings target, with imported British programmes such as *To the Manor*

Born and *Yes Minister* drawing the ABC's biggest audiences. In 1984, the new director of television, Richard Thomas, set about reaching this new target by building connections to the independent sector thereby leveraging Australian Film Commission (AFC) funding which increased the number of hours, although as Inglis notes, by 1991 local content was still only 56 per cent of the schedule (Inglis 2006b: 70–1; 208).

During the late 1980s, when people meters replaced diaries as the method of recording television viewing, ABC ratings rose, indicating that diarists had 'understated their watching of ABC programs' with Sydney's 11.5 per cent in 1989–90 rising to 15.7 per cent in 1990–1. With local productions becoming the ABC's most popular programmes, the ratings rise appeared to vindicate Whitehead's push for local content. The policy continued under David Hill (1986–94), who articulated his goals as getting 'more Australian programs on television and more people watching them' (Inglis 2006b: 207; 148).

By 1994, the ABC's prime-time ratings were shifting between 12 and 16, with weekly reach rising to 70 per cent and with 90 per cent of Australians tuning in every month. The locally made, romantic drama-comedy *SeaChange* provided the ABC with a ratings hit in 1998–9 as two million plus viewers tuned in to see how the city-barrister turned country-magistrate, Laura, played by Sigrid Thornton, was faring in her love life. It was a rare coup in which the national broadcaster trounced Channel Nine's *Sixty Minutes* in the ratings. From 2002 to 2005, the local comedy series *Kath and Kim,* about the exploits of a mother and daughter in deepest suburbia, achieved similar ratings success for the ABC before moving to Channel Seven. By 2007, the ABC's average prime-time rating share was 17.6 per cent (ABC 2007a).

Although the struggle to strike a balance between minority and mainstream interests – between complementarity and competition – to boost ratings while still serving diversity and quality is the main story regarding the ABC and its audience, the more recent and compelling sub-plot for ABC management is audience renewal and the need to build its youth audience. In the 1970s and 1980s, the ABC had considerable success in winning youth audiences. Following on from the early popular music series Johnny O'Keefe's *Six O'Clock Rock*, the ABC launched *Countdown*, fronted by Molly Meldrum in 1974. *Countdown,* which provided an hour of pop singers miming their own songs, was the most popular programme in the 10 to 17 age range, winning an audience of two million and reaching three million at its peak (Wilmoth 1993: 249). With *Countdown,* television gained primacy over radio as the medium that broke new music, and in that leading position the ABC was able to gain first option on music video clips to the angst of commercial broadcasters. When the era of CDs and music videos ultimately killed studio music shows on television, the ABC was unable to reinvent *Countdown's* popularity.

Since 2000, there have been fewer local drama and documentaries in prime-time, with the prioritisation of youth interests bringing an increase in local comedic offerings, often studio-based: *The Glass House,* a panel-based talk show featuring comedians; *The Chaser's War on Everything,* commentary on current affairs combined with skits by a team of comics; *Summer Heights High,* a mockumentary set in an high school in which creator Chris Lilley plays three dysfunctional characters; *Spicks and Specks,* a popular music quiz in which regulars are joined by performers/entertainers; and *The Gruen Transfer,* a quirky exploration of the world of advertising.

Non-Commercial –Struggling to Stay Pure

When it was first established Australians initially paid a licence fee for the ABC. While such an arrangement is commonly seen as offering greater autonomy from government, its abolition in 1974 changed little, for the ABC had in reality been financed from general revenue since 1948. Annual appropriations requiring yearly submissions involved considerable amounts of staff time and resources and frustrated long term planning. After protracted lobbying, triennial advance funding was fully established under the Hawke Labor Government (Inglis 2006a: 337; 2006b: 104). This alleviated political pressure on the ABC, providing freedom from the immediate threat of financial penalties. Nevertheless successive governments of both sides of the political divide have slashed ABC funding, driving an internal culture of doing more with less. The performance of ABC television is increasingly validated by comparisons with commercial stations in terms of programme cost, staffing and ratings points (Withers 2002). Unsurprisingly, in response the institution has explored alternative forms of subsidy – sponsorship, subscription, an international service, merchandising and licensing to varying extents – yet remains a non-commercial channel:

> The ABC remains one of the few major public broadcasters in the world not to seek revenue from private equity, paid advertising or the sanctioned sponsorship of programs… Whatever the ABC's flaws, faults, failings and pretensions, which are undoubtedly many and are freely admitted, the aspect that most sets it apart from other broadcasters is its lack of a commercial imperative. (Dempster 2000: xiv)

Under the Hawke and Keating Labor Governments' embrace of neoliberalism many public sector institutions such as the Commonwealth Bank were privatised. The survival of the ABC as a public service institution is attributed to determination of the Minister, Michael Duffy. Accommodating the ideological ethos and the economic climate of the times as the Australian dollar dropped, the ABC was downsized instead. Prime Minister Bob Hawke openly displayed his disdain for the ABC: making his Address to the Nation on the commercial broadcaster, Channel Nine, when attempting to stall the dollar's decline; and proposing to amalgamate the ABC and SBS, creating a new broadcasting entity as a cost saving measure (Inglis 2006b: 100–29).

The Hawke Government's decision to finance a communications satellite, Aussat, also impacted on the ABC, bringing a five per cent reduction to the ABC's 1985–6 budget and a one off cut of AU$20 million. ABC staff promptly campaigned for the reinstatement of the AU$20 million, imposing a ban on the use of Aussat. When the Minister, Gareth Evans, subsequently established a Review of National Broadcasting Policy, the ABC managing director, David Hill, declined to participate, instead launching the '8 cents a day' campaign to raise public awareness of the ABC's funding constraints and to hopefully frustrate the proposed cuts (Dempster 2000: 13–14). With ABC board support, the campaign controversially placed on-screen advertisements fronted by ABC presenters between programmes, successfully building public support. A survey soon revealed 50 per cent of the public would happily pay 35 cents.

The Minister's Review of National Broadcasting Policy released its discussion paper, *Funding the ABC*, in February 1988, offering three options but tacitly endorsing one that recommended the division of ABC activities into three categories – charter, non-charter and peripheral – in order to re-structure funding. Only charter activities, news, current affairs, drama, the arts, and children's and educational would be eligible for full government funding. Echoing the neoliberal thinking of the time, this market failure model would have marginalised the ABC. Having secured ministerial confirmation that ABC acceptance of the Review's proposals was not linked to government concessions – triennial funding and a reversal of the AU$20 million budget cut – the politically astute David Hill promptly announced the latter at his National Press Club address two days later. The ABC board subsequently rejected the Review's proposals, 'reaffirming its commitment to comprehensive broadcasting' (Inglis 2006b: 161–5).

The decline in ABC funding continued in the 1990s with the Hawke and Keating Labor Governments cutting ABC income by AU$120 million at the beginning of the decade. Elected in 1996, John Howard's Coalition Government imposed a further AU$55 million cut in the 1997–8 appropriation. A survey of ABC funding for the decade 1988/9 to 1998/9 revealed a decline of 20.3 per cent. The cuts prompted recourse to alternative sources of revenue, bringing mixed results. Through 'retailing, licensing, publishing, program sales and hiring ABC facilities', the ABC shops and ABC Enterprises increased income by AU$23 million from 1995/96 to 1998/99. While other strategies – sponsorship, pay TV, ABC International and the sale of ABC content to commercial online news providers – yielded new controversies and offered new leverage for the broadcasters' opponents (Dempster 2000: xv; 340–1).

In late 1994, the growing practice of 'backdoor sponsorship' in outsourced ABC productions was exposed on commercial television by Channel Nine's *Sunday* programme in a story titled, 'ABC for sale'. A subsequent enquiry into 'backdoorism' instigated by the ABC board found breaches of editorial guidelines in sponsorship deals involving both in-house and out-sourced productions, and led to a review of editorial guidelines and the resignation of the director of television, Paddy Conroy. The exposé also led to the establishment of a Senate Select Committee into ABC Management and Operations to investigate 'backdoorism' and other matters. Broadcaster and former staff-elected director on the ABC board, Quentin Dempster, recounts management victimisation of a key whistleblower, John Millard, then a reporter, and the separate enquiry that denounced the prejudicial treatment Millard received as a result of his efforts to defend editorial independence at the ABC (Dempster

2000: 138–70). Millard's case signals the role of in-house *corps d'esprit* in upholding public service values in the face of management pragmatism. Finding breaches of ABC procedures regarding backdoor sponsorship, the Senate Committee acknowledged that long term under-funding had encouraged the practice, but stopped short of recommending any increase in appropriations, opting instead to advise against any decrease (Inglis 2006b: 345–7).

Proposals for 'corporate underwriting' or sponsorship recurred throughout ABC history. The issue was raised in the Dix Report in 1982, then by the Department of Finance in 1984, again by the Minister of Finance, Peter Walsh, in 1985 (Inglis 2006b: 105; 107), and by Evans' Review in 1988. The proposition of sponsorship or commercial funding for the ABC built strange alliances – with the ABC advisory councils, listener and viewer group Friends of the ABC, and commercial television and radio broadcasters, all united in their abhorrence of the idea. Ultimately opposition from the powerful commercial sector and public antipathy make this form of public cost saving politically unwise. While ABC Online has also been kept free from advertising, concerns were voiced regarding advertising on the ABC's mobile platform on the ABC's own *Media Watch* programme in September 2008. Although subsequently dismissed by ABC management as part of existing licensing arrangements, the *Media Watch* website later noted management confirmation that 'ABC Commercial is developing commercial sites in partnership with third party companies' (ABC 2008c). The re-branding of ABC Enterprises as ABC Commercial has presumably been undertaken to ameliorate damage to the ABC's independent status, to ensure more rigorous separation from the corporation's non-commercial arm.

The ABC's most adventurous commercial initiatives began in 1992 with Australia Television International (ATV), a broadcasting service into Asia, and a pay TV venture, conceived as subscription television arrived on Australia's broadcasting horizon after years of resistance by the commercial television lobby.

Showcasing Australian culture across the Asia-Pacific region, ATV was launched in February 1993 with a seeding grant of a AU$5.4 million from the Keating Labor Government on the understanding that the venture would be self sustaining. With the ABC board persuaded that the editorial integrity of free-to-air services would be protected, and the ABC Act (1983) amended to permit corporate sponsorship, ATV began broadcasting English language programming – the ABC's back catalogue and news and current affairs – into fifteen countries, with the aim of serving 'Australians' interests in the region'. While the service was popular with Australian diplomats and opinion leaders across the region, unrealistic predictions of potential advertising revenue, which was slow to build, left the service threatening to become a drain on the ABC's domestic budget, prompting then Minister, Michael Lee, to instigate a review of ATV finances and prospects in 1994. However, with the 1995 report *Our ABC* from the Senate Select Committee's inquiry into ABC management operations supporting the ATV venture, both the ABC board and the government endorsed it (Dempster 2000: 98–105). Following the John Howard led Liberal-National Coalition victory in the 1996 election, the new Minister, Senator Richard Alston, announced ATV would be sold to a commercial network, a decision duly confirmed by the

Howard Government's review of the ABC, *The Challenge of a Better ABC*, undertaken by businessman, Bob Mansfield. While under Channel Seven's control from 1998 to 2001, ATV continued to receive government funding; the service returned to the ABC when Seven chose not to bid in 2001.

The ABC's plans for pay TV were also handicapped from the beginning by rigid terms imposed by government with the Prime Minister, Paul Keating, refusing to mandate the ABC as a provider of subscription services which would have obliged the government to fund it. Reducing the ABC's proposed four channels to two via satellite, Keating offered set-up costs of AU$12 million conditional on additional finance being raised through the private sector. Envisaging a 24-hour news channel and a children's and family entertainment channel, the ABC established a subsidiary company, Arnbridge Proprietary Limited, which held the pay TV licence and sought commercial partners for Australian Information Media (AIM), a joint venture company in which the ABC was to retain 51 per cent. The other AIM partners were the Australian news media company, Fairfax Holdings, and Cox Communications, the American cable company, along with CNN and Viacom through content arrangements.

To make its pay service commercially viable the ABC had to 'bundle' its content with that of commercial providers for a 'proportion of the subscription revenue'. Even though entry into pay TV promised to expand news operations, ABC staff resisted the venture, eventually forcing a management guarantee of editorial separation from the public service arm, something that was nevertheless problematic given a single managing editor had oversight of all ABC news and current affairs. On 31 July 1995, when AIM directors were assembling to sign the agreement, News Limited chief, Rupert Murdoch, cancelled Foxtel's involvement without explanation, scuttling the deal. On 22 September, Murdoch and Channel Nine Network chief, Kerry Packer, announced a joint venture, *Sky News Australia*, a non-exclusive local pay TV news channel to be launched in early 1996. On 29 September 1995, AIM was formally wound up, its high tech digital news centre shut down and over 100 staff hired to operate the service sacked (Dempster 2000: 116–34).

There were various reasons underlying ABC involvement: ensuring plurality by continuing Australia's dual system across all broadcasting sectors; resisting the dominance of imported content; and generating income to subsidise free-to-air services. However, it seems likely the commercial direction taken would have invoked greater opposition from both media rivals and ABC supporters alike. The relatively slow uptake of pay TV in Australia and the ABC's contemporary lead in new media services has subsequently revealed that this was not a necessary bridge to the multichannel era, as then assumed.

Prior to the release of the report of Mansfield's government review, the ABC's managing director, Brian Johns (1995–2000), who knew of the Howard Government's plans to reduce ABC finances, released his own report, *One ABC*. Proposing re-integration of radio and television in preparation for digital convergence, embracing the notion of contestability in anticipation of pressure for increased outsourcing of production, and promising financial economies through job cuts to the tune of AU$27 million, Johns arguably diminished the review's impact (Inglis 2006b: 391). The media also pipped Mansfield to the post, with the

Melbourne *Age* leaking the contents of a 1996 Cabinet submission. In it the Minister, Senator Alston, had advised that contrary to an election promise to maintain existing levels of funding for the ABC and SBS, the review would define a 'narrower focus' for the ABC. This would enable even more severe funding cuts but make them palatable to the public while also increasing government influence over the ABC (Tingle 1997). Although he declined responsibility for any directive for a 'narrower focus' in the Cabinet paper, increased control of the ABC came to be seen as Senator Alston's main agenda as Minister.

Ultimately the Mansfield report, *The Challenge of a Better ABC*, resisted assigning the ABC a market-failure narrowcasting role, recommending instead that the broadcaster should continue to serve 'all Australians' and provide a 'wide mix of programming'. Impressed by the ABC's public support (his review received 10,615 submissions), he confirmed the importance of public service broadcasting and recommended retaining rules against advertising and sponsorship. In outlining how the ABC should downsize to achieve its 'narrower focus', he recommended four strategies: 'more outsourcing, less property, no "non-core" activities, and better management', estimating that the ABC could then function on a budget of around AU$500 million. Choosing not to endorse ABC plans for digital multi-channelling, Mansfield advised only 'modest' government assistance for digital conversion, funding not included in the 1997/98 budget (Inglis 2006b: 396; 597). Making no formal response to the report, Senator Alston left the ABC Charter as it was (any amendments to the ABC Act opened the possibility for a challenge in the Senate), but he did advise the board that any funding for digitalization was dependent on ABC property sales and increased outsourcing. The abolition of in-house production feared by protesting staff did not ultimately eventuate, with production space incorporated into new purpose-built central city facilities at Ultimo in Sydney and Southbank in Melbourne.

By the late 1990s, as noted earlier, departmental production budgets had declined dramatically across all genres, from AU$28 to AU$17 million in drama, leading to increasing proportions of imported British content in the television schedule during the eleven years of Howard Coalition government. The 1990s also saw the departure of several popular ABC shows to commercial television networks. There was also a dramatic decline in the number of staff employed at the ABC with a fifth departing over the two year period 1997/98 (Dempster 2000: 253). The ABC's managing director from 2000 to 2001, Jonathan Shier, a past Liberal Party member widely regarded as a political appointee with a brief to downsize the broadcaster, had an abrasive management style that saw a number of high level staff departures, but nevertheless secured the ABC's first funding increase in 17 years. The ABC's next managing director, Russell Balding (2001–6), took a different tack in handling the funding shortfall, requesting an independent audit to validate ABC efficiency and hopefully elicit increased funding. Widely leaked in the media, the subsequent 2006 KPMG Report on the ABC's funding adequacy and efficiency, although commissioned by government, was never made public. However, the Minister, Senator Coonan, did confirm on ABC television in March 2006 that the Report had found the broadcaster 'both efficient and chronically under-funded'. She went on to use the opportunity to raise the prospect of advertising on the ABC, something later dismissed by the Prime Minister. According to one leaker, the KPMG report 'provided a scathing assessment of funding levels and said funding after indexation needed to rise AU$48.1 million in 2008–9 in order for the ABC "to sustain its present outputs"' (FABC 2008).

Accountability

In the new millennium, accountability has become a battlefield for the ABC. Accusations of political bias brought pressure to prove impartiality in news and current affairs. On the other hand, the expectations of the diverse charter goals – to deliver wide-ranging specialist programming and Australian-made drama along with mainstream audience reach – have become increasingly problematic as resources diminish and costs rise with the need to engage in new technologies. Pursuing television audience ratings as a strategy for proving performance has invoked a fair amount of criticism for its threat to 'quality' and diversity (Dempster 2005: 101–7; Moore 2008; Jacka 2004: 18–23; Salter 2006: 4). In December 2008, the ABC announced its highest rating year on record, 'a prime-time free-to-air share of 17 per cent', anticipating no doubt that this would improve its prospects for increased funding in the next triennium (ABC 2008c).

In 2005, Quentin Dempster identified ten separate internal and external accountability regimes to which ABC journalists and programme-makers are subject: the ABC Act; the ABC board of editorial policies; the ABC code of conduct; defamation and contempt laws; the Internal Complaints Review Executive; the Independent Complaints Review Panel (ICRP); the Australian Broadcasting Authority (since restructured as the Australian Communication and Media Authority, ACMA); Audience complaints; Parliamentary scrutiny via Senate Estimates and questions with and without notice; ANAO audits of ABC accounts and corporate governance. While contradictory to their intent, this multiplicity of mechanisms offers government ample opportunity to pressure the ABC.

Procedures for assessing complaints and measuring performance themselves raise questions regarding transparency, PSB values (Moore 2008), and journalistic freedom (Nolan 2005). A letter leaked to the media in January 2000 written by the Minister, Senator Alston, to the ABC Chairman, Donald MacDonald, revealed a tacit agreement between the two to a number of new 'performance measures and benchmarks' not yet agreed to by the board, including: an annual meeting between the minister and the board to review performance; the setting of targets for ratings as a measure of programming accountability; and the establishment of a monitoring unit to enhance editorial responsibility. Then managing director, Brian Johns, denounced the measures as a push for 'tied funding', undermining ABC independence, and in breach of public accountability (Inglis 2006b: 460).

Accountability issues for the ABC during the eleven years of the Howard Government included allegations of 68 incidents of anti-American bias in ABC Radio National's coverage of the Iraq war in 2003, levelled by the then Minister for Communications, Senator Richard

Alston, and widely seen as a witch hunt. Writing in *The Australian* on 16 October 2006, Mark Day summarised their investigation: 'An exhaustive process involved the ABC's Complaints Review Executive (which upheld two of the 68), the Independent Complaints Review Panel (which upheld a further 17) and ultimately the former Australian Broadcasting Authority (which found a further four breaches of broadcasting codes)'. Following release of the ABA report, David Nolan reflected on the fairness of its findings in *The Age*:

> If one follows its logic, journalists should present information from press briefings, but should not question the motivations behind them. 'Spin', so central to modern warfare, can only be presented as information, even in a current affairs program – if, that is, it comes from our side. Presenters cannot, it appears, ask probing critical questions to elicit information and analysis from those 'on the scene', whether guests or journalists. Rather they must ask them to simply describe what they see, without touching on critical issues at stake. (Nolan 2005)

Other problems regarding accountability have included: the stacking of the ABC board through the appointment of politically partisan directors; the removal of the ABC staff-elected director from the board; the 2006 appointment of a new director of editorial policy to report directly to the managing director; and the decision of ABC Enterprises (now ABC Commercial) not to sell news footage of a Minister's remarks about asylum seekers to a documentary maker on the basis that it was for 'an advocacy or cause' (a ruling later withdrawn following protests by Australian documentary filmmakers). While public accountability is a critical marker for public service media organisations, differentiating them from commercial media companies, excessive monitoring and policing has the effect of intimidating staff, resulting in a culture of self censorship and timidity that is counter-productive. Ongoing accusations of leftwing bias at the ABC under the Howard Government appear to have had this effect:

> Senator Alston's attack on *AM* served as a salutary warning. The ABC has been muted in its criticism of government policy in Iraq ever since. It is now aware of the dangers of 'going too far'. On Iraq, ABC television is now more likely to conduct an interview with Christopher Hitchens, who knows next to nothing about the Middle East, than it is with Robert Fisk, a journalist of strong views but also a profound understanding of the region. (Manne 2007)

Another similar trend detected was a 'careful blandness' in ABC news and current affairs, as managers succumbed to 'pre-emptive buckle' and staff morale fell:

> It is not a question of left versus right as some critics of the ABC feebly contend. Nor is it a question about balance in the air-time allocated to adversarial voices. It is rather, a question of the lack of enough rigorous analysis, resourceful reporting and fearless exposure of what has been concealed. (Dempster 2005: 106)

In October 2008, the Minister, Senator Stephen Conroy, announced an overhaul of the appointments process for the ABC board based on the Nolan Rules used by the BBC. Board positions at the ABC and SBS would be widely advertised as they become available, and an independent panel at arms length from government will apply merit based criteria to short list candidates for the Minister, who may also make his own appointee with the proviso that he justifies this to Parliament. The Rudd government has also committed to restoring the position of the ABC staff-elected board director.

Reinvention for the Digital Future

By 2010, the ABC had expanded to three free-to-air channels, ABC1, ABC2 and ABC3, delivered via the DTT platform Freeview, with ABC4, a 24-hour news channel due in midyear. Nine years after the transmission of DTT began in Australia, the national broadcaster was at last being encouraged to develop narrowcast channels and online initiatives, pursuing what many have long seen as its natural role. While DTT and the Internet offered so many possibilities for enhancing and expanding public service broadcasting, it was politics and ideology rather than technology that held sway.

The take-up of digital television in Australia has been a slow and laboured process, with a lobbying war dominated by the powerful association of free-to-air broadcasters, Free TV Australia, driving policy-making. Having been granted additional free spectrum during the analogue/digital simulcast period, Free TV Australia (then known as FACTS) convinced the Howard Coalition Government to mandate high definition television (HDTV), a more 'spectrum-hungry' form of digital transmission, which in limiting the availability of spectrum for new media services also constrained the emergence of new competition for advertising revenue. Following protests from aspirant new media companies, the 1998 HDTV decision was adjusted in 2000, with a change to the technical standard for HDTV to accommodate standard digital television as well, to enable new service providers to enter the market via DTT as licensed 'datacasters'. However, the interests of commercial broadcasters were protected again, at the expense of both SBS and the ABC, by the imposition of restrictions on the kinds of content genres and their durations that could be provided by these new datacasters. While both the ABC and SBS eventually secured the right to 'multichannel' rather than simply datacast, in the Broadcasting Services Amendment (Digital Television and Datacasting) Act (2000), there were also limitations imposed on this. The public broadcasters were not allowed to broadcast any 'national news, sport or drama programs (other than "occasional stand-alone drama programs")', although a helpful 'laundry list' was given of the kinds of permitted content along with the advice that there were still 'innumerable opportunities for innovative broadcasting'. When DTT was launched in Australia in 2001, all free-to-air broadcasters were required to meet a quota of 20 hours per week of HDTV within two years, but there was no new additional content to attract public take-up, and the custom built set-top boxes cost AU$699 (Given 2003: 140–86). To facilitate the roll out, the government invested AU$1 billion in digital transmission facilities for the ABC and SBS but offered no additional funding for programming.

While government policy manoeuvring and lack of funds appeared intended to keep the ABC out of digital television, ABC managing director, Jonathan Shier, opted to launch two digital channels, ABC Kids and Fly TV (a youth channel), in the ultimately vain hope of forcing extra funding from government. Up and running in late 2001, the first year of digital television transmission in Australia, the channels were funded via a 'series of one-off savings'. Reaching 500,000 and 300,000 viewers respectively, ABC Kids and Fly expanded the ABC's delivery of Australian-made content and provided a training ground in digital technology for 35 new staff. When the ABC board decided to close the two channels, Senator Alston, for whom the closure represented some embarrassment given they offered the only new content available on DTT, intimated that it had been presumptuous of the ABC to expect extra funding for them (Marriner & Needham 2003).

In 2006, with household digital uptake at only 30 per cent, the Howard government finally acted to improve the situation, announcing their Digital Action Plan to 'drive take-up of digital television', and nominating a DSO date of 2010–12. Among other measures the plan *Ready, Get Set, Go Digital*, enabled the addition of an HDTV multichannel by removing the requirement to simulcast HDTV programming, and removed the genre restrictions on multichannelling by both the ABC and SBS (DICTA 2006). This relaxation of the constraints that had been implemented to protect the commercial sector renewed hopes for a dedicated children's channel, which ABC management proposed as ABC3 in 2007.

Finally seeing the role the ABC could play in driving digital uptake, the Howard Coalition Government promised dedicated funding for the children's channel if returned in the November elections. With ABC funding firmly on the 2007 election agenda, the Labor Party committed to 'ensuring adequate funding' for 'high quality broadcasting services, free from political and commercial interference', and also importantly promised to 'ensure that the national broadcasters are able to exploit the full potential of new technology to deliver attractive and innovative content over digital television and the internet' (Rudd 2007). In June 2007, ABC managing director, Mark Scott, released a document titled *The ABC in the Digital Age – Towards 2020,* in which he proposed a 'suite of six channels'. In making a case for expanding the ABC, Scott outlined six ways it would continue to serve the public interest: by reflecting Australia; as a universally available service; as a site for local issues; delivering quality and diversity; being innovative; and engaging with international concerns. The proposed suite of six channels forecast a re-branding exercise with the main channel renamed ABC 1, while ABC2, then largely a catch-up channel was to be re-focused on factual, comedy, arts and entertainment, with at least 50 per cent Australian content. The new proposed channels included: ABC3, a non-commercial children's channel, also targeting at least 50 per cent of Australian content from all genres; ABC4, a news and public information channel screening press conferences and parliament plus news; ABC5, an educational channel, with English language instruction, and connecting to digital resources for schools; and lastly ABC6, offering the best of international programming (Scott 2007). In April 2008, at the Prime Minister's *Australia 2020 Summit*, Scott again promoted his plans for more digital production for ABC2, for the commissioning of ABC3, and floated the concept of the suite of six digital channels, outlining what constituted a leading role for the ABC in driving public take-up of digital television. The ABC children's channel and the development of ABC online as 'a virtual platform for the delivery of the arts in society' were among the ideas noted in the *Australia 2020 Summit Report,* and picked up by the government for further exploration in a review of public service broadcasting (Commonwealth of Australia 2008: 201).

Senator Stephen Conroy, the new minister responsible for broadcasting, announced a review of the ABC and the SBS in October 2008, publishing a discussion paper, 'ABC and SBS: Towards a digital future', and calling for public submissions. The timing of the Review was very significant, with the 2009–12 triennium funding for both broadcasters to be announced in the May 2009 budget. The discussion paper raised a number of issues under seven broad themes: the role of public broadcasting; the place of new technologies and how they should be used; the possibility of facilities sharing between the ABC and SBS; the relative importance of informing and entertaining with regard to the ratio of imported and local content; education, skills and productivity; social inclusion and cultural diversity, presenting Australia to the world; and the efficient delivery of services. Attracting over 2,400 submissions, the Review signified the continuing importance of PSB to the public, although the number was markedly down on that received by the Mansfield Review in 1996.

Despite the impact of the global financial crisis on federal government revenue, the 2009–12 triennium funding brought the ABC long awaited funding relief with an additional AU$167 million (Conroy 2009). This funding included: AU$67 million for a non-commercial, free-to-air, dedicated digital children's channel; AU$70 million to increase Australian-made drama to reach an annual target of 90 hours by 2012; and AU$15.3 million for 50 new regional broadband hubs – 'websites and portals that will operate as town squares…for local communities to communicate and where the ABC will encourage and assist user generated content' (FABC 2009).

Launched in December 2009, the children's channel, ABC3, which targets 8–12 year olds and broadcasts from 6:00 am until 9:00 pm, plans to be scheduling at least 50 per cent of Australian content within the next three years. With Australian made drama on the ABC having shrunk to only 17 hours in 2008, and previously been as low as only three hours in 2005, the increased funding was particularly welcomed by the production sector (Conroy 2009; Meade 2009), although it was also noted that this was down from the peak of 100 hours of first run Australian-made drama in 1993 (NLA c1994). The Screen Producers Association of Australia (SPAA) commissioned a paper in March 2009 to examine the economic benefits of just such an injection of funding, announcing, 'increasing the spend on ABC productions from 30 to 90 hours would create around 1000 full time jobs in the industry and a total of 2500 jobs across the Australian economy', noting too the additional benefits arising from increased skills (SPAA 2009). The funding for broadband hubs was particularly significant, acknowledging the ABC's new media role as being more than just a supplement to its broadcasting activities. In an ABC media release on the budget windfall, the managing director, Mark Scott, declared:

> The new funding for broadband content affirms the ABC's role as Australia's town square – a place Australians can come to speak and be heard, to listen and learn from each other. Broadband funding puts the ABC at the centre of the new digital revolution; using fast networks to communicate new content with audiences in different ways and allowing the ABC to host content the audiences create themselves…It represents a significant down payment on the ABC's future as a media innovator. (ABC 2009b)

The ABC initiatives that received the additional funding in the 2009 budget were all among items specifically requested in the ABC's submission to the DBCDE 2008 Review of the ABC and SBS (ABC 2008b). However, the funded items did not represent the complete list, with the public affairs channel, ABC4, envisaged as 'carrying live feeds of major events, press conferences and Parliament both online and on digital television' left unfunded. This reflected the surprising development of December 2008 when the ABC's digital ambitions took a knock with the Rudd Government signing a deal endorsing a privately-owned public affairs pay channel, A-Pac, apparently dismissing the ABC's proposal for ABC4 previously outlined at the Australia 2020 summit in April. A-Pac was launched in January 2009 by pay TV operators, Foxtel and Austar, with some suspecting the venture to be a gambit by the subscription sector to win additional spectrum from government post DSO. Described on its website as 'promoting discussion, democracy and debate', A-Pac provides limited downloadable resources for students on the Australian parliamentary system, and a link to a YouTube channel, Your Shout, inviting viewers/users to upload their thoughts on various issues on the promise that the best will be screened. It's not hard to imagine that the ABC would do this a lot better. As Margaret Simons observes, there is an implicit threat for the ABC in this precedent, one that has ramifications for its future digital ambitions (Simons 2009).

As digital technology transforms the business of television broadcasting, with the commercial free-to-air broadcasters facing falling advertising revenue as their audience share declines, the areas previously regarded as the ABC's special strengths are attracting new bidders. The government's deal with Foxtel and Austar was made despite the ABC's superior resources in news production – twelve international bureaux, 60 regional newsrooms, and a long history of being the country's most trusted source of news and current affairs.

Tensions between the ABC and the subscription television sector erupted again in March 2009 with the Sky News chief, Angelos Frangopoulos, indicating that Sky would be bidding for the Australia Television (ATV) contract when it came due in 2010. The international service has had a chequered history. When the commercial operator, Channel Seven, which had been running the service chose not to bid in 2001, the ABC took it over, re-launching it as *ABC – Asia Pacific*. Re-branded again as the *Australia Network* in 2006, the service continues to be funded directly from the Australian Department of Foreign Affairs and Trade, reaching 41 countries and 'twelve million viewers per month' across the Pacific and

Asia, including India (ABC 2007b). While such a service funded directly from DFAT raises potential issues for ABC independence, its outsourcing to Sky would set a precedence for further outsourcing. With Sky News chief, Frangopoulos subsequently calling for open tenders for all new television services such as the children's channel, it's an important political struggle for the ABC (Schulze 2009). The challenge from Sky prompted a speech on the value of 'soft diplomacy' by Mark Scott, who outlined ABC plans to extend ATV that would see the broadcaster: expand its news bureaux in the Asia Pacific to fourteen, 'more than either CNN or the BBC', making it the 'pre-eminent source of news and current affairs about and for the region'; expand its footprint to reach countries in Africa and the Middle East while also contributing additional bureaux; and to negotiate a new satellite deal to reach Latin America (Scott 2009). Undeterred by challenges from the subscription sector, the ABC announced in January 2010 that it would launch another digital channel, a 24-hour news channel to be broadcast on the ABC's HDTV spectrum later that year. The continuous news channel, which brings direct competition for Sky News, will run out of new studio built in the foyer of the ABC's Ultimo headquarters in Sydney.

While the struggle to expand spectrum rights and build on its portfolio of digital channels to better serve diverse publics is a politically fraught affair for the ABC, the broadcaster has played a pioneering role in the development of creative initiatives and innovations online. ABC Online hosts sites that address audiences according to age group, interests or geographical location, with content representative of every programme genre in addition to offering various sites for viewer/user participation. The first broadcaster in the country to podcast and vodcast, the ABC also provides catch-up services online via ABC iView, an application launched in July 2008 that delivered the country's first full screen, free-to-view television catch-up service. ABC Innovation also produces dedicated online projects one of which is Pool, a site for content sharing and social networking by Australia's creative communities. Following the devastating bushfires of Black Saturday in February 2009, ABC Innovation produced a media rich website and interactive documentary to document the events and the stories of survivors. Utilising the application ABC Earth, which uses geographical information software to overlay ABC content on Google Earth maps, the site serves as a record of the day, the progress of the fires, the media coverage and the survivors' stories. Incorporating audio clips, video clips, text and geo linked social media, the project migrated across several media forms. Video files integrated into the project later contributed a television documentary for the *Australian Story* strand, relating the recollections of two survivors, a brother and sister who lost their family and their home. As the producer of the project, which will in time become an historical archive, Priscilla Davies set out to experiment with new forms of digital storytelling to create meaningful, emotional engagement with the audience, but also to complement and build on the ABC's existing content and services for the affected communities (Davies 2009). The ABC has also begun releasing its archive online via the creative community site, Pool. As part of Creative Archive Australia (a programme of the Queensland University of Technology), which is exploring the possibilities for 'opening up' content from government institutions, the ABC has begun the slow release of content on selected themes from its archives (Simons 2009b). These and similar developments contribute to make the ABC a useful driver of broadband uptake for a government keen to see a national network established.

The remarkable achievement of the ABC is that despite its many trials at the hands of hostile governments from both sides of politics, it has kept its place in the centre of mainstream society. Market research in 2000 found the ABC to be the second most trusted organisation in the country (Inglis 2006b: 588). Managing director David Hill's maxim, 'doing more with less' – pursuing innovation despite the costs – in many ways typifies ABC management policy. It has probably been the ABC's saving grace, helping it to stay ahead of the new technology game, as now seen in Mark Scott's digital plans: a portfolio of six free-to-air digital channels; on-demand access to ABC programming via iView, the ABC's Internet television platform; along with a variety of online applications, some complementary to broadcast programmes and some dedicated new media content, inviting user generated content and social networking. The flaw in 'doing more with less' is, of course, that something has to give. That something has included locally produced drama, calculated as having fallen from 100 hours a year in its heyday to around 20 hours in 2007 (Manne 2007) along with a shift towards increased outsourcing. In 2008 the ABC announced 35 jobs would be cut from in-house production staff.

The ABC's increased funding for the next triennium announced in May 2009, along with support for ABC3, the broadcaster's second digital channel, and for 50 enhanced regional broadband hubs, signals official endorsement of the ABC's evolving identity as a multiplatform media provider. Although with much of the allocated funding actually withheld until after the 2010 election, there remains some uncertainty about the future of these initiatives. The Rudd Government's subsequent commitment to a National Broadband Network further strengthens the ABC's position as a principle player in the development of digital infrastructure. The declining quality of commercial media due to fragmentation, wider dispersal of the advertising dollar and the influx of private equity investors unprepared to take risks, has raised the value of the ABC's non-commercial service in the eyes of many. These circumstances pose rather different prospects for the future of hybrid funded public broadcasters like SBS, the subject of the following chapter.

Chapter 5

SBS – 'A Multicultural Service'

Introduction

When the Special Broadcasting Service (SBS) launched its television channel in October 1980, Australians were already served by three commercial television networks along with the Australian Broadcasting Commission (ABC). While the latter was screening mainly British programming supplemented with in-house current affairs, drama, special interest and children's programming in the spirit of a small scale BBC, the commercial networks were providing programming in populist, mainly US-style formats along with local news and mainstream sports coverage. Following the wave of immigration fostered by Australian government assistance in the post-war years, many new Australians from Europe and the Middle East found little they could identify with or understand on Australian television. Andrew Jakubowicz, a media academic and commentator who lived through the experience, described the ethnocentric viewpoint of the Australian electronic media in 1975: 'Accented English was unacceptable and sub-titled dialogue was permitted… only briefly…Where immigrants appeared they did so as objects…as problems to be solved' (Jakubowicz 1989: 108).

The Special Broadcasting Service, which began as a multilingual radio broadcaster, was intended to fill this gap. From the outset its supporters had divergent motives: lobbyists within the ethnic community were seeking both a political voice and cultural outlet; politicians hoped to woo the ethnic vote; and the government was looking for a way of integrating the ethnic community for reasons of social harmony and cultural enrichment. In addition, government support, Jakubowicz argues, was also motivated by a desire for greater social control (1989: 107). By the 1990s, the SBS had emerged as a nationwide alternative public broadcasting service, with the 'special' in its title subject to ongoing redefinition in response to social and economic change.

Balancing the role of multilingual narrowcaster with multicultural obligations (to reflect cultural diversity) and public service goals (to provide innovative, quality programming) has made defining the SBS target audience a delicate matter. With precariously low ratings, the institution's survival as the lesser of the country's two government funded broadcasters has been routinely threatened by talk of merger with the ABC. First proposed during the 1980s, when the Hawke government conceived it as a cost cutting exercise, merger with the ABC rose again during 2001 when Jonathon Shier mooted the idea during his short term as the ABC's managing director (Inglis 2006b: 134–5; 574). More recently the discussion paper – *ABC and SBS: Towards a digital future* – produced by the Department of Broadband

Communication and the Digital Economy (DBCDE) as part of the 2008 ABC/SBS Review, broached the topic again, questioning whether 'certain parts of the operations of the two national broadcasters' could be combined for greater efficiency 'without compromising their separate identities?' (DBCDE 2008: 41). While the final phrase signals government awareness of the broadcasters' essential differences, the ABC was sufficiently interested to commission the Boston Consulting Group to research the potential savings of amalgamation, subsequently announcing a merger was not being pursued (Harrison 2009).

Since 1991, SBS had been permitted to screen five minutes of advertising per hour in 'natural' programme breaks, resulting in the practice of 'block' advertising between programmes. In 2006, 'island' intra-programme advertising was introduced, sparking considerable public concern and the emergence of a lobby group, Save Our SBS. During the 2007 federal election campaign, the Labor opposition opposed in-programme advertising on SBS, describing it as serving to 'erode the fundamental tenets of public broadcasting', and following Labor's election victory the new Minister, Senator Conroy, requested a copy of SBS's legal advice on the matter (Cassidy 2007: 2008). In defence, the managing director of SBS, Shaun Brown, has highlighted how increased revenue has benefited local production, something that has been in scarce supply on both public broadcasters.

Operating like Channel Four along 'publishing model' lines with minimal in-house programme production, SBS television had to develop innovative strategies for programme sourcing and scheduling. These reflected both its brief to deliver a wide range of foreign language programmes and its low budget; SBS receives approximately a quarter of the amount of government funding that the ABC receives. In the 2009/10 to 2011/12 triennium, the ABC received AU$2.7 billion from the federal government while the SBS received AU$611 million (Conroy 2009). Since the late Eighties, the added costs of digitalization have brought pressure to increase entrepreneurial income. With its lean and hungry modus operandi and innovative approach, SBS has a flexible operating structure, which in the past appeared to offer some advantages in surviving the fragmenting digital environment, contributing a niche audience sensibility. However, with the global financial crisis of 2008/09 this advantage has been offset by acute demands on government revenue across society, raising the prospect of new financial constraints.

Still defined by its ethnic origins, the SBS Charter remains unchanged, although its interpretation has evolved to accommodate shifts in social and political values and management aspirations. Exploring the impact of this evolution on goals, audience, funding and accountability, the following discussion reflects on how such institutional flexibility is affecting SBS television's performance as a public service broadcaster in the digital era.

Breaking the Monocultural Mould

Ethnic broadcasting emerged from the joint efforts of ethnic community groups actively involved in developing the service and politicians conscious of the value of the ethnic vote. In 1974, having benefited from the ethnic community's election support, the Labor Government of Gough Whitlam initiated two non-profit radio stations, 2EA in Sydney and 3EA in Melbourne, to develop ethnic communities' English language skills and broaden their understanding of social services. With illiteracy another common problem for new Australians, the broadcasting platform offered solutions not covered by the ethnic press (Leong 1983: 7). Other factors identified as impeding integration were isolation and alienation, and broadcasting, enabling increased contact with home languages, offered a means of easing these. Formed in 1977 to administer the two community radio stations – 2EA and 3EA – the Special Broadcasting Service (SBS) eventually became an independent statutory authority in 1978, and was directed to provide 'multilingual broadcasting services and broadcasting for such special purposes as are prescribed' (Leong 1983: 8).

Ethnic television emerged from a 1977 election promise by Liberal Party Prime Minister, Malcolm Fraser, but initial plans for a pilot ethnic-TV broadcast on ABC downtime drew immediate opposition. The ethnic press feared competition for audience and advertising, while both Liberal and Labor politicians decried the expense of a second public broadcaster, and the ABC claimed it could provide the service more cheaply (Hall 1981: 85). The Victorian Ethnic Communities' Council also opposed the idea fearing government censorship and sought a service independent of SBS (Leong 1983: 9). Drawing poor audience response, the pilot broadcast prompted the Ethnic Television Review Panel (ETRP), established to report on how the service should be constituted, to adopt the concept of multiculturalism as a means of extending audience appeal. A second ETRP report revealed the SBS was widely perceived as a government propaganda organ, too vulnerable to government pressure and unable to deal even-handedly with politically controversial matters. The report recommended that a new Independent Multicultural Broadcasting Corporation (IMBC) be formed as a means of securing greater autonomy and long-term commitment to ethnic television. A senate committee subsequently ruling against the IMBC claimed the service would be a socially divisive 'electronic ghetto', recommending instead a second service for the ABC. Opting to proceed with his plans despite this rejection, Fraser oversaw the somewhat hasty launch of SBS television a mere six days before the 1980 federal election. The service was directed 'to complement and supplement the cultural and linguistic perspectives of other broadcasting sectors' and to 'give particular emphasis to meeting the specific needs of the ethnic communities', as well being 'accessible to the community at large' (ETRP cited in Leong 1983: 10).

Inadequate costing and rushed legislation created ongoing problems and left the institution vulnerable to government pressure. The application of public service employment practices, which was very much at odds with many of the organisation's goals, meant that new Australians were disadvantaged. Anglo-Australians dominated management and ethnic Australians were relegated to lower level, front line roles; one disenchanted employee noted the public service was:

Using SBS as an interesting place to send staff for work experience. Some of these people have been seconded from Parks and Wildlife, Fisheries and Immigration and Ethnic Affairs and have been moved into positions of authority over the television professionals. (Grenard 1982: 52)

In 1983, in response to poor staff morale and concerns of three Labor board members, a Committee of Review chaired by Xavier Connor was established to study the role and function of the SBS. Jakubowicz notes the opposing attitudes of the time:

One was a strategy which sought to resist change and encapsulate an often reactionary and patriarchal interpretation of a community's 'culture'. The opposing view argued that the SBS had a social role to play in aiding the participation of ethnic minorities in the social, economic and cultural life of Australia, and should be directly seeking to confront racism, reaction and conservatism. (Jakubowicz 1989: 115–16)

Established attitudes, however, by and large prevailed, with the committee failing to support an affirmative action programme for recruitment from cultural minorities. Although it did recommend the establishment of a new statutory authority, this decision was delayed for seven years.

The early goals of ethnic broadcasting were broadly twofold: to inform and educate ethnic groups about matters relating to the workings of Australian society and to ameliorate the sense of cultural isolation. 'Multiculturalism' added another dimension to these goals. It was the government's attempt to remould national identity into a form more acceptable for contemporary Australian society. Relinquishing Anglo-Celtic hegemony, the 'idea' of multiculturalism gradually accommodated second generation new Australians, paid attention to the culture of indigenous peoples, and began to acknowledge the nation's geographic situation and natural trading partners. For 20 years, the existence of non-English speaking Australians had been virtually ignored by television, their presence acknowledged occasionally through stereotypical characterisation in local drama. This 'electronic igloo' melted with the emergence of SBS (Jakubowicz 1989: 118).

The hasty launch of the television service and withdrawal of the IMBC legislation left SBS television without effective financial security, making long term planning impossible. Proceeding under guidelines established by the ETRP, SBS television developed a multilingual schedule that was 70 per cent imported programming, with English language local content – mainly in the form of news, current affairs and sport – making up the balance. The schedule was divided evenly between multilingual and English language programming, with all foreign language programmes being 'accessible' to the general audience through sub-titles. Despite public criticism, SBS-TV developed a loyal following in its first decade, largely due to innovative purchasing and scheduling strategies that served both minoritarian and mainstream multicultural objectives.

Serving the interests of ethnic fragments through homeland language programming was intended to sustain ethnic cultural identities. This was often compromised, however, by the need to reach a general audience to justify public funding. With some smaller communities receiving only one homeland language programme per year, the service was bound to leave some discontented. Low ratings among ethnic groups continued to threaten the identity of the channel which regularly faced criticism as catering for middle class, 'high brow' or cosmopolitan audiences. The spread of pan-ethnic, multicultural awareness provided a promising line of defence here and to this end, it was suggested that to engage more fully in the Australian multicultural experience SBS needed to open itself to a 'more authentic and critical immigrant voice' (Jakubowicz 1989: 125). By promoting the cause of multiculturalism, SBS has been able draw on a useful internal dynamic that enables 'it to continually transform itself, and permits it to develop a multipurpose character' (Kolar-Panov & O'Regan 1994: 142).

The growth of a second-generation immigrant population influenced social policy in the 1980s, contributing to the subsequent mainstreaming of multiculturalism. Marking a departure from its former ethnic focus, multiculturalism allowed the broadcaster to side step the difficult role of providing 'a forum for the neutral presentation of ethnic viewpoints' (Kolar-Panov & O'Regan 1994a: 166). Multiculturalism emerged as a policy under the Whitlam Labor Government when the colourful Al Grassby served as Minister for Immigration from 1972–74, and worked to establish ground rules for the human rights of new Australians from non-English speaking backgrounds (NESB), removing the remaining remnants of the White Australia policy. Known as the 'father of multiculturalism', Grassby was subsequently made first Commissioner for Community Relations under Whitlam, and pioneered the implementation of the Racial Discrimination Act of 1975. Under the Fraser Coalition Government, multiculturalism continued to be government policy but was given a much higher public profile under the Hawke Labor government after a shaky start. While this policy would ultimately advantage ethnic communities, subsequently eroding racism and discrimination, the fact that it was announced during cuts to the immigration intake – justified 'on the basis of economic rationalism' – outraged some in the ethnic community who viewed multiculturalism as bold political opportunism (Jakubowicz & Newell 1995: 140).

In 1986, when cuts to immigrant services and the proposal to merge SBS and the ABC prompted public protests, the Hawke Government, realising its political blunder, sought to remedy the situation by promptly announcing plans to develop an Agenda for Multiculturalism in consultation with the community. Launched in 1989 with the establishment of the Office of Multicultural Affairs, the Agenda provided the basis for new national goals for SBS leading to its reconstitution as a complementary, public service broadcaster serving interests and needs not met by the ABC. The Hawke Government's Agenda sought to mainstream multiculturalism in the interests of social justice, social harmony and economic efficiency, ultimately redirecting SBS towards a wider audience. Multiculturalism had been identified as the key to social harmony as early as 1981 when, addressing ethnic community leaders, Malcolm Fraser noted the concept's importance in preventing race riots like those that had set the inner cities of Britain alight that summer (Jakubowicz 1989: 107). By 1990, SBS had come to see its mission as:

> Contributing to a more cohesive, equitable and harmonious Australian society by providing an innovative and quality multilingual and multicultural radio and television service which depicts the diverse reality of Australia's multicultural society and meets the needs of Australians of all origins and backgrounds. (SBS 1990–3: 3)

However, there were underlying contradictions in this laudable goal. Of the three dimensions identified in the Multicultural Agenda, economic efficiency sat uncomfortably as a goal for public broadcasting. Much of the social policy that drove the development of SBS was essentially conservative and sought, through the promotion of multiculturalism and selection of board members, to control ethnic broadcasting, subverting class solidarity by appealing to other allegiances. Multicultural media policy promised cultural rights to minority groups. But rights were of two different kinds: (a) rights as an ethnic/minority fragment and (b) cultural rights as Australians to full participation in the social, economic and cultural life of the country (O'Regan 1994: 107). Delivery of the social justice dimension of multiculturalism was not necessarily compatible with building a 'cohesive, equitable and harmonious' society.

The new emphasis in the Multicultural Agenda had also been influenced by a review of National Broadcasting Policy, undertaken in 1988 by the Department of Transport and Communications (DOTAC) to determine future strategies for the multichannel environment promised by new media technology, which then referred to cable and satellite television. Having studied the effects of broadcasting deregulation in Italy and the United States and noted loss of programme diversity, the DOTAC committee recommended that the primary future role of SBS and the ABC should be to provide 'quality' programming, 'complementing' the commercial sector. It was also recommended that SBS's service reflect the multicultural character of the Australian community (Patterson 1992: 48).

Under the 1991 Act, SBS was established as an independent corporation with its own charter, which defined the principle function of the SBS as providing 'multilingual and multicultural radio and television services that inform, educate and entertain all Australians, and, in doing so, reflect Australia's multicultural society' (Commonwealth of Australia 1991: 6). Earlier ETRP-based policy had simply required that programming be 'accessible to all', which had been implemented through English subtitling. Adopting the ideals of the 1989 National Agenda for Multiculturalism, the 1991 Act directed the SBS to target all Australians. Thus, during its first decade, the role of SBS television shifted from providing multilingual, ethnic programming to delivering a nationwide, complementary, multicultural service.

An on-air marketing slogan in the 1990s – 'Bringing the world back home' – sought to capture the spirit of multiculturalism and to unite its disparate audience groupings – ethnic communities wanting programmes in their homeland language, cosmopolitan viewers wanting international 'high' culture, and various minority groups including indigenous Australians wanting special interest material relevant to their experience. In response to the government's mainstreaming of multiculturalism, SBS-TV changed its scheduling practice by dedicating two hours of prime-time (6.30 – 8.30 pm) to English language, actuality programming. This was justified as affording greater predictability for viewers and as affirmation of the Prime Minister's statement that SBS was for all Australians (Johns 1991: 18). News, current affairs and sport constituted most of the SBS's English language programming; the cost of drama, documentary and comedy being generally prohibitive, since SBS competed with prices paid by the far wealthier ABC. The policy change also of course had the great advantage of expanding the channel's potential audience, making public investment more politically acceptable.

Innovation has been the saving grace of this very meagrely funded television service, resulting in an international news bulletin that was regarded by many as the country's best. Unlike other Australian broadcasters who purchase from English language production organisations in the US and UK, the multilingual brief drove SBS to purchase foreign language programming from countries with no established film and television distribution systems. At international film and television markets, SBS also gained access to new sources of English language programming through PBS in the US and via Canadian and New Zealand broadcasters. When Channel 4 went to air in 1982, SBS offered a like-minded Australian destination for its documentary and drama productions (Ang et al. 2008: 176–89).

In representing local minority cultures, SBS invoked a more participatory style. In 1989, an Aboriginal current affairs programme, *First in Line*, was the first to give full editorial control to Aborigines and Torres Strait Islanders. SBS-TV host, Rhoda Roberts, became Australia's first Aboriginal presenter of a national prime-time current affairs programme. Dona Kolar-Panov notes, 'In presenting Aboriginal issues as cultural, inside a cultural political framework, SBS was able to pose Aboriginal cultural rights and articulate an Aboriginal politics outside public relations and welfarist standpoints' (Kolar-Panov & O'Regan 1994a: 158). Through news programmes like *Vox Populi*, SBS endeavoured to tackle 'the social justice issues of access and equity in multiculturalism' with locally produced items providing a forum for issues of concern to migrants and other marginalised groups such as gays, the disabled and the aged (Johns 1991: 18). The 'only multicultural and multilingual current affairs television programme ever produced in Australia', *Vox Populi* included some cringe-worthy moments but also helped to make the Special Broadcasting Service special, and in the words of producer, Voya Rajic, 'showing all Australia the Australians they never knew about'. Launched in 1986 and running for nine years, *Vox Populi* was not frightened of controversy, being 'among the first to investigate the issue of Aboriginal deaths in custody' and regularly exploring 'everyday racism, workplace exploitation and isolation' (Ang et al. 2008: 52–3). Through the practice of naturalising broken English in news and current affairs programming, SBS supported the growth of a cross-ethnic Australian identity (Kolar-Panov & O'Regan 1994: 139).

In 1996, almost ten years after Hawke first announced his Agenda, the Howard led Coalition Government disbanded the Office of Multiculturalism. The 'm' word fell victim to the 'culture wars', with the social policy subsequently replaced by the adjective 'multicultural' in the 2007 SBS Annual Report and 2007–12 Corporate Plan (Dawson 2008: 9). No longer the active designated agent of government policy, SBS shifted gear as its board assumed more commercial aspirations under the rubric of reflecting cultural diversity. In redefining its role during the years of Howard Government, SBS commissioned two extensive research surveys. The first, *Living Diversity* (2002), explored trends in multicultural Australia, while the second, *Connecting Diversity* (2006), investigated the experiences and attitudes of young Australians from diverse cultural backgrounds. The latter helped to legitimate pursuit of the youth audience, a strategy announced in 2003.

The existence of SBS alleviated pressure on other broadcasters to represent minority groups. While this slowed the breakdown of stereotypical representation on mainstream commercial television, SBS, as a symbol of multiculturalism has won wider social acceptance of cultural difference as 'normal'. On screen, SBS reflected a very different look to other broadcasters, lacking the staid, Anglo-ethnocentricity that characterised much of the programming on ABC television and the consumerist, American television culture of the commercial networks. SBS helped to make multiculturalism attractive, encouraging and enabling Australians to embrace their country's contemporary social reality with pride.

During its first two decades, SBS television sought to steer away from the comfortable and familiar, endeavouring to provide an alternative to mainstream programming. The authors of *The SBS Story* relate the role played by Bruce Gyngell, a professional manager from the commercial television sector who was appointed to set up the new television service, and subsequently had a profound influence on both the look of SBS television and its programming philosophy. Establishing early on the need for presenters from non-English speaking ethnic backgrounds, Gyngell oversaw 'SBS Television's visible commitment to multicultural diversity by showing non Anglo-Celtic faces on screen'. He also identified ways of attracting a broader audience, targeting a group he called Australian-born 'early adopter innovators' alongside ethnic communities. Understanding that in the Australian television sector, SBS as a multicultural broadcaster would need a distinctive 'channel identity' that set it apart, Gyngell developed a counter-programming strategy to give viewers a real alternative to other television services (Ang et al. 2008: 34–7; 94). Part of this SBS programming strategy has been packaging cheap and available material around 'issue' based timeslots. In this way, the *Eat Carpet* series provided a timeslot for locally made, creative short films that had previously had no television outlet. When funding was available, SBS initiated series on multicultural themes. *Through Australian Eyes (1983)*, an on-going, low budget documentary series, gave young directors a chance to tell their stories. Similarly, *Under the Skin (1993)*, a twelve part series, enabled directors from various cultural backgrounds to produce drama on a multicultural theme. SBS also ran seasons of feature films with homosexual themes and public television forums on Aboriginal issues and politics, and produced an 'Aboriginal Sesame Street', *Manyu Wanna* (SBS 1994: 23–33). Expedient and innovative scheduling of imported programming around 'themes' such as the acclaimed *About Women* series of 1989, 'incorporated different ethnic fragments into a common women's way of life' (SBS 1994: 141). By block scheduling programming under broad subject themes, feature films, plays, documentaries, sport and comedy from different countries were linked. This maximised opportunities for audience crossover, catering for more than one audience grouping at a time and sometimes for a general audience. Introduced in 1988, the programming philosophy of theme weeks has changed over time. Noting early themes included *About Women, Strangers in the Land* and *About Men,* Ang et al. (2008) describe how the concept, as 'an experimental programming space' served via its 'cumulative effect' to 'deepen understanding through diverse perspectives, voices and representations', representing 'contradictory and conflicting positions' alongside each other (Ang et al. 2008: 113).

To realise SBS goals, television schedules also needed genre diversity in local content to fully represent Australian multicultural experience to a mainstream audience. In 1994, a commissioning arm, SBS Independent (SBSi), was established under the Keating Labor Government's Creative Nation programme, initially receiving seeding funds of AU$13 million over four years. SBSi sought to increase the amount of programming from Australian independent producers that screened on SBS. When the Creative Nation monies expired in 1998, the Federal government committed ongoing funding. From 1994 to late 2007, SBSi commissioned a wide range of work – low budget features, drama, comedy and experimental productions, with almost 1,200 hours of local programming produced by 2006 (Long 1995: 19; SBS 2006: 3).

During its thirteen year existence, SBSi applied a funding model similar to Channel 4's FilmFour. Film commissioning at SBSi produced a host of award winning Australian films including: *Floating Life* (Clara Law 1996), *The Boys* (Rowan Woods 1998), *Radiance* (Rachel Perkins 1998), *Mall Boy* (Vince Giarusso 2001), *Yolngu Boy* (Stephen Johnson 2001), *Walking on Water* (Tony Ayrs 2002), *The Tracker* (Rolf de Heer 2002), *Look Both Ways* (Sara Watts 2005), *Noise* (Matthew Saville 2007) and *Ten Canoes* (Rolf de Heer 2007). Managed by experienced independent producers contracted as commissioning editors, SBSi played a key role in nurturing emerging filmmakers, a goal reflected in the detailed information and generous resources on its website, and in its policies of co-funding series of short dramas and half hour documentary strands with state and federal government film and television funding agencies. In 2008, the SBSi website was taken down and an in-house commissioning team now administer the AU$7 million of federal government funding earmarked for local production. The change in management echoes the broadcaster's shift to more commercial priorities, addressing the need to increase audience ratings, and putting the onus of risk in testing new talent, back on the industry.

As a complementary public service broadcaster directed to 'contribute to the diversity of Australian Television and Radio services', the future of SBS is inevitably linked to that of the ABC. Yet as a hybrid funded publisher/broadcaster, the SBS's low-budget structure has in the past constituted a threat to the ABC. As already noted, amalgamation with the ABC was posed as a logical rationalisation of resources and a solution to rising costs more than once. Yet the two services have performed distinctly different roles. The ABC, as discussed in the previous chapter, has a comprehensive and complementary remit, targeting both special interest and general audiences, complementing and competing with the commercial networks as part of Australia's dual broadcasting system. In contrast, SBS television's complementary service has aimed to offer something for everyone across the week, delivering on audience reach rather than ratings, providing mixed special interest programming of the kind that offers a higher level of engagement to niche audiences. As a publisher/broadcaster, SBS television also broke with the constraints and elitism of broadcasting professionalism, pioneering more experimental programme forms.

Ethnic – Cosmopolitan – Young

Instituted as a narrowcast, multilingual service, and as the first broadcaster using the ultra high frequency bandwidth (UHF), SBS television had limited audience reach when it first went on air. Some saw the service as a cynical political strategy to open up UHF broadcasting for commercial interests. Certainly, because of the cost and the location of ethnic communities, it was not originally intended to extend coverage beyond the main urban centres – Sydney and Melbourne initially, then Canberra. National coverage was deemed too expensive and in the long term unnecessary. The television service was launched on both VHF and UHF bandwidths as Channel 0/28, as a temporary measure intended to help establish an audience while educating the public about new UHF capable TV sets or videocassette recorders (VCRs), and how to install new antennae to receive the UHF (line of sight) signal. In January 1986, when the VHF transmission ended and SBS television became a totally UHF service, many ethnic viewers dropped away, some believing transmission had ceased and others unable to afford a new TV set or the aerial required to receive UHF (Kolar-Panov & O'Regan 1994a: 162). Operating on UHF undoubtedly limited SBS's potential audience. As the pioneer of UHF transmission in Australia, SBS was left to deal with a multitude of technical difficulties involved in insuring good reception for its viewers, while also shouldering sole responsibility for research, educating the public about UHF and lobbying for the expansion of its actual coverage area.

The system did, however, eventually begin to expand later that decade. The launching of AUSSAT, Australia's first domestic satellite in 1986, enabled the SBS network to extend its reach more cost-effectively. At the same time, the Hawke Government's Agenda for Multiculturalism heralded a grander role for ethnic broadcasting, while a new policy for regional equalisation, applying the principle of equality across television services, expanded the transmission infrastructure for SBS (Kolar-Panov & O'Regan 1994: 137). Slowly the service expanded its potential audience: in 1994, only 74.3 per cent of the population covered by SBS transmission were able to receive UHF signals, with only 53.3 per cent receiving a clear picture (SBS 1994: 131–2). Over the next decade, development of the transmission system expanded analogue coverage to 95 per cent of all Australians and digital coverage to 80 per cent.

The ethnic groups served by the SBS have changed over time to accommodate new waves of migration. The initial objectives were to provide multilingual entertainment, news and other information programmes and to offer equitable services across all language groups, independent of size. The service began targeting migrants from southern and eastern Europe, and later those from Asia and then the Middle East, groups who were identified as being more culturally distanced from Australians than people from the UK or northern Europe. Most came to Australia after World War Two, were largely working-class and spoke languages other than English (LOTE). The problem of serving over sixty language groups was originally resolved by apportioning programme time according to community size. From the beginning, programme quality varied. There were difficulties in finding programmes of sufficient technical standard amongst some language groups. By prioritising entertainment genres for multilingual programming, SBS accommodated the requirement to avoid political partisanship, and incorporated general appeal. The addition of English sub-titling enhanced the possibility of drawing cosmopolitan English-speaking Australians and a cosmopolitan pan-ethnic group. Television subtitling was considered a risky venture when first introduced in Australia in 1979. It has subsequently not only enabled SBS to make its multilingual programming accessible to a wider audience, but has also introduced the Australian public to a previously untapped rich resource – the mass of quality, foreign language films and programmes hitherto unscreened on Australian television. In this way SBS has extended Australians' understanding of 'high' culture beyond the formerly, ethnocentric, Anglo-Celtic viewpoint (Ang et al. 2008: 74–82).

The first programming success for SBS television was the international world news, inaugurated in 1980 as *Worldwide News*. Having monitored the number of satellite-feed news stories utilised by other networks, SBS staff discovered that nine to eleven were unused on a daily basis. Combining these with weekly tapes from overseas government broadcasters and a small amount of locally produced news, SBS offered a service that was more international and diverse than more expensive bulletins on other channels. SBS *Worldwide News* contributed a cachet of quality and difference to the broadcaster's reputation and brand. Sport provided similar opportunities and increased audience share. Noting popular international sports not covered by other channels, SBS purchased television rights for soccer, cycling and motorcycling, subsequently attracting and building new and appreciative audiences. The Tour de France and the Soccer World Cup remain among the greatest ratings successes of SBS (Patterson 1992: 43–8; Ang et al. 2008: 176–88).

As part of its charter, the SBS is also obliged to reflect the changing nature of Australian society. With the changing profile of Australia's immigrant communities, SBS's target audience changes and grows. While the mainstreaming of multiculturalism on SBS television failed to satisfy left wing critics who had hoped for more active ethnic community participation and debate, ethnic groups were nevertheless better represented by the broadcaster's emphasis on social issues rather than exotic difference. SBS television helped to deliver social justice by exposing shared concerns and experiences between cultures, undermining the supremacy of mono-cultural viewpoints and thereby eroding the bases of racism and prejudice. Once predominantly European, migrants now come mainly from Asia, the Middle East and the Horn of Africa, representing new language groups for the multilingual broadcaster, while second and third generation new Australians for whom language is no longer an excluding factor have developed different more cosmopolitan tastes to those of their parents and grandparents.

Audiences have been defined according to the availability and affordability of programming, accommodating SBS television's chartered objectives. This originally consisted of multilingual and special interest programmes – primarily feature films and documentaries – targeted to niche audiences with English sub-titling, ensuring optimum accessibility for the 'broader Australian community, along with English language programmes serving the multicultural interests of all Australians' (ETRP 1980). In 1991, the SBS Act made specific mention of the rights of indigenous Australians and the inclusion of other non-ethnic cultures, and multiculturalism entered everyday language as an umbrella term inclusive of wide ranging special interest groups sharing a common identity through experience. Through an eclectic mix of local and imported programming, the SBS helped to change public perceptions about Aborigines, gays and ethnic Australians, and contributed to ethnic community solidarity, raising the local profile of Australia's ethnic cultures and developing a more cosmopolitan awareness amongst the general audience. Representing Italians through opera, the films of Fellini and their love of cycling and soccer, for example, SBS television created more engaging public images than the caricatures of previous media stereotypes.

During the 1990s, three groupings were identified within the target audience of SBS television – the ethnic, the minoritarian, and the cosmopolitan. Crossover between the ethnic and cosmopolitan was facilitated by English subtitling and the growth of an ethnic cosmopolitan audience with a pan-ethnic identity as the children of migrants have grown up and inter-married. Foreign language, 'art house' films have been instrumental in increasing the audience share of the SBS, although these have also been criticised for privileging middle class, English speakers at the expense of the migrant homeland language group for whom they were supposedly purchased. As an editor of a migrant newspaper noted, 'most migrants come here from working-class backgrounds and they watch these films because they like to hear their own language spoken. But do working-class French people go to watch the movies of Truffaut and Godard?' (Grenard 1982: 54). The minoritarian audience is also problematic because groups as diverse as gays, the disabled, religious minorities, Aborigines, and arts and cultural groups, seek not only to share common experiences amongst their group, but also to build wider social understanding and tolerance through cultural exchange with the wider community.

In its first two decades, SBS did not pursue a mass audience in the same way as other Australian television broadcasters, resisting the scheduling tactics of other networks devised to hold viewer loyalty. Preferring to measure its success by weekly audience reach rather than programme ratings, SBS was quoting a weekly viewership of 4.2 million per week out of a possible 15 million in 1995, and calculated its cost per viewer at five cents per day (SBS 1995). The question of what constitutes a viable audience size for a free-to-air broadcaster remains a critical one for SBS. Lingering at 1.8 per cent for its first seven years (SBS 1994: 52), SBS audience ratings rose to 3 per cent during the 1990s, reaching stasis at around 5 per cent by the new millennium and climbing to 6 per cent in 2007 (SBS 2007).

In 2003, SBS television management identified two specific target groups – youth and females – in the hope of making the channel more attractive to advertisers in a bid to increase on-air advertising revenue. While this has arguably helped to increase revenue, it created considerable concern amongst Australia's ethnic communities for whom it represented another move to hijack SBS to serve the mainstream interests of Anglo-Australians. While this change of direction constitutes no real obstacle to the promotion of multiculturalism as a celebration of difference and diversity, it does threaten the separate identity of SBS as an independent corporation, representing the involvement and participation of the multicultural community.

Innovating on a Shoestring

Launched during an economic downturn in 1980, funding, or rather lack of it, has remained SBS's greatest problem, with Government appropriations always disproportionate to the stated objectives of the remit. Originally a non-commercial service, SBS television was granted the right to take advertising and pursue other commercial revenue in the 1991 SBS Act. Competition from commercial broadcasters and from satellite and cable subscription services since the mid Nineties, along with its multicultural brief, constrains potential advertising income. The combination of the publishing-house production model and hybrid funding have been described as, 'the model structure for the new conservatism's public corporation, combining the stimulus of market forces with the maintenance of political control by the government'. Together they pose obvious conflicts with public service goals (Jakubowicz 1989: 113).

Initially considered when the service was being planned, funding from advertising was abandoned following opposition from the commercial networks and the ethnic press who feared the competition. During its first eleven years, SBS revenue comprised annual government appropriations supplemented by programme sales. After 1991, however, SBS began to raise money from entrepreneurial activities, limited advertising sales, and began a pay-TV venture. This represented a step back in the government's commitment to the service, signalling reluctance to continue as sole funder. Further deregulation of the telecommunications industry in 1992 laid out new, relaxed ground rules for broadcasting, facilitating the development of subscription television. Following the launch of its first subscription service, Multilingual Subscriber Television (MST) Limited, the then executive director, Malcolm Long, intimated plans for co-ventures with local cable companies. The launch of MST Limited to provide multilingual subscription services 'to better meet the communication needs of people who seek broadcasting services in languages other than English' returns profits to SBS' free-to-air service (SBS 1994: 2). MSTL also performs another useful purpose through its investment in Pan TV, the company that produces the World Movie Channel for Australia's subscription television market, contributing to the international reputation of SBS in the field of English language sub-titling, a function that assists the broadcaster in securing free-to-air broadcast rights for foreign language movies for SBS (Jolly 2007). In 2009, SBS increased its holding in Pan TV to 100 per cent.

Although Australia's privately owned commercial television networks were entitled to screen fifteen minutes of advertising per hour, the 1991 Act restricted SBS on-air advertising to five minutes per hour, and only during 'natural' programme breaks. At the time, the commercial free-to-air broadcasters were in crisis following the economic downturn of the late 1980s, with plummeting advertising revenues showing no promise of recovery (Cunningham & Turner 1993: 38). In competition with three commercial networks, SBS television advertising and sponsorship income has covered only a small proportion of operating costs. In 1993–94, SBS earned AU$10.7 million from sponsorship and the sale of advertising as opposed to AU$85.5 million from government appropriations (SBS 1994: 90).

Operating as a publisher/broadcaster, SBS keeps production costs and overheads to a minimum while the uncertain future of government funding maintains pressure for cheap programming. This means that SBS pays the lowest price on offer for independent product in Australia. In 1983, a number of film importers complained so bitterly to the government about SBS undercutting their prices by going directly to overseas producers that the Department of Communications set up a committee to investigate SBS purchasing policies (Kolar-Panov & O'Regan 1994a: 159). Despite the high cost of local drama, novel solutions were found. 'Six Pack', a studio-based series on a multicultural theme, utilised student directors and scriptwriters from the Australian Film, Television and Radio School (AFTRS) (O'Regan 1994: 161). In the 1990s, sponsorship and co-productions with the federal government-funded Film Finance Corporation increased local drama content. SBS was proactive in developing cooperative funding initiatives and local documentaries were often funded through multiple government agencies. The Aboriginal current affairs series, *First-in-Line*, was funded by the Department of Aboriginal Affairs and a number of other government departments. This kind of composite funding, however, sometimes compromised editorial control or entailed other drawbacks. As Tom O'Regan observed, 'underfunding to some extent made SBS uncompetitive, as it became a last resort for filmmakers with eccentric product or product the ABC was unwilling to take' (O'Regan 1994: 161). As noted earlier, the role played by SBSi in nurturing emergent Australian filmmakers between 1994 and 2007 appears to have been abandoned in 2008 with its closure (Debrett 2006).

Accountability

SBS is ultimately accountable to the public through the charter enshrined in the 1991 SBS Act. Translation of the charter into operating policies is the responsibility of the SBS board, which is accountable through its Annual Report to parliament, a triennial corporate plan and the SBS codes of broadcasting practice. A community advisory committee and public complaints procedures offer more direct forms of public accountability.

Charged with implementing the Charter, the four to eight non-executive board members are required under the 1991 Act to collectively represent the culturally diverse audience of SBS. Under the Rudd Labor Government's proposed reforms the board will be appointed according to the Nolan rules and will include a staff representative. The board must now also include an approved employee representative (DBCDE 2008). The Act entitles the Minister to direct the board on matters of 'national interest' but not 'in relation to the content or scheduling of programs to be broadcast'. The Board's duties include: maintaining 'the independence and integrity of the SBS'; ensuring that 'SBS…news and information [programs] are accurate…[and] balanced over time and across the schedule'; that SBS is 'aware of and responsive to, community needs and opinions on matters relevant to the charter'; and that SBS's complaints policies are publicised. The Board is also required to 'co-operate closely with the ABC to maximise the efficiency of the publicly funded sectors of Australian broadcasting' (Commonwealth of Australia 1991: 4).

The codes of practice translate the goals of the charter into programming guidelines. Acknowledging that programmes will sometimes be offensive to some groups, SBS defines an 'alternative' approach similar to Channel Four's, interpreting audience interests as being best served by unobstructed exposure to a wide range of cultures, values and perspectives. Thus the challenge for SBS television is to present diversity in a responsible manner, which includes ensuring a balance of diverse views over time (SBS 1994a: 7). The codes of practice provide guidelines on a range of issues: prejudice, racism and discrimination; appropriate language; the right of self identification for groups and individuals; and policies for covering violence, sex and nudity. The policy on racism stipulates that SBS will 'avoid broadcasting any programming which clearly condones, tolerates or encourages discrimination', and commits to the elimination of racism from Australian life. Arguably seeking 'to correct the distorted pictures of cultural communities and issues of race', the codes of practice provide the basis for public monitoring of SBS performance, and detail procedures for the handling of complaints (SBS 1994a: 10).

The Community Advisory Committee (CAC), which is appointed by the board, was established under the 1991 Act to advise on 'community needs and opinions'. Criteria for membership of the CAC, 'an understanding of' or 'interests relevant to' the constituencies of SBS, falls short of the community participation envisaged through the state consultative committees recommended by the Ethnic Television Review Panel (ETRP). The second report of the ETRP in 1979 had indicated that public access was important, and expectations of community access lingered in the ethnic community. SBS was, however, also directed 'to avoid political partisanship', something that would be very difficult to monitor with public access. This issue was resolved to some extent with the birth of Community Broadcasting in Australia in the late 1980s (Jakubowicz 1989: 109). The CAC's terms of reference include the needs of newly arrived migrant groups, community consultation and community education, and the promotion of SBS to 'our multicultural communities' (SBS 2009). However, despite this mechanism community access has not always been equitable:

> More it is the voices of the community representatives who actively court a hearing with SBS regarding particular requests or complaints which are heard. As a consequence it tends to be the well-organised and vocal groups who exert an influence. (Ang et al. 2008: 45)

Fundamental ideological differences within ethnic or other cultural groups will always complicate the issue of democratic representation and consensus on what constitutes equitable programming. Selecting imported, multilingual, ethnic programming on the apolitical bases of language and culture eschews such divisions within ethnic communities. In the area of news and current affairs, however, avoidance of controversy is more problematic, and in 1985 a former news producer called it 'ghetto news' (Ang et al. 2008: 54). Two initiatives in the mid 1980s identified the need for better engagement with issues that ethnic communities found controversial. When several 'progressive ethnic activists' were appointed to the board in 1983–4 they established an Advisory Committee on Combating Racism, and subsequently produced a report outlining how SBS could 'combat racism through education' (Ang et al. 2008: 55). This coincided with the 1985 report of the Committee of Review of the Special Broadcasting Service, which criticised avoidance of controversy in news and current affairs coverage of migrant issues. One of these activist board members, George Zangalis, a trade unionist, backed the notion of consultative, community-based committees. The plan stalled due to difficulties with the election process and was abandoned when Zangalis' term finished. In Marrickville, Sydney, five thousand angry members of the Greek community attended a meeting following leaks that SBS programmes were vetted by the Greek Orthodox Archdiocese. Although unanimously supporting the idea of a committee, the meeting failed to agree on who should be on it and was adjourned in disarray (Jakubowicz 1989: 116–17).

Although many have found SBS wanting in terms of the community participation anticipated at the time of its launch, prescriptive social criteria for board members and chartered requirements to reflect diverse constituencies did initially build closer community ties and more open accountability than other national broadcasters. The most common complaint levelled against SBS's servicing of ethnic community needs is reflected in comments made by the National Forum for Equal Access to Public Broadcasting in 1990, that SBS had been 'hijacked away from the ethnic communities it was set up to serve, in favour of English-speaking people' because its 'trendy French and German programmes, which appeal to Anglo-Celtic yuppies get highly favoured treatment' (Kolar-Panov & O'Regan 1994a: 155). By 2004, the broadcaster's relationship with ethnic communities was being tested by SBS management's priorities, with the SBS board, chaired by businesswoman Carla Zampatti, endorsing the redirection of SBS towards more remunerative mainstream audiences.

An episode in late 2003 offered SBS management a reminder of the special relationship with ethnic communities. Many Vietnamese Australians expressed outrage when SBS television began broadcasting *Thoi Su*, a 'news services sourced from Vietnamese state television', in the morning *WorldWatch* timeslot dedicated to foreign language news. Community demonstrations in Sydney and Melbourne following 'crisis talks' eventually persuaded the board that 'demonstrable "community hurt" was a legitimate reason to suspend the broadcasts' (Ang et al. 2008: 43). Most Vietnamese Australians arrived in Australia as refugees escaping the Hanoi communist regime that now governs a united Vietnam. As former South Vietnamese, they regarded *Thoi Su* as government propaganda and claimed that just the thought of SBS broadcasting Vietnamese state news bulletins evoked traumatic memories. The decision wrankled with Vietnamese viewers who wanted to watch *Thoi Su*, and also with SBS staff who saw it as threatening their professionalism. SBS subsequently amended its code of practice to reference the importance of consultation with the 'language community' in choosing current affairs programming (Ang 2008: 43). This scheduling about-face reflects the ethical/professional conundrum of an institution directed to consult diverse community groups. Ultimately any public broadcaster's integrity depends on editorial independence.

Reinvention for the Digital Future

As a broadcaster that has always regarded itself primarily as an aggregator rather than an originator of programming, SBS is better placed than many other broadcasters to benefit from the multi-channel possibilities of DTT, drawing on the vast range of existing international content. With the advent of both digital television and broadband Internet, SBS now has an opportunity to reinvent itself as a multiplatform media provider to serve its diverse audiences more effectively via additional digital channels and interactive media-rich services online. However, government policy choices and underfunding have so far frustrated the realization of this potential. Despite these obstacles, SBS managing director, Shaun Brown, signalled his determination to pursue this path despite the lack of additional funds, re-launching the digital channel SBS Two in June 2009 – offering foreign language news in the daytime and international programming and films in the evening. The move was perhaps timed to take advantage of the government's April 2009 injection of AU$6.7 million to promote digital take-up. In 2010, SBS television services available on the digital platform Freeview included SBS One (the main channel), SBS Two, and SBS HD, along with on-demand television content on SBS online.

The roll out of digital terrestrial television in Australia has been slow, complicated by political lobbying from the influential commercial sector, as discussed in the previous chapter on the ABC. The ABC and SBS were the joint recipients of an additional government investment of AU$1 billion for digital transmission but received no additional funding for programming (SBS 2008c, 8–9). When the Howard Coalition Government finally relaxed the constraints on multi-channelling by the public broadcasters in 2006, there was still no additional funding granted to develop content for additional channels. As a result, the take-up of DTT remained slow.

In response to the Rudd Labor Government's 2008 ABC SBS Review, held in the run up to the 2009–12 triennial funding decision in the May 2009 federal budget, SBS submitted a proposal for a suite of four channels, pending sufficient finance. In addition to enhancing local production and sports broadcasts on its main channel, the accompanying document, 'SBS Plans for the Future', proposed the re-launch of the existing World News channel as SBS World, screening international programming with an Asia-Pacific emphasis, and including children's programming in both LOTE (languages other than English) and English. The proposal for four SBS channels by 2013 offered two options: one differentiating between the channels on the basis of genre; and the other differentiating on language, but with both offering programming mostly in LOTE with English subtitles. Under the genre option SBS 3 was described as 'Stories that go deeper', a mix of factual content of various kinds, while SBS 4 was described as 'Unexpected stories' – 'international comedy, animation, short film, soap opera, quirky game and lifestyle shows, "cult" and new international movies'. Under the language option SBS 3 was described as 'Asia focus' and offering 'new and exciting stories from our region' – Indian film, Japanese anime, Korean soap opera, plus 'current affairs and documentary on the issues relevant to our region'; while SBS 4 was described as 'Europe focus' – European comedy, soap opera, 'cult movies and new movies, current affairs and documentary' offering a 'deeper view of the social, cultural and political issues' (SBS 2008b: 4; 5).

Prior to the Treasurer's triennial funding decision, Brown announced that SBS would re-launch its digital channel as SBS Two in June 2009, regardless of the funding outcome. The channel was to screen 'quality, diverse content including documentaries, in-language programming, films, major sport, news and current affairs'. The triennial funding rounds proved a disappointment for SBS with the government committing an increase of only AU$20 million, a long way short of Brown's bid for an additional AU$70 million. This rebuff was made more painful by the ABC's success in achieving an additional AU$186 million to launch its children's channel, ABC3, and regional broadband hubs. This disappointment followed widespread complaints from SBS viewers about changes to advertising policy at SBS which had also drawn the critical attention of the Minister and prompted the establishment of the web based organisation, Save Our SBS, by former SBS staff.

When Shaun Brown as recently appointed head of SBS television announced increased audience ratings as a key priority in 2003, many SBS viewers and staff members were outraged. Brown's pursuit of better ratings across the youth and female demographics was seen as a betrayal of the broadcaster's multicultural origins and goals, a commercialisation and 'dumbing down' of the unique character of SBS. Brown, who became the managing director in 2005, was unapologetic, arguing that better ratings in these demographics would enable an increase in advertising rates and reap much needed additional revenue. While the more affluent, 'high brow', middle-class audience once constituted the major portion of SBS-

TV's audience profile, drawing in corporate sponsorship, now programmes like the populist US series, *Mythbusters*, and the UK's BBC2 ratings success, *Top Gear,* along with the quirky American animation series, *South Park*, are attracting bigger youth audiences. SBS, as noted earlier, connected this audience to its charter via two academic audience research projects, 'Living Diversity' (2002) and 'Connecting Diversity' (2006), studies which set out to 'explore the role the media play in the lives of young people from culturally diverse backgrounds' (Ang et al. 2006: 75).

This change in policy also reflected a change in the composition of the SBS board, which began with the appointment of fashion designer and businesswoman, Carla Zampatti, as board chair in 1999. During the eleven years of Howard Coalition government, the SBS board under Zampatti became increasingly business oriented as directors from NESBs were replaced by those from Anglo and largely business backgrounds, a situation echoed at senior management level where 'only one person on…the 12-member executive was of non-English speaking background' (Ingram 2009). This was in marked contrast to the ethnically diverse composition of the previous board under the founding chairman, Sir Nicholas Shehadie, a man 'deeply committed to multiculturalism', who headed the board for the corporation's first 18 years (Ingram 2009).

The commercial direction pursued by management since 2003 eroded key aspects of the broadcaster's distinctiveness, leading ultimately to some public embarrassments for Brown and the SBS board. First among these was the departure of the respected news anchor, Mary Kostakidis, one of the broadcaster's founding staff, and widely admired as 'the face of SBS'. Kostakidis apparently voiced disagreement with the introduction of spot advertising and changes to the early evening bulletin including its expansion to an hour, and left following disagreement with management about her role. In 2007, having taken the corporation to the Federal Court for a breach of contract, Kostakidis received an out of court settlement. Another embarrassment that followed Brown's changes at SBS was the loss of the popular hosts of the long running *Movie Show*, Margaret Pomerantz and David Stratton, whose frustration with changes at SBS led to their defection to the ABC.

Although the 2007–8 financial report showed advertising revenue following the introduction of spot advertising, with the total amount of AU$56.8 million up from AU$41.7 million in 2006/07, this result also reflects the limited commercial possibilities for this innovative multicultural service. With pay-TV and on-demand television available online eroding the audience share of all free-to-air broadcasters, the battle for audience is on in earnest and the advertising income for SBS is unlikely to increase much in the short term. The controversial introduction of spot advertising in 2006/7 produced a small gain in income, but with Australia's overall advertising spend likely to decline further in 2009–10 following the global recession, government appropriations – AU$190.3 million in 2008/09 – seem set to continue as the major source of annual revenue for some time. With government funding also likely to remain tight for some years to come, the integrity of the service will continue to depend on the ingenuity of SBS staff in maintaining programme quality while working with minimal budgets.

Expectations and beliefs about what actually constitutes the interests of any ethnic community will always be contested from the outset and will also shift with generational change. To fulfil its multicultural brief, SBS needs to navigate these differences and changes as they arise. Suggesting that a new vision statement in the 2004–6 SBS Corporate Plan – Communicating Australia's Living Diversity – embraced a 'popular multiculturalism', Ien Ang, Gay Hawkins and Lamia Dabboussy observe in their book, *The SBS Story*, that SBS now 'reflects neither the old-style ethno-multiculturalism of traditional ethnic communities, nor the more intellectual and internationalist cosmopolitan multiculturalism of Robert Hughes' (Ang et al. 2008: 50). The observation acknowledges that two former loyal audience groups have been superseded by 'a more mundane and everyday multicultural spirit…a joyous affirmation of Australia as an irrevocably multicultural nation, warts and all' (Ang et al. 2008: 50). Alongside the pursuit of the youth demographic, this shift signals a new interpretation of the SBS remit. The concept of a 'popular multiculturalism' being conflated with 'cultural diversity' is ambiguous and apolitical, and avoids any engagement with the hardships of new immigrants and refugees still arriving on Australian shores. Interpretation of the phrase 'all Australians' as a mass audience, in the quest for increased revenue, has threatened the principal function of SBS 'to provide multilingual and multicultural broadcasting services' as outlined in the SBS Charter. In the SBS Corporate Plan 2007–12, this shift was evident in the four strategic priorities: 'Provide content that is relevant to all Australians'; followed by, 'focus attention on growing revenues'; adapting to the 'rapidly changing media environment'; and lastly, 'building stronger relationships and partnerships with stakeholders', the last of which refers to the independent sector and 'strategic partners' rather than ethnic or cultural communities.

In 2005, George Zangalis, as President of the National Ethnic and Multicultural Broadcasters Council (NEMBC), publicly criticised SBS in a press release following rumours the broadcaster was about to enter a commercial agreement with the commercial network Channel Nine:

> Programming in community languages has shrunk, while English programming has grown. Advertising has increased and become increasingly strident. Rather than focusing on different cultures, the SBS seems to be moving towards mainstream sports like cricket and now AFL. There is plenty of this type of programming on the ABC and the three commercial channels. (Qtd. in Cassidy 2008a)

Later in an interview for the authors of *The SBS Story*, Zangalis noted the ethnic communities' 'love affair' with SBS had come to an end (Ang et al. 2008: 247). As racism has become more prominent as a public issue in the Australian media following the Cronulla riots of 2005 and violent attacks on Indian students in 2009, so has criticism of the new direction being pursued by SBS. In October 2008, a Melbourne *Age* report, 'Fraser laments decline of "multi" in SBS culture', noted the former prime minister who launched SBS, had, in the company of other prominent Australians, endorsed a statement on the Save our SBS website warning that SBS 'was in danger of losing its way', with 'mainstream replacing multicultural'. Noting the introduction of advertising was driving SBS in a more 'generalist' direction, the statement raised some specific concerns – the commissioning of a local version of the high rating UK programme, *Top Gear*, and the loss of English language teaching programmes on television. Such public reprovals spurred a renewed emphasis on ethnic community services and English language tuition in the SBS submission to the government's ABC and SBS Review in November 2008.

That same year the federal parliamentary member for Kooyong, Petro Georgiou, also spoke out about the need to reclaim space on SBS television for that minoritarian ethnic audience, to reinvigorate SBS's multicultural agenda:

> The manner in which we have made multiculturalism part of the character of our national broadcasting is a uniquely Australian achievement. But I am mindful that many who should be among its staunchest supporters feel concerned at how its $180 million annual budget is spent. I share these reservations. I don't begrudge the pleasure many viewers get from shows like *Top Gear* and *South Park*. But where, for example, is the investment in programming to encourage and facilitate the learning of English? The purposes for which the Service was established remain relevant to our evolving multicultural society. I believe that we need an independent and comprehensive review of how successfully SBS is meeting its intended purposes of the furtherance of English and language learning, the facilitation of settlement, the right to maintain a cultural identity and the promotion of mutual understanding between diverse communities. (Georgiou 2008)

While multiculturalism remains part of the Rudd Labor government's commitment to 'social inclusion', its focus has shifted from cultural to religious diversity. Reflecting on the subject, Georgiou noted the 'perceived conflict between obedience to laws enacted by parliament and the dictates of religion', taking issue with those who blame multiculturalism as 'mushy', observing that 'respect for the rule of law enacted by parliament has always been a non-negotiable and central tenet of the policy of multiculturalism', and quoting former Prime Minister, Malcolm Fraser:

> Multiculturalism is concerned with far more than the passive toleration of diversity. It sees diversity as a quality to be actively embraced, a source of social worth and dynamism. It encourages groups to be open and to interact, so that all Australians may learn and benefit from each other's heritages. Multiculturalism is about diversity not division – it is about interaction not isolation. It is about cultural and ethnic differences set with a framework of shared fundamental values which enables them to co-exist on a complementary rather than a competitive basis. It involves respect for the law and for our democratic institutions and processes. Insisting upon a core area of common values is no threat to multiculturalism but its guarantee, for it provides the minimal conditions on which the well being of all is secured. (Georgiou 2008)

In the run up to the federal government's Review in November 2008, SBS moved quickly to reassure the ethnic lobby about its commitment to charter goals. The Federation of Ethnic Communities Councils of Australia (FECCA) subsequently lodged a submission endorsing the broadcaster's bid for increased funding, and its plans for a 'new SBS World multichannel with predominantly LOTE programming, including children's LOTE programming and English language tuition programming'. However, on a more cautionary note, FECCA commented on the need for better reflection of cultural diversity on the SBS board, something many had observed had become overly commercial in both outlook and composition (FECCA 2008: 1). Speaking at the FECCA conference in 2009, Brown acknowledged that SBS 'was falling short' on its 'multilingual objectives', and promised community consultation having identified two broad groups for special development via digital and online services: the top ten language groups which are underserved relative to their size; and recently arrived migrants with high needs, including refugees from war zones (Brown 2009). It has been observed that the ethnic lobby is no longer the unified force it once was in the 1980s when SBS was born (Ingram 2009b). Nevertheless reflecting and serving multiculturalism as social policy offers SBS its best strategy for distinctiveness alongside the ABC, and is likely to increase in importance in the event of both PSBs sharing transmission facilities, as mooted by the government in 2008.

Alongside the new commercial emphasis, SBS television continues to represent multicultural Australia in ways no other broadcaster does, delivering some groundbreaking local drama centred around the lives of cultural minorities: *The Circuit* (2007), which focused on the members of a legal team and others involved in the travelling court system servicing the Kimberly region in northern outback Australia offered a site for reflection on the difficulties Australian Aboriginals face when caught between two laws; *East West 101* (2007), a Sydney-based police drama centred around a team of detectives – an Australian Muslim of Middle Eastern origin, an Anglo-Australian, and a Samoan-Australian – similarly offers a canvas for representing issues of racial and religious intolerance, and has won awards locally and internationally in 2009 and 2010. Stepping up more directly to the challenge of reflecting diversity, the documentary series, *The First Australians* (2008), another 2009 AFI award winner, offered a seven-part account of the history of relations between white settlers and Aboriginals, offering for the first time 'the story of the nation from an indigenous perspective' (Neill 2008). A similar series on Australian multiculturalism is scheduled to go to air in 2010.

The influence of SBS on Australian society has been much greater than its audience share would suggest. Breaking the mono-cultural blandness of Australian media, the broadcaster facilitated the development of an Australian national identity that is more in tune with its place in the Asia-Pacific region and more accepting of its multicultural populous. While the apolitical skew of its multicultural brief sometimes inhibited SBS as a 'site for controversy', limiting its ability to inform viewers on political matters, being represented in diverse forms and contexts enhanced both self awareness and social tolerance for many previously marginalised groups. While its hybrid funding and specific brief constrain its role, SBS has found solutions that suggest new sustainable approaches for public service broadcasting. As a multicultural broadcaster, SBS has pioneered ways of bridging a national and international public.

The Rudd Labor Government's April 2009 promise to fully fund the National Broadband Network (NBN) promises benefits for Australian audiovisual media providers and new scope for multiplatform content. While the costs will only emerge in time, the prospect of widespread broadband Internet connection offers SBS relatively affordable possibilities for delivering diverse interactive services, such as its plan for online hubs for every one of the 70 plus language communities catered for by SBS services – 'a public square of content, discussion and news created in every language' (SBS 2008b: 8). Although many are likely to be excluded, falling on the wrong side of the digital divide, SBS online offers the underfunded broadcaster a new opportunity to re-build bridges with ethnic communities and, as noted in its submission to the DBCDE Review, 'to leverage its cultural connections, expertise and relationships with communities often "left out" of national conversations to truly broaden Australian public debates online' (SBS 2008b: 8). The NBN potentially offers SBS an affordable platform to meet the divergent objectives of its charter: to better serve newly arrived migrant groups with programming and media content in their home languages; to engage them in active participation in online communities; to directly connect them to relevant government services and community and non-governmental organisations in the spirit of the digital commons; and to better serve pan-ethnic second and third generation migrant groups, and the cosmopolitan audience, by making international and locally produced multicultural programming available as on-demand content online. However, while relatively affordable, these kinds of services are not yet achievable. In 2010, the organisation Save our SBS was requesting SBS viewers to write to the Treasurer urging the allocation of additional funding for the development of SBS online.

In 2009, the SBS website was remodelled around the idea of 'story', the result of 'an 18 month research project to re-design and contemporise' that led to the redefinition of the onscreen identity with the phrase 'Six Billion Stories' – a matching acronym reflecting the current world population. Although likely unintended, the tagline 'Six Billion Stories and counting…' also signals the dominance of linear media content in the brand identity of SBS, and the absence of the networking and public participation in evidence on ABC Online. While SBS online offers some highly developed supplementary programming sites such as those for its two prime-time current affairs shows, *Dateline* and *Insight,* which offer an archive of on-demand television content as well as blogs and online discussion around the various issues, the potential for similarly focused multilingual sites is presumably beyond current budgetary limits.

SBS innovation has occurred largely through its scheduling, which has accustomed SBS viewers to a more eclectic programme mix than that of other mainstream broadcasters. This has led to idiosyncratic successes such as *Costa's Garden Odyssey,* in which the exuberant host embarks on down-to-earth eco-gardening projects that gently subvert the lifestyle shows of privately owned commercial television. The experimental programming space of

SBS programme seasons and the prominence given to documentaries in the SBS schedule, along with a habit of counter programming has driven the broadcaster's involvement in collaborative ventures such as 'Why Democracy?', in which ten documentaries about contemporary democracy were screened simultaneously by forty broadcasters around the world in conjunction with a website, chat rooms, podcasts and other participatory initiatives (Ang et al. 2008: 113–15).

While current funding inhibits the speed of development of additional digital channels, Brown has signalled his determination to pursue this path despite the lack of additional funds, re-launching the digital channel SBS Two in 2009 – scheduling foreign language news in the daytime and international programming and films in the evening, and announcing a new pay TV channel focusing on arts and entertainment and operated by Multilingual Subscriber Television Limited for 2010. In 2010, Senator Conroy, the Minister responsible for broadcasting, moved to return AU$250 million of licence fee revenue to commercial free-to-air broadcasters, apparently in consideration of the decline in advertising revenue; it was a controversial move in an election year and one that must have wrankled with SBS management.

Chapter 6

American Public Television – 'A Non-Commercial Service'

Introduction

In most Western countries, public service broadcasting developed from the perceived need to manage limited spectrum resources in the public interest as the wider social implications of broadcasting emerged. In America, however, public broadcasting developed in the wake of the free market commercial system and was relegated a subordinate role. Established to repair the inadequacies of programming on commercial networks, it was never intended to challenge commercial domination. Neither a fourth network nor a truly participatory local system, lack of a cohesive structure and failure to secure independent funding have persistently undermined the effectiveness of public broadcasting, leaving it vulnerable to divisive internal pressures, corporate influence and government interference.

Originating from a loose, collaborative association of educational and community stations broadcasting on UHF, public television was initiated by President Johnson in 1967. The development of numerous local stations into an interconnected, nationwide, publicly funded system followed the recommendations of the Carnegie Commission on Educational Television, which had released its report in January 1967. Stressing the importance of independence from direct governmental influence, the Commission had recommended a public trust funded through a tax on the sale of television receivers. The Act, however, designated annual funding through the federal budget appropriations process leaving public television at the mercy of political vicissitudes.

Rising dependence on corporate sponsors, increased corporate visibility through 'enhanced underwriting', and the on-screen pursuit of donations through membership subscription drives have all diminished public television's credibility as an 'alternative' service. The reluctance of Congress to relinquish its financial power has limited public television's ability to tackle controversial subjects, restricting it to a primarily educational role thus limiting its general appeal. During the 1980s, the 'systematic deregulation of broadcasting' by the Federal Communications Commissioner, Mark Fowler, relaxed restrictions on cross media ownership, enabling media conglomerates to consolidate cultural hegemony. Fowler also eliminated the Fairness Doctrine, which had required broadcasters to cover controversial issues, along with the 'equal-time rule, which stipulated that opposing sides be fairly treated' (Kellner 1990: 64). While these changes arguably increased the significance of public television's role as a forum for democratic public debate, growing competition from niche channels delivered via cable and direct broadcast satellite, along with the hostility of a Republican dominated Congress, further imperilled the system's survival.

The audience for public television has changed and declined in recent decades; with the arrival of cable television and niche channels many who had previously been public television viewers switched to pay-TV because of its apparent diversity. While the Internet has further increased competition for audience, particularly for younger viewers, it has also brought public television new ways of reconnecting with its lost audience groups through various forms of participatory local media. It is the regional structure of public television that best differentiates the system from others and is central to its mission. While funding remains problematic for all public broadcasters, it is particularly so for American public television which necessarily gleans revenue from multiple sources – government appropriations, corporate sponsorship and audience membership subscription, along with assistance through various institutional affiliations. As a decentralised and localised system, public television is well endowed with procedures for public accountability through both formal and informal mechanisms, although individual stations can still be vulnerable to capture by single interest groups. The restrictions of space in a book such as this limit the scope of reflection on the system's regional diversity. This chapter will explore public television through its purpose, audience, and structures for funding and accountability before finally discussing its plans, preparations and prospects for the digital future.

Corrective to the 'Great Wasteland'

At a time when commercial broadcasting 'was in a state of almost delirious prosperity', the Public Broadcasting Act of 1967 became one of the final pieces of Johnson's Great Society Programme and served as a palliative to a public divided by the Vietnam War. The Public Broadcasting Bill faced remarkably little opposition in Congress and incorporated most of the recommendations of the Carnegie Commission, with that one notable exception, the trust required to fund it (Barnouw 1990: 357). Unreliable funding and political tinkering with its internal structure, particularly during the Nixon years, undermined the primacy of the public television mission, limiting its ability to represent dissenting viewpoints or to provide genuine programme diversity.

Apart from a brief period during World War One when the navy controlled radio, the development of broadcasting in the United States was left to private interests. Through their early purchase of key patents, major corporations – American Telephone and Telegraph (AT&T) and General Electric (GE) – dominated from the start, forming the Radio Corporation of America (RCA) with the United Fruit Company in 1919 (Kellner 1990: 25–6). The libertarian philosophy of the times saw no incompatibility between private and public interests, and the popularity of early commercial broadcasting reinforced this stance (Rowland 1993: 158). While criticism of the monopoly in broadcasting prompted a federal antitrust lawsuit in 1924, resulting in AT&T's withdrawal from that sector, the enhanced status of RCA as the remaining dominant force reflected a misplaced faith in the notion of socially responsible private enterprise. By 1927 there were three commercial broadcasting networks in operation when the Federal Radio Commission (FRC) – reconstituted as the Federal Communications Commission (FCC) in 1934 – was formed to regulate spectrum use. Although broadcasting was initially deemed a public trust on the basis of its use of a public resource – with public interest clauses included among obligations for radio licensees – the FRC reallocated the best frequencies to the largest commercial interests and reserved the 'less powerful, and thus less desirable' frequencies for educational stations (Kellner 1990: 31).

While limitations were initially set on radio advertising, sponsorship had emerged as a controlling force by the 1930s, with sponsors choosing programme content to maximise ratings. The networks that controlled radio broadcasting moved naturally into television as the numbers of receivers proliferated in affluent post-war America. Television soon proved the perfect conduit for promoting consumer society, with advertisers paying for the new 'free' mass entertainment medium, hence legitimating their control (Kellner 1990: 34).

Widespread criticism of the commercial system eventually prompted the federal government to support the construction of non-commercial facilities with the Educational Television Facilities Act of 1962 (Rowland 1993: 191). Fred Friendly, former CBS News head, addressed the problem of funding non-commercial television on a national basis in 1965. Newly appointed to the Ford Foundation to develop its work in broadcasting, Friendly proposed granting ownership of recently developed satellite transmission to non-commercial television to provide a source of revenue that was non-threatening to the commercial networks but which would enable the service to grow. While the FCC was still considering this proposal, the Carnegie Commission published its report – 'Public Television: A program for action' – in 1967 (Somerset-Ward 1993: 82). Coining the term 'public television' and defining what looked very much like public service goals, the Commission recommended the establishment of a Corporation for Public Broadcasting (CPB) to promote the development of a non-commercial system.

The Carnegie Commission's vision for a 'public' system became widely accepted as an ideal model for non-commercial broadcasting in the United States. As a corrective to commercial television fare, public television was to serve neglected audiences and reflect the heterogeneity of the American public, providing 'excellence in the service of diversity' and programming that 'can help us see America whole in all its diversity', serving as 'a forum for controversy and debate...providing a voice for groups in the community that might otherwise be unheard'. Seeing the system's potential for revitalising democracy, the Report asserted that programming on public television:

> Can deepen a sense of community in local life...It should bring into the home meetings, now generally un-televised, where major public decisions are hammered out, and occasions where people of the community express their hopes, their protests, their enthusiasms, and their will. (Carnegie Commission 1967: 14; 92)

During its research the Commission visited 92 of the 124 educational television stations and localism subsequently emerged as the framework for its vision. Accommodating

American aversion to state control, interconnection of the educational stations under their existing licensees became the basis for the system. The non-profit CPB was to co-ordinate the business of interconnection and programme production. The latter was to be achieved through funding at least two national production centres, the contracting of independent producers, and support to local stations for local production as appropriate. The operational costs of local stations were to be met by the Department of Health, Education and Welfare (HEW).

The Public Television Act, passed ten months later, made two significant adjustments to the Carnegie Commission's recommendations. The Board was expanded from twelve to fifteen members, all of whom were to be nominated by the President, with no more than eight from the same political party thereby ensuring dominance by the government of the day. Secondly, following lobbying from television set manufacturers, the system was left directly dependent on the federal government, ignoring the Commission's expressed concern. Lyndon Johnson promised long-term politically insulated funding would be developed later once the Act had been passed, but his decision not to contest the next election left this promise in limbo.

Intended as a corrective for the inadequacies of American commercial television, which FCC Chief Commissioner, Newton Minnow, had famously referred to as a 'great wasteland' in 1961, public television was defined as 'non-commercial' and 'alternative' rather than as a public service (Barnouw 1990: 300). The mixed motives of the administration that had nurtured the Act were evident in two ways: through the modest appropriation of $4.5 million, granted for the first fiscal year, a fraction of the $40 million anticipated by the Carnegie Commission; and through Johnson's selection of CPB board members whose unsuitability was typified by the first chairman, Frank Pace Jnr., a former Secretary of the Army, who enthusiastically greeted the task with the idea of using public television for riot control (Barnouw 1990: 398). Never intended as another network, the educational emphasis and local station structure effectively constrained public television's audience reach and limited it to a marginalised system unable to achieve the national or cultural centrality of public service broadcasters elsewhere. Initially, however, the service thrived. In the five years following the passing of the Act, the number of stations doubled and the audience grew, responding to programming of a quality unavailable on commercial television. BBC productions like the *Forsyte Saga* (1967) and *Civilisation* (1969), and the establishment of *Masterpiece Theatre* drew record ratings for prime-time on public television, while the innovative *Sesame Street* improved the levels of literacy amongst children from low socio-economic groups (Somerset-Ward 1993: 85).

The nucleus of educational television stations around which public television grew was originally funded by the telecommunications industry through university engineering departments as part of industry research and development. From the early days of broadcasting, these stations began making and distributing programmes that went beyond simple lecture formats and some became popular enough to attract support from the networks. In 1949, when the FCC imposed a freeze on the issuing of television licences until

1952 for the purpose of reformulating policy, one of the Commissioners, Frieda Hennock, argued for the rights of educational users, and frequencies for 242 educational television stations were subsequently reserved.

American traditions of philanthropy funded the foundations of public television. In addition to the contribution of the Carnegie Commission in 1967, the Ford Foundation played a leading role in the early development of educational television, funding the Educational Radio and Television Centre in Ann Arbor, Michigan, which later moved to New York, where it was renamed National Educational Television (NET) (Smith 1976: 227). NET began a campaign for a national system of interconnection to improve its method of distribution, which then entailed posting programmes to stations. The federal government eventually lent support with the Educational Facilities Act of 1962, which authorised $32 million for transmitters and studios. As a result of Newton Minnow's efforts, educational television gained a much needed station in New York, securing the license for the hotly contested Channel 13 despite more impressive bids from commercial contenders. Minnow also had a key role in persuading Congress to mandate UHF capability on all television sets made after January 1963, thus enhancing the future coverage of UHF educational stations (Barnouw 1990: 302).

With continued Ford Foundation support, educational television production grew during the 1960s, with NET in New York supplying seven and a half hours of programming each week to over one hundred stations across the country. Broadening the definition of education, its mix of public affairs, cultural and children's programming suggested a possibility of something akin to the BBC model of public service television, despite the structural differences.

Given NET's early nurturing role in the development of public television, the continued educational emphasis is hardly surprising. Educational and instructional programming fills a large proportion of public television schedules, and along with the development of special services like closed captioning technology for the deaf introduced in 1980, Descriptive Video Service (DVS) for the blind in 1988, and Spanish translations on the Separate Audio Programme (SAP) has come to dominate its public profile. With many stations owned and run by colleges and universities, the system's relationship with educational providers has always been strong. Educational programming covers all levels and targets all ages, from pre-school to vocational training, and is both formal and informal in style. Programming includes college degrees and formal catch-up courses for adult students who could not otherwise afford them, along with pre-school programming.

The educational emphasis, however, has been criticised as a policy of minimal risk, which delivers educational 'product' to an audience of passive learners and backs away from actively engaging viewers in any 'forum for controversy and debate' of the kind that would extend their abilities as citizens. Although the Carnegie Commission was careful to distinguish between educational and public television, that distinction became blurred in the interests of financial survival. Much state and local government funding is tagged for educational support. Educational television has been noted for its tendency to stress consensus over controversy, and for prioritising 'definitive' programmes staidly framing 'objective truth' rather than subjective viewpoints that engage the viewer actively in further thought and debate. Cummings, a historian who worked on a WGBH/British co-production, *Korea: The Unknown War*, observed, 'In the end WGBH wanted an appearance of probity, a semblance of objectivity, a package that would not offend, and a position in the "middle" of television's fictive consensus' (Hoynes 1995: 112). Commercial networks readily supported the Public Broadcasting Act, with CBS pledging $1 million to the CPB (Carnegie Commission 1967: 86). The prioritising of education and other non-profitable programming for the new non-commercial system promised to ease onerous 'public interest' obligations on commercial broadcasters, and the stipulation that the new service was not to be a fourth network confirmed its subordinate role.

The decentralised structure of public television accorded with American faith in individualism and the philosophy of federalism. Public service systems, viewed as state-owned, conflicted with the libertarian philosophy of the free market system. Federalism promised a more representative and participatory system that provided a structural alternative to existing networks. It resulted, however, in an unwieldy bureaucracy and dislocated management structure that thwarted unified national policy, and diverted public television from creating the much needed 'site for controversy'. As the recipient of direct government funding, the CPB's isolation from station operations, production and scheduling was justified as necessary to maintain distance from government. As the executive body, it was neither broadcaster, sole programme commissioner nor genuine regulatory controller. Most of its responsibilities were to some extent shared with other organisations. With no authority to operate the interconnection between stations, since this was seen as giving it power equivalent to a 'fourth network', the CPB, in association with the Ford Foundation and station managers, conceived the Public Broadcasting Service (PBS), a private membership organisation representative of all public television stations and governed by a board representing station managers, CPB, NET and the public (Lashley 1992: 31).

The Carnegie Commission had stressed the role of the local stations as being critical to the system's commitment to diversity and the nation's differentiated audience (Carnegie Commission 1967: 33). But localism hampered the implementation of the system's national mission, giving local stations the right to refuse programmes funded and supplied through CPB and PBS (Somerset-Ward 1993: 138). Although decisions for the National Programme Service (NPS) were subsequently centralized through a programme 'czar', the Chief Programme Executive (CPE), in 1992, the stations retained their right to reject programmes within the NPS (Somerset-Ward 1993: 98). This tension between local programming and a national service remains a source of frustration for PBS. In the interests of greater cost efficiency, PBS has endeavoured to get local stations to sign a 'declaration of interdependence' to support a stricter 'common carriage policy', giving them less freedom to opt out of the National Program Service. While facilitating cost efficiency in overall programme production, the arrangement was also viewed as undermining the localist system (Ouellette 2009: 185).

Station variation in staffing numbers, production output, historical origins and management ethos complicates the executive's role in formulating national policy. Friedland's five-tier typology, developed in his study of the Wisconsin Collaborative Project, details the variation and possibilities for collaboration. The first tier, 'major producing stations' comprises the three 'flagship' stations – WGBH Boston, WNET New York and WETA Washington DC. In the period 1990–3, these contributed 73 per cent of all programming in the National Programme Service (NPS), some of which was contracted out to independent producers. The second tier, the 'larger community stations', contributed a total of 21 per cent, while the third tier stations, the 'state networks and university stations', contributed 5 per cent of the NPS during the same period, but also produced instructional programmes that are not part of the NPS. The fourth tier are the locally producing stations which keep producers on staff but rarely contribute to the NPS (0.73 per cent between 1990–3), although they do produce an above average amount of local programming and take part in occasional regional co-productions. The fifth tier are the consuming stations which may produce some local programming each week but fill most of their local schedule with the NPS. There is also a wide variance within each of these tiers (Friedland 1995: 138).

Described variously as a 'crazy-quilt' structure and a 'hodgepodge of organisations', the decentralised structure of the public television system has been cast as both its greatest strength and intrinsic weakness (Rowland 1993: 184). Its history of educational and community involvement has been the foundation on which the public system was built, but its funding and structure constrained its development as a genuine citizen based system. Presuming access via fibre optic cable or DBS, the Twentieth Century Task Fund's future scenario for public television as a 'multimedia public library with its own electronic town square' involved a more vital role for local stations, with 'interactive' citizen participation (Somerset-Ward 1993: 110), one that digital terrestrial television and the Internet again seem to promise.

The decentralised local station structure is also expensive. Of the $1.2 billion spent in the public television system during 1992, approximately 75 per cent was used for station operations. The replication of multiple production facilities and overlapping competing stations are often seen as inefficiencies the service can ill afford, although Somerset-Ward noted in 1993 that the CPD estimated only 11 of the 351 stations actually overlapped (Somerset-Ward 1993: 4; 164). The Twentieth Century Fund Task Force recommended that federal funding should be reserved for national programmes and that communities support their own stations. While the first offers a solution to the problem of funding worthwhile programming that's unlikely to attract sponsorship, the second is more problematic given the wide range of station types and the communities they serve. Federal funding of facilities has been critical in terms of delivering national coverage, a vital public service goal, but now comprises only 17 per cent of overall CPB income with membership and private funding making up the lion's share at 60 per cent (CPB 2008: 2).

While the local station structure is staunchly defended as the basis for a truly participatory forum for democratic discourse at local, regional and national levels, it inevitably undermined the development of coherent national policy and diverted funding to facilities rather than programming. The separation of management, programme commissioning and transmission weakened the executive's authority and this was further compounded by station variation.

To complicate matters further, the public television system also endured successive administrations tinkering with the structural balance between the CPB and PBS. The executive powers enjoyed by the CPB under the Johnson Administration were eroded during the Nixon era (Lashley 1992: 29–37). With anti-Vietnam War protests raging, the Nixon Administration became increasingly sensitive to the changing tide of public opinion expressed through the media. Vice-president Spiro Agnew's 1969 speech on bias in the media, and the White House's subsequent 'TV Blitzkrieg', as Variety magazine termed it, marked the first of the Nixon's attempts to silence dissenting voices on television (Barnouw 1990: 445). During 1970–1, public television scheduled a number of controversial documentaries produced through NET and the National Public Affairs Centre for Television (NPACT), public television's production centre attached to WETA-TV in Washington (Hoynes 1995: 3). Viewed by the White House as 'anti administration', the programmes prompted a prolonged campaign of retaliation. White House adviser Clay Whitehead argued that public affairs programming had no place on public television and complained that public television was becoming a fourth network (Smith 1976: 231). Stopping short of political censorship, Nixon added more layers to the bureaucracy, giving the Executive Office of the President (EOP) greater discretionary powers and creating the Office of Telecommunications Policy (OTP) to manage the broadcast spectrum and provide facilities and policy oversight. NPACT, which was later merged with WETA in 1973, was to be responsible for broadcasting the full 51 days of gavel-to-gavel Watergate hearings which led to Nixon's impeachment. While NPACT had regularly produced 'television of record' documenting public hearings, this was the first time it proved a ratings winner, prompting the commercial networks to get involved.

The EOP made it clear that the CPB's future funding was contingent on restructuring on more decentralised lines. The CPB board demurred. On June 30th 1972, President Nixon vetoed the CPB's authorisation bill arguing that public television had become too centralised (Lashley 1992: 50). Local station executives endorsed the drive for increased localism. CPB and PBS relations were strained during this conflict, and in response to presidential pressure PBS relinquished its programming function to the Station Programme Cooperative, ceding stations responsibility for their own schedules.

The veto and the changes it imposed led to the resignations of the chairman, the president and the director of television on the CPB. With eleven Nixon appointees on the CPB board, the much vaunted return to 'the bedrock of localism' actually diminished public television's credibility. Smith notes a Ralph Nader report on Mobil Oil commercials was dropped after the multinational contributed $1 million to public television, while a segment on FBI informers was cut from the *Great American Dream Machine* following government pressure (Smith 1976: 233). The Nixon Board withdrew funding to NPACT and to all public affairs programming except *Black Journal*, and reduced the power of PBS by taking over programme acquisition and production grants, and responsibility for monitoring objectivity and balance, tasks previously performed by PBS. The autonomy of local stations was increased at the expense of the national system. By changing the make-up of the board, adding to the bureaucracy and altering the balance of power between local stations and the executive, Nixon also weakened the CPB (Lashley 1992: 50–5).

The Nixon Administration's restructuring and funding cuts marked the system's transition from a forum for cultural diversity to one of cultural elitism (Lashley 1992: 52). The potential of PBS's National Programme Service (NPS) as a site for critical public discourse was crippled by lack of funds, increased station autonomy, and vulnerability to political pressure often in the form of self censorship. Increasing dependence on corporate underwriting dollars drove the NPS in the direction of corporate preferences for non-controversial programmes catering for middle-class audiences.

The Ford and Carter Administrations consolidated the structural changes made under Nixon, confirming the increased autonomy of the local stations at the expense of the Corporation's authority. The matched funding formula, introduced by Ford and adjusted under Carter, whereby every federal dollar was dependent on the acquisition of two dollars from external sources, prompted an increase in corporate underwriting as a means of funding programme production, along with a drive for viewer membership to fund station operations. Both these sources of funding had potential to conflict with public broadcasting goals, namely editorial independence and content diversity.

Media deregulation under Reagan brought about further decentralisation, served the interests of media monopolies and promoted the growth of cable companies. In 1981, under Chief Commissioner Mark Fowler, the FCC systematically dismantled the regulatory structure built up over several decades, eliminating social responsibility requirements. Deregulation was particularly damaging to children's television where the integration of merchandising meant commercials sometimes account for as much as 20 minutes of a 30 minute programme (Kellner 1990: 64; 196–202). In 1984, relaxation of the FCC guidelines on corporate underwriting facilitated increased commercialisation of public broadcasting. In the same year, the Cable Communications Policy Act ceded operators greater control of the services they offered.

PBS took a sharp right turn during the Reagan/Bush years becoming 'dominated by conservative political talk shows and pro-business programmes', prompting public calls for 'at least one weekly programme addressing the public interest agenda – consumer, labour, ecology, peace, civil rights'. Broadcasters were no longer deemed 'trustees of the national interest' and television was treated as a business like any other. Although controls on commercial television were relaxed, Reagan actually increased regulatory monitoring of public television, enforcing the right of rebuttal against left wing viewpoints without extending this right to appeals against right wing bias (Kellner 1990: 202–3).

The attack from the right was relentless, and in 1992 the Centre for Media and Public Affairs, a conservative institution in Washington, published a report titled, 'Balance and Diversity in PBS Documentaries'. The report found that overall programmes 'fell short of the standard of diversity by failing to give voice to excluded groups', and also asserted that 'the balance of opinion tilted consistently in a liberal direction' (Somerset-Ward 1993: 136). That same year, Congress directed the CPB to define national programming standards for public broadcasting, to monitor stations and to make future grants conditional on compliance with these standards. The rescission of the Fairness Doctrine, as noted earlier, left commercial television free from any such strictures. Legislated in 1946, the Fairness Doctrine required broadcast licensees as public trustees to represent controversial matters and to do so in a manner that was balanced and fair (Lashley 1992: 18). Conservative critics drew on the criticisms of a lack of balance to argue for the withdrawal of public funding (Lashley 1992: 18). Thus in representing alternative viewpoints, public television had opened itself to charges of liberal or leftist bias, risking federal funding and corporate underwriting. Yet neglecting alternative programming also drew criticism from both sides that it was elitist and failing its mission.

Under Served and Unserved Audiences

The preferences of corporate underwriters inevitably drove public television down a low risk path, alienating many of the 'under served and unserved groups' within its target audience, and drawing criticism that it looked like commercial television. Bill Hoynes notes the significance of the funding issue in the cancellation of the public affairs programme, *Kwinty*, hosted by investigative journalist, Jonathan Kwinty. Featuring a more equitable balance between representatives of the public and official/governmental/authority guests than found in many public affairs programmes that favour governmental and corporate sources, *Kwinty* offered an alternative viewpoint unmatched by any other channel (Hoynes 1995: 106). Yet Kwinty lasted only one season on public television because of its failure to attract a corporate sponsor. Hoynes records a similar development with the series, *South Africa*, a programme that met most public broadcasting goals but which, on having failed to attract a corporate underwriter, was dropped from the schedule.

The Carnegie Commission had cited 'excellence in the service of diversity' as part of the mission of public television. Limited funding and lack of independence exacerbated the tension between these two goals. Excellence interpreted as 'quality' became 'a code for elitist, highbrow programmes' which conflicted with the risk-taking aspect of programme diversity (Hoynes 1995: 152). Safely appealing to corporate funders and the wealthier section of the public who comprise public television's potential subscribers, this identification of quality with 'high culture' tends to exclude innovative programming that challenges conventional ideas and forms. While employees within the system came to see this kind of 'quality' programming as alternative on the basis of its difference from commercial television, it was not the forum for alternative viewpoints that remains the hope of those jaded with commercial television. Resenting the lack of diverse viewpoints and the surfeit of safe non-controversial programming, many of the 'under served and unserved' audiences that public television had been directed to serve came to believe their interests would be better represented by independent producers. Although public television screened the long running *Black Journal*, and included stations run by and for ethnic and/or minority audiences, multicultural programmes were nevertheless erratic on the NPS.

During the Ford and Carter Administrations, a 'symphony of dissent' decried public broadcasting's failure to represent minority viewpoints and to comply with EEO requirements (Lashley 1992: 54). A barrage of protests from groups as diverse as the FCC, the National Organisation of Women and the National Black Media Coalition pointed to the absence of women and minorities from positions of authority throughout the system, and their under-representation in programming. A major cause of dissent was the acquisition and investment in foreign programmes, specifically BBC productions. Independent producers protesting this trend formed the National Coalition of Independent Broadcasting Producers to lobby for more access to public broadcasting funding. The result was the establishment of the Programme Fund in 1978, whereby the CPB annually committed funding to independent broadcasting producers (Lashley 1992: 74). The Programme Fund, however, also made grants to public broadcasting entities and had no percentage allocation for independent producers outside the system.

During the Reagan-Bush Administrations, public broadcasting lost support both within Congress and from traditionally supportive lobby groups. Some were disappointed with the system, describing it as a 'country club for broadcasting professionals' and an 'old boy network'. Others qualified their support during congressional subcommittee hearings, making it dependent on the implementation of the employment and programme diversity mandate (Lashley 1992: 62). Black activist groups also challenged the EEO performances of several public television stations by filing against their license renewal.

Calls for action on the diversity mandate were finally heeded in 1988 when independent filmmakers, along with other minority groups who had been lobbying since the 1970s for more access to programme funding, were granted independent funding allocations within the CPB budget. Hawaii's Senator Inouye, summarised the purpose of these measures at the hearings in 1988:

> Congress is not satisfied that the CPB has allocated sufficient funds to smaller independent producers…blacks and Hispanics alone constitute 30 per cent of our nation's population… the need for programming addressing those audiences, including foreign language programming, should be a primary concern of public radio and television stations and the CPB. (Lashley 1992: 64)

By 1989, the Independent Television Service (ITVS) had been formed to coordinate programme grants to independent producers to foster a wider range of programme voices (Rowland 1993: 165). The significance of the ITVS was reinforced through the addition of a paragraph to the Public Broadcasting Act of 1967:

It is in the public interest to encourage the development of programming that involves creative risks and that addresses the needs of unserved and underserved audiences, particularly children and minorities. (Lashley 1992: 64)

Directed to expand diversity and innovation across public television programming, the Independent Television Service (ITVS) echoed the broadcast publishing house model pioneered by Channel Four. However, the avowed intention of ITVS to produce risky programming that stations were unlikely to produce themselves highlighted the difficulties of localism. Regional differences in public taste and station management attitudes led to broad variance in tolerance for non-mainstream programming. The stations operating out of New York, Pittsburgh, Washington and San Francisco are known for their liberal 'bias' or broad level of tolerance of 'alternative' programming. Differences in tolerance became obvious in 1989 when *Tongues United*, an ITVS documentary about black homosexual experience, was turned down by 111 PSB stations that normally carried the POV series in which it was scheduled, following agitation by the Reverend Donald Wildmon's American Family Association. A month later another controversial programme, *Stop the Church*, about the occupation of St Patrick's Cathedral in New York, was dropped from the series, drawing criticism from viewers of liberal persuasion (Somerset-Ward 1993: 135). The tendency for localism to encourage parochialism, depriving minority groups of their right to be heard, undermines public television's remit to reflect the homogeneity of American society.

Controversy, diversity and innovation were largely lost in the struggle for survival, and programming on public television came to be characterised by educational worthiness, and 'quality' production values; for many this equated with the 'alternative' brief. Deregulation under Reagan removed the FCC guidelines on news and public affairs content, dramatically reducing public affairs programming and coverage of social issues and increasing reality programming, which cost less but attracted similar ratings (Kellner 1990: 183–4). In the deregulated, commercial environment created under Reagan, the need for an 'alternative' broadcaster had never been greater, as programming with a public interest agenda declined. But as the variety of services available on cable fragmented the television audience, public television confronted new challenges for survival, further confounding any revitalisation of its original mission.

As a non-commercial, educational system, public television was originally directed to strive for diversity and excellence rather than targeting mass audience in pursuit of high ratings. However, subsequent congressional directives to develop alternative funding sources have inevitably made audience ratings and demographics important. In 1991, a decision was made to reject the Markle Foundation's proposal for 'The Voters Channel', a series of election specials according major party presidential and vice-presidential candidates the opportunity 'to communicate directly with the electorate'. Although airtime would also have been granted to other perspectives, the project was dropped despite available funding, because the stations didn't want programming with such narrow appeal (Somerset-Ward 1993: 134).

The importance of audience ratings increases as viewers are lost to cable, driving the system towards self promotion and populist programming in the bid to compete. Clearly an unsatisfactory measure of success for a service committed to 'diversity and excellence', audience share nevertheless has an unavoidable impact on the system's credibility. Commenting in 1993 Somerset-Ward observed the earmarking of $6 million by PBS and the CPB for a 'more broadly popular series' to deliver better prime-time ratings (Somerset-Ward 1993: 134). Emphasis on the national schedule, a key to promoting the PBS brand, needs to be carefully balanced with the alternative localist remit.

During the 1980s and 1990s, cable companies moved into programming for audiences that public television had previously had to itself, targeting children and lovers of the arts and documentaries. This initially came through the Arts and Entertainment Network (A&E) – a joint venture by RCA, Hearst and ABC – which competed for the purchase of BBC productions, pushing prices up in the process (Somerset-Ward 1993: 93). The later emergence of the Disney Channel, Nickelodeon, the Discovery Channel, the Learning Channel, CNN, C-SPAN and Bravo, provided competition for the entire public television schedule, delivering children's programming, documentaries, news and current affairs and cultural programmes of the kind previously ignored by commercial broadcasting. Public television's monopoly of formal instructional and educational programming was broken by the emergence of Whittle's Channel One and Jones Intercable's Mind Extension University, both of which provided accredited degree programmes – a blow to the heart of public television (Rowland 1993: 170).

Preoccupied with lobbying for funding and the constant need to justify purpose, public television was slow to recognise and respond to the threat presented by cable. Its past record in specialist programming and access to multiple broadcast television frequencies should have given it an edge in the competition for niche audiences and delivery of complementary programme services. However, initial complacency born from the assumption that cable competitors would ultimately fail negated any advantages. Between 1987 and 1991, the public television audience declined by 12 per cent. This decline is attributed to both the impact of cable and the spread of VCRs (Somerset-Ward 1993: 94). Public television eventually resorted to seeking alliances with cable companies through 'arts and special interest ventures' (Rowland 1993: 170).

Funding – The Unfulfilled Promise

Public television operates on a tiny fraction of the revenues of the commercial broadcasting and cable sector – calculated as 2 per cent in 1998 (Rowland 2002: 12). The lack of the promised insulated funding system recommended by the Carnegie Commission has remained the system's greatest impediment. At the mercy of government, vulnerable to political censorship, unable to formulate long-term plans because of short term funding allocations, public television has increasingly sought funding elsewhere. Today viewer subscriptions and commercial sources exceed federal grants and other tax based funding from local government. While private funding enables public television to continue, it is also seen by many as eroding the integrity of a supposedly non-commercial system. Having failed to achieve any secure form of revenue from the federal government, public television staff have fallen back on membership pledge drives, corporate sponsorship and philanthropy to fund programme production. The PBS Foundation invites donations of $1 million or more for four categories of 'platform neutral' content, offering 'recognition' in return in the form of a hyperlink on the PBS Foundation web page (PBS 2009).

Under the Johnson Administration, three federal agencies were involved in the distribution of funds for public broadcasting, making the system particularly bureaucratic. The biggest funding problem continues to be dependence on the annual budget round that involves public broadcasting staff in an intensive, yearly lobbying contest that is time consuming and expensive. In the 1970s, the financial crisis precipitated by Nixon's veto induced the CPB to increase corporate funding. Oil corporations seized the opportunity to buy cheap publicity and improve the industry's image – damage control in the face of rising environmental awareness. Corporate underwriting, as it is known, carries the entitlement to substantial tax deductions. Mocked as the 'Petroleum Broadcasting System', this association of PBS with oil sponsors damaged the image of public television as a non-commercial service.

Under the subsequent Ford and Carter Administrations the federal funding system was improved bringing relative financial security to public broadcasting (Somerset-Ward 1993: 89). Ford instigated a new system that guaranteed federal authorisations for five years in advance and appropriations for three. Carter, however, cut the authorisation period from five to three years and the appropriation period to two. As noted earlier the setting of a matched funding formula prompted an increase in corporate underwriting and an annual drive for viewer membership.

Reagan's veto of bills proposing extending CPB funding authorisation to five years were sustained by Congress and left the corporation without federal authorisation from 1984–6 (Katz 1989: 201). The Republican-led Congress under Reagan also reduced the national budget deficit by cutting government spending, slashing appropriations from $172 million in 1982 to $137 in 1983, and halving the facilities programme. Although the situation eased during the administration of George Bush Senior, authorisations continued to fall and public broadcasters were required to lobby during federal budget hearings. While capital equipment allocations were more generous with a three-year satellite replacement programme ensuring retention of existing coverage, relentless lobbying took its toll on the organisation:

The very mechanisms of the federal funding process, as much as the inadequate amount, almost guaranteed that public broadcasting would be capable of only the most modest reassessment of its goals and capacities. It could reorganise a particular national programme service office or align itself with a renewed interest in education, but it could not plan for, let alone implement, significant, far reaching changes in the entire range of services and national and local delivery means. (Rowland 1993: 179)

Republican antipathy continued under the administration of George W. Bush, which declined CPB requests for two-year advance funding and for additional digital funding for the financial years 2002–2011, although these were subsequently restored by the full House and Senate Appropriations allocations.

While state and local government support for educational and non-commercial broadcasting is declining in proportion to private funding, it has always far exceeded federal government funding. State government contributions are frequently seen as investment in education. Enthusiasm for distance learning, signalling ways in which new technology can be used in education, helped to legitimise close ties between many stations and the education sector.

Corporate underwriting ('enhanced underwriting') foundation grants and membership subscriptions account for over half the annual revenue for public broadcasting. The second most significant source of funding is that raised by the annual membership pledge drives. The expansion over the years of five-second 'underwriting acknowledgements' into 30 second commercials has angered many, as a contradiction of the non-commercial service legislated in the 1967 Act. Corporate funding originated with the Ford Foundation's early support of educational television, and was already a respectable form of funding when public broadcasting was conceived. As the audience for public television became identifiably upscale, corporate underwriting offered unique marketing opportunities that were unavailable elsewhere. Somerset-Ward records that enhanced underwriting 'had an immediate effect, increasing income from business and corporations from $38 million in 1983 to $56.6 million in 1984'. Introduced in 1981, 'enhanced underwriting' drew caustic comment for its close similarity to the advertising on commercial stations, with industry magazine *Broadcasting* noting in November 1991:

> We know they're only 'extended sponsorship credits', but somehow the difference between a 15-second sponsorship credit featuring say the name and logo of a car manufacturer and video featuring the latest sports car, and a 15-second commercial featuring the name and logo of a car manufacturer and video featuring its latest sports car, escapes us. (Somerset-Ward 1993: 96)

Accountability

The CPB is publicly accountable to government for its implementation of public broadcasting's mission through regular appearances at congressional budget hearings. As already discussed, the CPB's role has been routinely redefined over the years. While responsibility for regulating the system has been largely constant although shared with the

FCC, the distribution of federal funding through the facilities programme and programme commissioning has been variously shared with the PBS, individual licensees, the Office of Telecommunications Policy (OTP), the Independent Television Service (ITVS) and the Chief Programme Executive (CPE). Under the original structure of public broadcasting, the CPB was deliberately distanced from station operations and the National Programme Service (NPS) to protect the system from direct government influence. However, with direct dependence on Federal government funding along with presidential nomination of the CPB Board members, such concerns appear tokenistic.

The application of balance across the schedule rather than within each programme was urged by the Twentieth Century Task Force. Given the freedom afforded commercial broadcasters with the lapse of the Fairness Doctrine this would be a more equitable arrangement, and one that would enable public television to function more successfully as a forum for diverse viewpoints. Under the present federal funding system, however, it remains dependent on the goodwill of the government of the day, and the optional nature of the NPS means it can be undermined by local licensees.

Owned and operated by station licensees, the PBS is a membership organisation that manages the interconnection between stations. In 1974, following restructuring by the Nixon administration, a 'partnership agreement' was negotiated with the CPB. This directed a percentage of the CPB funds directly to local stations and returned programming supervision to the PBS through the Station Programme Cooperative (SPC). In 1989, the creation of the post of Chief Programme Executive (CPE) helped to centralise production for the NPS, streamlining the decision-making process thus helping to make the national schedule more responsive to change and to audience tastes and programming opportunities. It also facilitated advance funding for international co-productions like the WGBH/BBC 26-hour series *The People's Century*, which enabled the production of more innovative programmes and made rapid rescheduling possible. The effectiveness of the latter was demonstrated in 1991 by televised coverage of the Clarence Thomas Hearings, 'conducted by the United States Senate Judiciary Committee to investigate Professor Anita Hill's allegations of prior sexual harassment by Supreme Court nominee Clarence Thomas'. Capturing public interest, the televised hearings came to symbolize 'a public referendum on sexual harassment and other gender inequities in late twentieth century America', and drew a record audience from October 11–13 in 1991 (Beasley 1995). The number of stations committing to full participation in the National Programme Service subsequently increased from 59 per cent in 1991 to 82 per cent in 1992 (Somerset-Ward 1993: 132).

Controlling advertising and promotion, the CPE, with assistance from a public relations company, tailored a more coherent identity for public television and made the system more cost efficient, with the increasing popularity of the NPS enabling reductions in local programming. This, however, had its downside. When the successful Children's Television Workshop (CTW), producers of *Sesame Street*, eclipsed locally made children's programming which could not compete with CTW's superior production values, it highlighted the tendency for diversity to be overshadowed by excellence. The dilemma of a system based on localism is balancing national goals with local needs. Another function regularly raised in discussions of public television's performance, public participation, reflects back to the conflicts inherent in its structure. While localism was idealised as a means of facilitating community involvement in the service, the community boards established to formalise this have registered only limited influence. Somerset-Ward notes that a WGBH community board recommendation not to drop the local news was overridden by the advisory board. While membership pledge drives offer a rather different form of public participation, the responsiveness to local needs envisaged in the 1967 Act has been better served by initiatives like the Nitty Gritty City Group. Formed in 1989, the group represented 15 urban stations that pooled resources to tackle inner city problems, using airtime to develop solutions to particular problems through discussion of shared experiences. The group's programmes, accompanied by closed circuit teleconference workshops, brought together participating networks in a collaborative approach to resolving social conflict. Another past community initiative, the National Campaign to Reduce Youth Violence, united 100 local stations through a partnership with Public Television Outreach Alliance, the Nitty Gritty City Group and Bill Moyers Public Affairs Television, with co-sponsorship from the Department of Education, demonstrating the system's potential as a forum for community involvement in addressing social issues (Somerset-Ward 1993: 128–131; 172).

Reinvention for the Digital Future

With the switchover to digital terrestrial television in the United States on 12th June 2009, the channel capacity of public television stations was commonly expanded to four channels. This is reflected in national programming delivered via PBS networks which now include: PBS World; PBSKIDS; PBS KIDS Sprout; PBS HD; PBS Satellite Service and Create, the last of which carries programming from another public television distribution service, American Public Television, formerly known as the Eastern Educational Network.

The decision to convert terrestrial or 'over-the-air' (OTA) television transmission to digital was undertaken in 1997 with the US congress authorising the recommendations of the FCC, initially setting the date for analogue switch-off at 31 December 2006. The date for digital switch-over was subsequently adjusted three times and eventually achieved under the Obama Administration on 12th June 2009, with an estimated 3 per cent of OTA dependent households left without a television service – 11 per cent of all television households are OTA dependent (FCC 2010). Congress approved a temporary scheme offering coupons for converter boxes to assist disadvantaged groups in the transition to digital. Converting OTA to a higher quality system had been the subject of FCC investigation since 1985 when the government, having previously agreed to adopt the Japanese standard for HDTV, had a change of heart following objections from the European Union and US companies with an interest in the matter. In 1987, during the Reagan Administration, the FCC appointed an Advisory Committee on Advanced Television Services (ACATS) to 'explore how to make a transition to a new system of television broadcasting'. ACATS opted to hold a competition inviting relevant firms and research laboratories 'to produce prototypes of advanced TV systems'. In 1993, ACATS reported that none of the final three systems submitted were superior, all having shortcomings of some kind, and subsequently invited the three competing groups to merge into a 'super team' to resolve the remaining problems. Having agreed on an all digital system incorporating 'computer-like features to television sets and set-top boxes', the competing groups merged to form a 'Grand Alliance' to work through the issues involved in developing a compatible standard across various platforms and technologies (Hart 2010: 8).

The size of the cable and satellite market in the United States made the experience of digital transition rather different to that of many other countries. With around 80–5 per cent of the population receiving cable or satellite services, the proportion of households the government had to encourage to switch to digital was relatively small. On the other hand, the transition to digital was more politically complex because of its ramifications for the 'must carry rules' which applied to cable operators. An early *quid pro quo* arrangement whereby cable operators were required to carry OTA services in return for the use of public space in the laying of cable, the must carry rules bought new tensions between cable operators and OTA broadcasters. Many OTA broadcasters, having been granted additional spectrum to simulcast their services in analogue and digital during the transition period, were also choosing to use the allocated HDTV channel to multicast. This expanded the amount of space that cable operators would have to allocate to carry OTA services. For satellite and cable companies, which were delivering HDTV by 2002/3, the new services were unwelcome, representing more competition. While the cable industry fought vehemently to overturn the must carry rules, the FCC opted to retain them, making some concessions for smaller cable companies and placing limits on the proportion of space a cable or satellite operator could be expected to set aside for OTA services.

For public television, the costs of digital conversion and programming for additional channels brought additional financial pressures to an already cash strapped system. In 1995, Senator Larry Pressler proposed that the funds raised from the planned auction of the spare spectrum, those frequencies freed up after analogue switch off (the digital dividend), an estimated $14 billion, should be used to establish a trust fund for public broadcasting. However, with a Republican majority in congress and opposition from the National Association of Broadcasters, the proposal was dropped (Hart 2010: 13). While public broadcasting secured federal government agreement to fund 45 per cent of the projected transition costs of $1.7 billion (about $5 million per station), by the end of 1999 less than $30 million had been allocated. As additional fund raising ventures to cover the costs of digital conversion, PBS announced plans to raise $1 billion from 'foundations, state governments and viewers', and in August 1997 PBS sought FCC permission for public television stations to use the additional channels for commercial purposes – 'from leasing them to commercial broadcasters, home shopping networks, or infomercial producers to offering PBS programming for a monthly subscription fee' (Starr 2000: 165–6). In 2001, the FCC ruled that public television stations could make money from their digital channels through advertising and ancillary services (Aufderheide 2001). This ruling followed a decade of creeping commercialisation, documented in Jerry Starr's book, *Air Wars: The fight to Reclaim Public Broadcasting*, during which many public television stations had fallen captive to partnerships with corporate interests and commercial broadcasters in the quest for production investment.

Certainly the online environment and the added element of interactivity that characterises digital media has contributed a vast new and rich dimension to the educational content in which public television excels, with separate pathways for children, parents and teachers detailed on the PBS site. However, as new opportunities arise, so do new problems – the digital divide which frustrates universal access, along with the added cost of clearing rights for online multiplatform content, in addition to the costs of producing more content for the expanded network. In 2005, PBS released its Digital Future Initiative, described as a 'latter-day Carnegie Commission', identifying 'lifelong education' as the number one challenge, describing America's educational system as one in crisis. Reaffirming the system's emphasis on the key tenets of education and localism, the Digital Future Initiative (DFI) outlines steps for transforming public broadcasting into public service media. While the scope and scale of the plans are impressive, it is the means by which their development will be funded that has drawn comment. Acknowledging the unpredictability of federal funding, the DFI proposes the establishment of a Digital Future Endowment to be funded through the PBS and NPR Foundations, increasing the system's dependency on private funding. With public television originally defined as a non-commercial service, this proposition is a controversial one.

Bringing new funding pressures and opening new threats to the system's non-commercial status, the advent of digital television inevitably impacted on local stations' ability to make local programming. In 2004, Jerry Starr noted that 'less than 5 per cent of all public TV programming is local' (Starr 2004: 3). As a corollary to this, digitalization led to a higher profile for PBS, as Pat Aufderheide observes:

At the beginning of the 21st century, economic, political, and technological forces finally converged to refocus public television's role. PBS attained a clearer agenda-setting role within the diffuse bureaucracies involved in public television, effectively controlling the national schedule and radically revising its prime-time line-up for the first time in two decades. It aggressively branded the public television environment as 'PBS' by such measures as creating websites for all programs but refusing to show competing websites on air; carrying the PBS 'bug' on channel feeds; outreach and educational campaigns and materials; and public relations with opinion-makers…Producers within and for public television more frequently entered into co-productions internationally, both with public service and commercial partners, and worked harder to retain intellectual property rights.

The challenge of developing and programming digital channels has created new financial pressures and new business plans. (Aufderheide 2001)

But despite this decline in local production across the public television system, Aufderheide adds, 'At the same time, stations have individually experimented with local partners, with extended educational services, including distance learning, and with becoming nodes of community networks' (2001).

Certainly KQED in San Francisco is one public television station that has developed these kinds of the relationships and connections amongst the community, as evidenced by the comments of Richard Winefield, then Vice President for Interactive Educational Services, KQED, San Francisco.

At KQED, the concept of localism means far more that local programming, and outreach and community engagement go beyond the expediency of media production:

> We are a very, very grassroots outreach team. Our people are in schools, they are in childcare centres, they are in adult learning centres, they are in health centres, they are in child nutrition programs, head start centres…because our customers for education are not KQED viewers or listeners. Our customers are low socio-economic, low income, low education, underserved communities. It's the people least likely to be KQED viewers, listeners or members. That's our mission…All of our services are provided free of charge. It's all about public broadcasting which started 50 years ago for a series of purposes, and one of those purposes is to service underserved communities. Nobody is doing that, we are the only ones doing that. (Winefield 2006)

Having decided to focus on stories from its own geographic region, the Pacific rim, rather than compete with East Coast stations, KQED, which is situated in relatively close proximity to Silicon Valley, was also one of the first stations to embark on the development of dedicated web content, viewing the Internet as a third platform offering the benefits of interactivity and on-demand access and not just a supplement to radio and television.

Judging PBS more a follower of commercial media than a leader in its employment of interactive platforms, Laurie Ouellette observes public television's exploitation of the new branding opportunities of the interactive digital environment:

> PBS's employment of user-generated video and social-networking websites ties interactive fundraising to participation and fandom. On PBS's YouTube channel users are invited to watch teasers of current PBS programs, post and read comments, and follow links back to PBS in order to sign up as donors/members. Similarly the official Facebook PBS fan site encourages visitors to fill out PBS surveys, participate in PBS polls, upload photos and link their personal Facebook sites to PBS, in addition to pledging financial support. In both cases the energy of interactive users is channelled into the health and vitality of PBS with minimal cost – the logic of efficiency. (Ouellette 2009: 193)

While the individual ventures of specific stations offer multiple examples of engaging, inventive, interactive cross-platform projects serving educational goals, public television's capability to deliver on its original mission is ultimately tied to the way that its brand is developed and used. If civic participation is to remain a key component of those goals, PBS must endeavour to create a space for genuinely open political debate, something that seems unlikely to be achieved without a more secure source of public funding.

Re-directing responsibility for funding local programming back onto the local stations reflects 'self-service democracy' as Ouellette observes:

> When public service is envisioned as technology for equipping individuals to overcome diminished material resources, it is not surprising that the cultural enlightenment goals of the 1960s – such as exposing citizens to the arts or mobilising them to vote on televised debates – seem less significant or urgent. (Ouellette 2009: 198)

While the Carnegie Commission's goals for Public Television included catering for specific audiences, the 'underserved and unserved', the system has faced increasing criticism as a service for an 'upscale' and elitist audience from 'well educated and upscale lifestyle clusters' (Ouellette 2009: 186–8). Citing 2007 Nielsen Media research, the PBS website claims an average '1.2 primetime rating during the 2007–8', with a weekly reach of 'more than 61 million people in 39 million households' and a monthly reach of over '124 million people [who] access PBS content either on-air or online' (PBS 2009a). The traditional public television audience is popularly cast as middle class, mainly white, wealthier, more 'cultural' and better educated than the general public. It is this audience that attracts corporate underwriters for whom sponsorship represents ambush marketing, reaching those consumers who are generally suspicious of advertising. However, this upscale group also comprises those most likely and most able to support public television as membership subscribers, a source of revenue that now comprises a significant proportion of total annual revenue (Ouellette 2009: 190–1).

Public television became caught in a vicious cycle as commercialisation intensified, with Starr reporting in 2004 that, 'five second underwriting acknowledgements have expanded into 30-second commercials, including pitches on children's programs for junk food and theme parks' (Starr 2004). However, between 2002 and 2008 audience ratings declined from 1.8 to 1.2 per cent (Ouellette 2009: 187; PBS 2009a), while public television membership also fell by 20 per cent between 1993 and 2002 (Starr 2004). In his book, *Air Wars*, Starr had declared public television at a crossroads in 2000, noting a changed mentality in the system. In 1999, PBS hired two commercial broadcasters to develop a plan to address the issue of overlapping public television stations and the duplication of programming, then perceived as a financial drain on the system; the resultant plan was PBS-2:

> A three-night-a-week service consisting of programs from sources such as the BBC, Buena Vista, Columbia, Tri-Star, Twentieth Century Fox, Warner Brothers, and CBS… older cheaper programs [which] can be purchased for $20,000 an hour, on average…old

episodes of *Sixty Minutes*, *On the Road with Charles Kuralt*, and CBS war documentaries… The target is males from twenty-five to fifty-four years of age, 'an audience that has enormous disposable income and [is] highly desired by prestige advertisers'. (Starr 2000: 264–5)

Later that same year, Starr reports, a 'scandal erupted over PBS stations selling and trading donor lists'. The practice, he notes, has become relatively common in the non-profit sector, adding, 'underfunded and urged to be ever more entrepreneurial PBS stations had simply followed suit' (Starr 2000: 266). PBS signed up for the Nielsen ratings for the first time in 2009.

Future prospects of even more television channels and increased competition for special interest audiences drew renewed attacks on the public television system. On the premise that multichannel capacity would ultimately contribute to programming diversity, it was posited that public television's mission could be better served by the 'democratic' system of market response. Calls for the privatisation of public broadcasting began in the early nineties under the Republican dominated Congress. Seeking to reinvigorate the system as a non-commercial one, a group of viewers established Citizens for Independent Public Broadcasting (CIPB). Headed by academic and media activist, Jerry Starr, CIPB launched a campaign for a Public Broadcasting Trust to replace the 'politicized Corporation for Public Broadcasting' and to 'take over the satellite distribution systems now administered by PBS and NPR' (Starr 2000: 276). The CIPB proposes the trust be funded through various taxes on commercial broadcasters who do not pay for their use of the airwaves, and on spectrum auctions (Starr 2004). While the idea offers a way to resolve the decline in local programme production and the trend towards commercialism and the under-representation of dissenting voices, the trust funding mechanism takes on a very formidable opponent, the National Association of Broadcasters.

The absence of those dissenting political voices on public broadcasting marks its failure as a forum for controversy and debate and has been linked to Americans' low level of political engagement, as evidenced by statistics on voter turnout. The gap the CIPB would have public television fill in countering the dominance of right wing media such as Fox Network and Christian Broadcasting Network is now being taken by other media groups. Foremost of these is *Democracy Now!*, an independent syndicated news based programme that is aired by about 700 radio and television networks across America. Founded in 1996 in New York by a group of journalists including Amy Goodman and Juan Gonzalez, who present much of the show, *Democracy Now!* aims to be 'the exception to the rulers', Goodman's slogan for the show, and serves a growing audience, as New York based community broadcasting specialist Nan Rubin observed:

She [Amy Goodman] has probably a couple of million people who watch or listen to the program every day. More than Channel Thirteen [New York's public television station]… But Amy represents some of what people I think would like to see more of in terms of public service type reporting and production. She is on five days a week. The programme is an hour. It's extremely topical, she interviews a lot of really topical people, they do reports…they will take material from producers…There are a couple of community based public television stations in the United States that…do put Amy on. But in New York…it's on one of the public access channels. (Rubin 2006)

This development indicates a niche that public television might serve and one definitely within its mission, with cross platform delivery via web-based content, UGC and podcasts providing a way of winning the interest of younger viewers and driving a more participatory news service. Nevertheless, representation of political dissent and controversy remains difficult. In 2004, it emerged that the conservative thinking CPD chairman, Kenneth Tomlinson, had hired an outside consultant to monitor bias in the PBS public affairs show, *Now with Bill Moyers*, without the authorisation of the CPB. That year the CPB announced its withdrawal of funding for the show, and when Moyers departed after the 2004 elections the show's length was cut to half an hour. Following an internal investigation into his activities as Chairman in 2005, Tomlinson left the CPB. In 2007, Moyers, a journalist and commentator who has been very critical of the US media, reprised the long running PBS show, *Bill Moyers Journal,* which had run for a decade in the 1970s. When he declared plans for retirement, however, PBS took the opportunity to announce replacements for both *Bill Moyers Journal* and *Now*, programmes described as 'two of the hardest-hitting shows on public television' by the organization Fairness and Accuracy in Reporting (FAIR):

> The two shows stand out as examples of what PBS public affairs programs should be: unflinching independent journalism and analysis. The shows have covered poverty, war and media consolidation – not to mention serious discussions of subjects taboo elsewhere, like the case for impeaching George W. Bush. (FAIR 2010)

The other long running public affairs show on PBS, the *Jim Lehrer News Hour*, had previously, in 2006, been criticised for lack of diversity by FAIR, an assessment with which the PBS Ombudsman agreed. However, PBS has also produced some hard-hitting documentary public affairs shows. One innovative public affairs series, *Exposé* (originally titled AIR – America's Investigative Report) is a collaboration between New York's Channel Thirteen/WNET and the non-profit organisation, Centre for Investigative Reporting, which launched in 2006. The series screens half hour documentaries that revisit the public interest exposés of investigative journalists gleaned from across the media, giving them a national audience (PBS 2010a). Another is the long running *Frontline* produced by Boston's WGBH, which is accompanied by an impressive media-rich website that provides background research and resources that build prolonged relevance into any documentary project. Documentary strands such as this provide the opportunity for in-depth social and political analysis that is in scarce supply across the commercial media; inevitably more moderated and reflective, they represent public affairs rather than current affairs, which is by its nature more the province of live talk-based shows. While many suggestions have been made for how public television might improve its public affairs programming, with more live participatory coverage directly engaging viewers at a local level, this weakness is likely to continue. Ultimately, public television's funding mix of viewer subscriptions, corporate underwriting and federal appropriations necessarily invokes caution in the coverage of current affairs and a need for ratings, pressures which together frustrate the system's remit to provide a forum for public debate.

Avoidance of controversy, increasing commercialism and the pursuit of a prosperous demographic of the kind likely to contribute during public television's fund raising 'pledge week' have left localism and education as the standout enduring strengths of the public television mission. While local production initiatives still emerge and are likely to continue to do so, as noted earlier, it is through its services to education that public television increasingly defines and justifies its existence. The creativity and rigour with which some public television stations approach this is reflected in the comments of Richard Winefield, former Vice President for Interactive Educational Services at KQED in San Fransisco:

> We have a firm that we use to evaluate all of our educational projects longitudinally…they document how people feel about our workshops. They follow a sample of people over time longitudinally to find out, Ok a year ago you went to a KQED workshop, are you continuing to use that content in your classroom? Are you seeing any impact on student achievement? We didn't always do that…five years ago we got a small grant from someone…and what we found was not only does it help us improve our programs, because when we get feedback from teachers or from childcare providers, community people, we can use that to modify our programs. But also potential funders absolutely love that evaluation stuff and it really does add credibility. So when we go out looking for money, when we put that down in front of them and say, here is what an independent evaluation expert has said, and please call them if you would like…that's gold. (Winefield 2006)

Educational content on public television spans the full gamut of possible genres, and while KQED specialises in community outreach and engaging interactive content targeted to children still in school, the system also produces a considerable amount of documentary programming and associated cross-platform content that might also be termed educational for a general audience. At WGBH in Boston, which along with Channel Thirteen/WNET in New York produces 60 per cent of PBS's prime-time programming, institutional history and proximity to universities such as Harvard and the Massachusetts Institute of Technology (MIT) has spawned longstanding relationships with leading US researchers across a range of fields. This serendipitous situation has resulted in the production of multi-platform projects integrating television programming and online content that contribute what WGBH Interactive Producer, Howard Cutler, refers to as the library aspect of media:

When you are spending enough money to make the television program, it's usually one of the few times you are going to amass the critical amount of content that would actually enable you to do it. So maybe once every decade you have this kind of opportunity to take a major subject…we just did the first 25 years of the AIDS pandemic. That's not going to happen again for a while. So if you can make that project and then translate it to the web, you have got a whole generation that can look at that history and deconstruct it in different ways, and make what they need of it because you have placed it where it's continually available…Our funding model is a national funding model, but there's no question when you publish to the web, that we are publishing internationally and there's no question that our audience is international because we can see it in the stats that come back. The search engines rule. The search engine is the single most important invention after the web itself, and it's a natural ally of what we do. (Cutler 2006)

Production staff at WGBH interactive have been gratified to discover their projects routinely top the Google search engine rankings, reflecting both popularity and relevance. Such discoveries herald a new purpose for public television productions, and along with a digital archiving project, Preserving Digital Public Television, which is being undertaken with the Library of Congress, indicate the liberating possibilities of on-demand platforms for public broadcasting. PBS documentary strands such as *Nova*, the PBS science series, *American Experience*, a history series, along with the public affairs strand, *Frontline*, provide ideal foundations for various forms of cross-platform content and participatory opportunities. *We Shall Remain,* a five-part television documentary series for about Native Americans, was one such cross platform project, with a website offering Native American communities workshops and the opportunity to participate through uploading short films made on mobile phones. The website also links viewers to a National Library initiative encouraging community libraries to get involved in running events and activities to engage public interest in Native American culture and history (PBS 2010b).

The 2010 decision by the Obama Administration not to fund PBS educational partnerships undertaken with the Department of Education – Ready to Teach and Ready to Learn, suggests that the system may in future have to look more to its more general educational programming, its cultural and historical productions to define its place in the broadcasting environment (CPB 2010). In the face of continuing commercialism, a soft political line and an increasingly homogenous audience, this high quality documentary and cross platform content, characterised by extensive background research and careful crafting of both television narrative and interactive structures, seems likely to consolidate its place as the distinguishing feature of public television. In the seriousness of its intent, productions of this kind contribute to the diversity of television content across the sector and given the long term accessibility assured through online digital archives overcome elitist categorisation.

Chapter 7

Television New Zealand – 'A Crown Owned Company'

Introduction

Although New Zealand state broadcasting was originally modelled on the BBC, the tyranny of size and distance constrained its emulation of the British broadcaster and despite white-settler ties to the 'mother country', the concept of public service broadcasting was never totally embraced for a variety of reasons. Colonial 'cultural cringe', population size and the economics of broadcasting were all contributing factors in the history of compromise that led to TVNZ's current conflicted hybrid identity.

As part of widespread neoliberal 'reforms' in 1988–9, TVNZ was remodelled as a State Owned Enterprise and directed to return a dividend to government. Coinciding with the introduction of commercial competition which ended 28 years of state monopoly television, the restructuring saw TVNZ shedding most of its former public service aspirations as it was transformed into a highly profitable business. In November 1999, the Labour Government of Helen Clark was elected on a platform of resuscitating public service television. While subsequently restructured as a Crown Owned Enterprise (CROC), and eventually accommodated with a public service charter, TVNZ was still expected to perform as a successful commercial business, delivering a biannual dividend to government. In 2008, the National Party Government of John Key was elected on a promise of scrapping the TVNZ Charter. Claiming that 'the charter hasn't worked', Key later announced its abolition in April 2009 (*Otago Daily Times* 2009). Given its turbulent history, TVNZ is an apt final case study for this book, reflecting several potential directions and strategies for reinventing public service media along with the dangers of too many radical reversals. With privatisation an ever-present spectre since the 1990s, TVNZ's path has taken some unexpected turns. Digitalization, first abandoned to the private sector then reclaimed by the government, led to the expansion of TVNZ's coverage with the launch of two additional non-commercial niche channels. While it is primarily its funding system – the 'cash cow' model of public broadcasting – that makes TVNZ a suitable final case study here, the broadcaster's many restructurings also challenge perceptions of public service goals, audience expectations and public accountability, evoking an ABC staff slogan, 'if public service broadcasting is lost it can never be reborn' (Dempster 2000: 255).

A System in Flux

Small society conformity, the dislocation of rural lifestyles, and predominantly mono-cultural values placed social harmony above social justice and left New Zealand with a relatively underdeveloped public culture. Maintaining an ordered society and a stable workforce was deemed necessary for economic growth, and the control of dissenting voices was part of this. Early monopolistic control of the print media by proprietorial interests worked to silence radical viewpoints. National interest tended to be defined in terms of economics rather than public freedoms and as such was an established priority for the media when broadcasting arrived. The pioneering spirit of this former British colony had contributed a habit of resourcefulness that prioritised practical solutions over theoretical concerns. Thus, financing a national transmission system for New Zealand's small, geographically dispersed population and rugged terrain became the dominant feature of early broadcasting policy. The most cost effective means of securing this was through state control (Butterworth 1989).

The New Zealand government was the first in the world to legislate for the state control of radio broadcasting with the Wireless Telegraphy Act in 1903 (Butterworth 1989: 147). As a diversity of voices began to be heard with the growth of private operators, the government tightened its hold. Even to own a receiving set required a declaration from a Justice of the Peace, and in 1923 broadcasting 'propaganda of a controversial nature' was prohibited. The privately run New Zealand Broadcasting Company, a loose association of private 'A' radio stations, was transformed by the National Government in 1932 into the New Zealand Broadcasting Service (NZBS), with all power subsequently vested in the state. The primary objective of the NZBS was to develop a national service (Gregory 1985: 24)

As the service became established, Robert J. Gregory observes, the pragmatics of political convenience soon outweighed those of cost. In 1935, elected on a platform of wide ranging social and economic reform, the Labour Prime Minister, Michael Joseph Savage, assumed control of broadcasting, abolishing the board set up by the previous government and taking on the new ministerial portfolio himself. Savage used the antagonism of a conservative business-oriented press to justify continued 'suppression of dissonance', announcing his intentions for broadcasting in 1936: 'What the newspapers neglect to do, the Broadcasting Service will do. The government is going to be the master of publicity' (Gregory 1985: 18).

Labour's pre-election promise that popular, independent provincial 'B' stations would be given the right to take advertising was made conditional on their state purchase and eventuated in a new state run commercial service. The dual system, which comprised the non-commercial National 'YA' service and the commercial National 'ZB' service, was administered by a government department under direct ministerial control. Aspects of the BBC model were selectively transplanted according to government needs, and the YA service was conceived in high moral, Reithian terms by the first Director of Broadcasting, Professor James Shelley:

Broadcasting should bend its efforts to develop a spirit of trust and tolerance, and not succumb to the temptation to provide the superficial excitement of petty strife. (Qtd. in Gregory 1985: 30)

The Reithian ideals of unity and control served the interests of the Labour government with its paternalist concerns for public welfare. As Minister of Broadcasting, Savage used radio to promote his programme of social and economic reform. Through his 'Sunday Evening Talk' and parliamentary broadcasts, he became a popular radio personality and cemented support for his policies. Despite past criticism of the previous National Government for suppressing coverage of controversy on radio, the Labour Government continued the policy, restricting the opposition's access to parliamentary broadcasts.

New Zealand's television service grew from public demand rather than government initiative, with little consideration given to the possible social effects of the medium. As with radio, the costs and practicalities of securing national coverage assumed primary importance. The first service began in 1960 under the NZBS, but this was replaced in the 1962 Broadcasting Act with a public corporation, the NZBC, primarily to accommodate television. Although posited as bringing greater independence from government, some doubted the efficacy of a state owned corporation given New Zealand's intimate political environment. Gilbert Stringer, who drafted the legislation and became director-general, planned a triumvirate structure designed to ensure operating autonomy. However, the intended balance of power was dependent on the chairman of the board upholding his role as an independent intermediary, protecting the director-general from the minister. In reality, the established practice of government interference tended to overrule any constitutional constraints, with the board of political appointees generally endorsing government policy.

Between 1960 and 1988, the television license fee was used to buy non-commercial days on television. Initially by way of compromise, half the week was kept commercial free; as costs rose non-commercial days gradually disappeared, reflecting the triumph of convenience over principle and 'basic uncertainty about what constituted good television or how to achieve it' (Farnsworth 1992: 198). The limit on advertising time, originally six minutes per hour, was raised to nine minutes in 1977 and then removed entirely when the industry became self regulating under the 1989 Broadcasting Act. Hybrid funding gave the corporation useful independence from government during its first fifteen years, but the added financial pressure of a second channel in 1973, the government's refusal to raise the license fee, and the economic downturn of the late Seventies, drove increased dependence on advertising revenue. Represented as the most practical means of delivering a national television service, this mixed funding solution became an obstacle to putting public interest first. Viewers accustomed to the compromises of the hybrid funding system were initiated with relative ease into the fully commercial era in 1988. With adroit sleight of hand, the government replaced what had once been called public service broadcasting with a small proportion of commercially viable, local programmes, courtesy of a publicly funded Broadcasting Commission (later renamed New Zealand on Air).

Thus technical considerations and costs prioritised from the beginning contributed a pragmatic utilitarianism that came to dominate state broadcasting policy. The early technical achievements of the national transmission system for TV1 and TV2 made broadcasting engineers the 'organisational heroes' of television, and their prestige outweighed that of producers and journalists within the corporation (Farnsworth 1992: 192). The prospects offered by new cable and satellite communications were represented as bringing inevitable and sweeping change, and played an integral part of restructuring and deregulation under the Fourth Labour Government (Rennie 1988: i). Thus the public was persuaded to accept technological and economic factors as key determinants and to believe that deregulation and competition would leave them better served.

The combination of radical structural change and economic pressure eroded the editorial independence of state owned television in New Zealand. Economic pressure has been variously applied over the years through controlling the purse strings for capital development, controlling the license fee, threatening private competition and demanding the maximisation of profits. Recurring structural change prompted routine shifts in presentation formats, creating job insecurity and undermining the development of professional standards in television journalism in New Zealand.

Making a relatively late arrival in New Zealand, television evoked a largely reactive response from government with party political and economic interests determining its course rather than committees of enquiry, as had been the case in other nations, as Gregory observes:

> The principles that did shape the introduction of television in New Zealand were based on general party philosophy towards the role of the state in the economy rather than on consideration of the political functions of public broadcasting in an open society. (Gregory 1985: 40)

Nevertheless television did revolutionise news reporting in New Zealand. As founding director-general, Stringer's major contribution was the establishment of New Zealand's first national news service autonomous from government. Until its arrival, radio news bulletins had lacked any pretension to journalistic analysis or investigative reporting, consisting of announcers reading from newspapers, government releases and items from the BBC. Challenging this passive spectator role, television brought a greater public profile to news. By 1969, a strong independent voice had emerged with *Gallery*, a current affairs programme that entered new controversial territory. For the producer, emigrant Irishman, Des Monaghan, one of the functions of the programme was to hold politicians to public account. When the Head of the Security Intelligence Service (SIS), Brigadier Gilbert, demanded the withdrawal of an interview he had done with journalist, Brian Edwards, the NZBC ran the programme as scheduled in an unprecedented strike for independence (Gregory 1985: 64–71).

Tensions between television journalists, the BCNZ Board and parliament were ongoing during television's first fifteen years. Interventions and 'reproofs' were usually justified on the grounds that journalists had failed to present 'proper balance' or 'due impartiality', claims that were difficult to dispute (Gregory 1985: 53). While director-general Stringer's stand on the Edwards' interview with Brigadier Gilbert staked a claim for independence, later political interventions were more successful in silencing dissent. In 1966, Gordon Bick, a journalist with another current affairs show, *Compass*, resigned when his investigation of possible price rises with the changeover to decimal currency was pulled from the schedule. The problem was that 'proper balance' could not be met because representatives of the Decimal Currency Board were unavailable (Gregory 1985: 74). The incident reflected both the Board's preparedness to self-censor in the interests of harmonious relations with government, and the ease with which officialdom could sabotage a story it didn't like.

Used as 'political football', television was restructured six times between 1973 and 2009. In 1972, the Broadcasting Authority, which was responsible for spectrum management, asked for applications for the second channel. The NZBC, initially resistant because of high inflation and the costs involved, but also fearing competition, proposed a non-commercial service funded by the license fee with establishment costs financed by NZBC reserves. This was the logical option where a commercial service cross-subsidising a non-commercial one would give viewers optimum choice and diversity. Yet in all the changes made to television broadcasting, this option was never tried. While the National Government favoured privately owned television and opted for the Independent Television Corporation (ITC), Labour's 1972 election win saw the decision reversed and broadcasting restructured.

Government interference in current affairs programmes had made independence a public issue. In January 1973, it was announced that the NZBC would be replaced by three separate corporations with a Committee of Inquiry, under the chairmanship of Professor Kenneth Adam (the Adam Committee), established to make recommendations on the proposed changes. The 1973 Broadcasting Act subsequently instituted three separate corporations – TV1, TV2 and Radio New Zealand (RNZ) – with a regulatory body, the Broadcasting Council, to collect and disperse the license fee.

A policy known as 'Guided Competition' was introduced under the recommendations of the Adam Committee. The guidelines stipulated that there should be no overlapping of key programming – news bulletins, current affairs, local productions or programmes of similar kind – and that common junctions be set across the different broadcasters (Adams 1973: 41). The Act afforded more power to those in creative roles, and claimed to signal a new independence for broadcasting, removing the ministerial portfolio. Underlying the decision to make the channels commercially competitive were plans to convert to colour by October 1973, the indebtedness of public commercial radio following the introduction of private competition in 1969, and the expense of the second channel (Gregory 1985: 4).

Two channel competition changed the way television presented itself to the public. The imbalance between services was a challenge for the disadvantaged TV2. While TV1 inherited the NZBC national network and the new production centre at Avalon, TV2 had only limited facilities and partial coverage, which prompted it to follow a populist approach, modelled on Australian commercial broadcasting. 'Guided competition' attempted to harness competition between the two corporations to stimulate commercial revenue and enhance local programme quality. It did both, but also promoted popular programming, conditioning viewers to new levels of commercial hype, which drew public criticism. Nevertheless, despite its new commercial look, the freedom offered by the three corporation structure did prove a creative stimulus for producers, and local production reached a high point during this era. The structure, however, was not cost-effective, with unnecessary duplication of services, staff and resources and no common pool of funds whereby commercial services could subsidise the less commercial.

Labour's defeat at the next election forestalled any real test of 'guided competition', with the National Government restructuring broadcasting yet again, reviving the NZBC and the ministerial portfolio. The latter was given new powers, the right to issue directives to the corporation, which in return was required to 'have regard to the general policy of the government in relation to broadcasting' (NZ Broadcasting Act 1976: 20[1]). Under the 1976 Act, the old NZBC structure was reborn as the Broadcasting Corporation of New Zealand (BCNZ), which was to act as a 'public trustee of the national interest'. The two channels were directed to be competitive but complementary with each being represented by its own Standing Committee, and reporting to the Board.

In addition to the upheavals of restructuring, the Prime Minister, Robert Muldoon, was a frequent adversary of the corporation from 1975 until 1984. His criticisms ranged from accusations of left-wing bias and incompetence amongst journalists to extravagance in *The Governor*, a landmark drama series about Sir George Grey, New Zealand's first Governor. Through his column in the weekly newspaper, *Truth*, and through refusing to work with particular journalists – television interviewers Simon Walker and Ian Fraser, and *Listener* columnist, Tom Scott – Muldoon challenged the BCNZ's credibility (Gregory 1985: 94). This hostility was further evident in his resistance to any rise in the licence fee, which made television increasingly dependent on advertising revenue.

State owned television underwent further restructuring when BCNZ chairman, Ian Cross, on assuming office in 1977, was confronted with the task of increasing efficiency during an economic downturn. Under the 1980 'Cross Plan', Television New Zealand (TVNZ) became a vertically integrated two-channel service. TVNZ was restructured into two divisions – the network service and the production service – with a national news operation based in Auckland. This removed expensive duplication although moving the news to Auckland was a controversial decision given past antipathy between Wellington's Avalon journalists and the Prime Minister. With Wellington also the seat of government, the move seemed to signal new priorities. Cross pursued a policy of complementary rather than competitive programming. Despite the static licence fee, he pushed informally for local content quotas, requiring a 38 per cent proportion of locally produced material on TV1 and 25 per cent on TV2. He also stipulated that 'programmes of substance' and locally produced programmes should not be scheduled against each other. Some minority interest programmes returned to prime-time from the late night and Sunday afternoon ghettos, as public interest priorities resurfaced; in 1980, a Head of Children's programming was appointed and a decision was made not to screen advertising around children's programmes. Cross also attempted a 50:50 audience split between channels to maximise advertising revenue. The integrated, dual system kept the purchasing costs of foreign programming to a minimum, removing the inflationary factor of competitive bidding.

The 'Cross plan' was viewed by some as an attempt to frustrate privatisation of one of the channels. Whatever its intentions, the reorganisation proved good for advertising sales, with BCNZ revenue increasing threefold from 1979–83 (Smith 1996: 12). As this new, merged TVNZ was launched in 1980, a third channel was proposed with private ownership mooted by both government and the BCNZ. Following protracted hearings, the third channel was eventually launched at the same time as TVNZ underwent its fourth restructuring.

When Labour came to power in 1984, the Minister for Broadcasting, Jonathan Hunt, established a Royal Commission of Inquiry into Broadcasting. Chaired by Professor Robert Chapman, the Commission was given a broad brief encompassing matters related to operations, technology and funding, along with independence and quality in programming and reflecting national culture to better serve all New Zealanders (Chapman 1984: 8). The Commission listened to 282 submissions, sat for 71 days, visited a number of BCNZ facilities and travelled to Japan, the United States, Canada and the United Kingdom in its study of different broadcasting systems, providing the most thorough investigation of broadcasting the country had initiated. Yet its recommendations for fine tuning existing structures, and regulations regarding local content and advertising, as well as cautions regarding new technologies were virtually ignored in the radical deregulation of broadcasting that began the following year.

The decision to allocate a third channel was endorsed by the Labour Government under Prime Minister David Lange, and the Broadcasting Tribunal hearings to consider submissions began in August 1985. The TV3 group, which had varying shareholdings from region to region, emerged as the victor when the hearings ended in 1987. The group's chief appeal was the involvement of successful broadcasters and its five year growth plan forecasting local content peaking at 40 per cent, a figure that shamed TVNZ's rate of 25 per cent (Smith 1996: 24).

Introducing private commercial competition, the allocation of the third channel paralleled other radical changes in broadcasting policy, which began in August 1987 when the new Minister for Broadcasting, Richard Prebble, requested a report on broadcasting from the Treasury and the Ministry of Trade and Industry (Smith 1996: 35). Supplanting the recommendations of the Royal Commission, the report provided the basis for reforms. The democratic consultative process was deemed too slow for the changes supposedly necessary to accommodate new telecommunications technologies (Cocker 1995).

Bringing the sector into line with the government's economic restructuring, broadcasting deregulation was legislated through three separate acts: the Broadcasting Corporation of New Zealand Restructuring Act of 1988, which transformed Television New Zealand and Radio New Zealand into State Owned Enterprises (SOEs); the 1989 Broadcasting Act, which repealed the 1976 Act, disbanded the Broadcasting Tribunal, lifted advertising limits and created two independent statutory authorities, the Broadcasting Standards Authority (BSA) and the Broadcasting Commission (later renamed New Zealand on Air); and the Radio Communications Act of 1989, which transferred responsibility for spectrum frequency allocation to the Ministry of Commerce through a market based system of frequency auctions (Smith 1996: 45). The final touch was added by the National Government in April 1991 with the Broadcasting Amendment Act, which abolished restrictions on foreign ownership, opening the way for TV3 to be wholly foreign owned.

In the deregulated three channel environment, TVNZ maintained a 70 to 80 per cent audience share, with TV3's achievements well below its 28 per cent target. By aggressive marketing, by poaching TV3 programming strategies, by superior programme purchasing power and through diversification into a number of associated businesses, TVNZ trounced its only free-to-air competitor in audience ratings and proved itself a highly profitable business, returning a NZ$66 million dividend to the government in 1996 (*Onfilm* 1996: 6). Past aspirations to a public service mission were reworded to accommodate TVNZ's new business ethic, which was spelled out in Section 4(1) of the State Enterprises Act (1986): 'the principle objective of every State enterprise shall be to operate as a successful business'. The telling omission of the phrase, 'to inform, educate and entertain', from the 1989 Broadcasting Act, left the way clear for a fuller embrace of commercial values with a vaguely worded 'social obligation' clause providing little impediment. TVNZ's new entertainment-centred news and current affairs focused on the human-interest stories and scandals about celebrities and royals that typified tabloid infotainment culture. The transactional dynamic of commercial broadcasting, whereby audiences are 'sold' to advertisers rather than 'served', was evident through programme and station promotions and the increase in advertising per programme hour, which rose to 25 per cent of prime-time.

As a State Owned Enterprise (SOE), TVNZ was directed to compete for audience in the newly competitive commercial environment, and to return biannual dividends to government. Far from the new business ethic releasing broadcasting from its historical dependence on the government, political interference persisted. The National Government's public admission that it 'does not believe it is the owner of a television network for the long haul', induced timidity at TVNZ throughout the 1990s (*Onfilm* September 1996: 5). The cancellation of plans for a current affairs pre-election programme on a key election issue, the Employment Contracts Act, suggested a serious loss of independence (Campbell 1996). Current affairs stories like the *Assignment* programme that exposed a tax evasion 'scam' in the Cook Islands became rare exceptions. With no legislative obligations on TVNZ to produce quality news and current affairs, advertisers' interests became paramount. Thus the expensive but vital public service role of providing news and current affairs was left to the discretion of profit driven broadcasters in an apolitical and commercially skewed sector. The independent agency, New Zealand on Air (NZoA), was delegated the responsibility for reflecting New Zealand identity and culture and representing the interests of minority groups.

The dearth of local content on New Zealand television, which has hovered between 20 and 30 per cent, has been attributed to two factors. Firstly, the average cost per programme hour for imported programming is far lower – estimated in 1988 as NZ$2,000 compared to NZ$53,000 for New Zealand productions (Rennie 1988: 35). The local industry cannot compete on an equal footing with broadcasters and production companies with widespread international distribution (Rennie 1988: 42). Secondly, as an English speaking nation where the dominant 'Pakeha' culture retained close ties to Britain (still referred to as home by many into the 1970s), there was a wealth of attractive available programming from overseas. Preference for British programmes was accompanied by a critical view of the local efforts, which in television's first decade had difficulty matching BBC standards. The resultant 'cultural cringe' kept programming costs down, with New Zealand estimated as 'the fourth highest consumer of imported television programmes' in 1970 (Stewart & Moss 1983: 283).

Local programming increased in quantity and diversity as local talent emerged throughout the 1970s alongside the rebirth of the New Zealand film industry. The enhanced power of producers and strong commitments to local production by both channels nourished local television drama. By 1976, TV1 claimed 75 hours of local drama in its first twelve months, more than the total output of NZBC's thirteen years (Gregory 1985: 149). The launch of New Zealand's first soap, *Close to Home*, in 1975 proved a valuable training ground for local drama, running for eight years. Local producers contributed children's programmes, drama, comedy and some special interest, magazine programmes in addition to local news and current affairs. TV2 also produced several drama series, the most notable being *Hunter's Gold*, a 13-part children's series, the first of many the corporation was to make. Sold to the BBC, which screened it twice, the series boosted confidence in local production. Local content reached a high of 34 per cent in 1974 before the economic downturn and controversy over the production costs of *The Governor* brought budgetary cuts. Following questions in parliament, a parliamentary committee was set up to look into budgeting and control of expenditure in television in 1977; Eventually revealing that *The Governor* had cost NZ$1.4 million, the Committee recommended that the BCNZ improve its budgeting procedures (Boyd-Bell 1985: 54).

With over two thirds of the schedule devoted to imported programming, the absence of local faces and voices became one of the distinguishing features of New Zealand television. The 1986 Royal Commission found local content was only 25 per cent of the schedule, the same level calculated in 1971 (Smith 1996: 119). By 1995, local content on TVNZ had declined further to 23.2 per cent, with sports coverage contributing nearly one third of this amount. The commercial imperative had almost entirely displaced the SOE's legislated social responsibility objectives, 'the provision of programmes which reflect and foster New Zealand's identity and culture', which had been largely devolved to the Broadcasting Commission (New Zealand on Air). Administration of the broadcasting fee, previously allocated to TVNZ, was delegated to New Zealand on Air (NZoA). After 1993, 13 per cent of this funding was allocated to a separate Maori broadcasting funding agency, Te Mangai Paho. A funding board with Maori members, Te Mangai Paho resulted from a legal challenge by Maori groups, who argued that the government had a responsibility to protect the Maori language and culture under the Treaty of Waitangi, signed in the early days of European settlement (Horrocks

1996: 55). The broadcasting fee was abolished in 1999, following a legal claim that the fee was an unjust tax, and substituted with equivalent funding from government coffers. NZoA administration of government funding for local television production (a cultural subsidy) meant public service funding decisions were made on a programme by programme basis, instead of being in the control of a single state broadcaster; TVNZ had to compete for the funds with the private/commercial broadcaster, TV3. With NZoA investment dependent on broadcasters' prime-time strategies, commercial values dominated and 'local content' displaced public service programming as the primary focus of public funding; minority interest programming was still funded but marginalised to ghetto time slots.

By the mid Nineties, a National Business Review poll 'found that two thirds of viewers were dissatisfied with television' (Smith 1998: 34). In 1999, elected on a platform of bringing back public service broadcasting, the Clarke Labour Government promised a charter to end TVNZ's commercial emphasis. The Government's avowed 'Third Way' ideology conflating public good with economic efficiency (Thompson 2004: 62) informed TVNZ's conversion from SOE to Crown Owned Company (CROC). As Minister for Culture and Heritage, overseeing the broadcasting portfolio, Prime Minister Helen Clark pre-empted reports from her own broadcasting task force, ruling out 'any prospect of exploring the possibility of commercial free-television' because of budgetary constraints (Thompson 2004: 62). The negotiation of the new charter extended into Labour's second term, revealing underlying tension between overlapping ministries, the Ministry of Economic Development (formerly Commerce) and the Communications and Broadcasting portfolios (Thompson 2003: 19). Launched in 2003, the charter addressed issues of national culture, the needs of Maori, children, and minorities, and the importance of contributing to citizenship and encouraging 'creative risk-taking' and also marked the fifth restructuring of state owned television (TVNZ 2003). The CROC structure retained the problematic requirement to return a dividend to government, stipulating that TVNZ continue to perform as a successful commercial broadcaster; the implication being that it must somehow maximise profits without infringing its chartered obligations. Media academic and commentator Peter Thompson describes this as the practical reality of the 'third way', which 'tends to promote the pursuit of social-cultural-democratic goals in whatever policy space remains after market imperatives have been accommodated' (Thompson 2004: 62).

Implanted on top of TVNZ's existing commercial enterprise, the charter was a symbolic public good, but was all but impossible to implement under the existing funding structure. A government allocation of NZ$13 million for charter programme funding did not even offset income lost from the sale of BCL (NZ$14.2 million in 2002), TVNZ's former transmission arm, which had been a separate SOE (Thompson, 2003: 5), and the Treasury's demand for a dividend of NZ$37.6 million from TVNZ in 2004 was subsequently revised (NZ$11.4 million returned) following the corporation's very public objections (Thompson 2005: 7). Yet problems besetting the charter's implementation went beyond matters of cost, exposing issues of accountability and whether charter funded programmes should be identifiable 'like sultanas in a fruit cake', or reflected throughout the schedule (Collins 2003: 3), whether it was legitimate for charter money to fund programmes also funded by NZoA, or for the charter to focus on 'local content', which is the designated role of NZoA (Thompson 2004). Instead of putting the state owned broadcaster on a solid public service footing, the confusing dual remit and special 'charter program' funding, along with programming funded by NZoA and Te Mangai Paho, led to disputes with government over the dividend payment. A media meltdown over newsreaders' salaries angered the Prime Minister and further alienated the public, as popular presenters were dumped.

Consumers, Citizens and Shareholders

TVNZ's 1989 transformation from state owned monopoly to State Owned Enterprise radically altered the public broadcaster's relationship with the audience. Primarily consumers targeted by advertisers, viewers were now delivered programming according to the dictates of mass interest taste; this was most obvious in transformation of *One Network News*, but was also evident in the dearth of intellectually engaging programming for older viewers and the relegation of minority interest programming to morning television.

Under the system of channel differentiation in the 1990s, TVNZ's two channels, branded as TV One and TV2, catered for different demographic groups through complementary programme schedules: live sport, news and current affairs, British comedies and drama, documentaries, and educational television on TV One; and a mix of entertainment, sport, music, movies, comedies on TV2 (TVNZ 1995). Following deregulation, in anticipation of commercial competition from TV3, the brand for each of TVNZ's channels was researched and existing identifiable trends were enhanced to signal their target audiences. As media commentator Paul Smith observes, the brands offered clear cut albeit limited choices: 'If TV One offered the sediment of serious viewing, Channel 2 provided the baubles and sparkle' (Smith 1996: 64). Complementary programming makes sense if the two channels are jointly owned, since it splits the potential audience base between them. But the fact that TV One's better ratings were out-paced by TV2's advertising revenue is a potential problem for a corporation driven to pursue an unshackled economic imperative. TV3 competes predominantly with TV2 for the younger demographic group that draws greater advertising revenue (18–49 year olds). The more cutthroat competitive environment thus saw the interests of the larger, older audience subordinated to those of the younger minority.

Under the SOE and CROC structures, TVNZ's primary relationship is with advertisers as clients, to whom it delivers audiences as consumers from appropriate demographics. The aspiration of public service broadcasting to serve viewers as citizens, to equip them with cultural and political resources for exercising their civic rights and electoral duties (Murdock 2005: 186), took a back seat to increasing profits. Unlike other commercially subsidised public broadcasters, advertising income is not reinvested in programme production and operations. The influence of audience ratings on TVNZ news and current affairs has been well documented by New Zealand media commentators (Atkinson 1994; 1999; 2002; Comrie

& McGregor 1992; McGregor 1996; Comrie & Fountaine 2005; Cocker 1995; Edwards 1992; Farnsworth 1992; Thompson 2003; 2005). News bulletins, which are prominently sponsored by banks, contain content framed to accommodate populist, entertainment values with dramatic or emotional sub-text subverting any ethic of impartiality. The business ethic similarly undermines the informing and educative role of other actuality programme genres, with cautious appraisal of a programme's ratings potential deterring the commissioning of serious styles and sub-genres, particularly for documentary slots (Debrett 2004).

The commercial makeover of TV One's Network News to increase its audience pulling power had a profound impact on news values. 'Winning the news' was deemed critical to winning top ratings in prime-time. In transforming the news into an entertaining show with wider audience appeal, American consultants transformed news content and presentation, replacing the single newsreader with a 'news family', who 'emoted' the news and interacted cheerfully on cue. Infotainment values prioritised pictorial stories with shorter sound bites, more humour, sensationalism and emotion (Atkinson 1994: 9–10). Depoliticised television news avoided serious analysis of social issues, reinforcing mainstream conformist values at the expense of minority interests in the quest of maximising audience share for advertising clients. Smith cites a case of a programme with a lesbian theme being rescheduled after a complaint by a company that had bought advertising around the timeslot (Smith 1996: 158).

Presenting minority issues in a format that serves both minority and general audiences has proved a problem for public service broadcasters everywhere, but is central to the concept of representing diversity. While ghetto slots are welcomed as better than nothing, they do little to broaden understanding between different social groups. Maori programming on TVNZ in the 1980s was largely supplied through three programmes: *Koha*, a weekly documentary series in English; *Te Karere*, a week-nightly Maori news bulletin in Maori; and *Waka Huia*, a weekly magazine programme on oral history, also in Maori. In 1990, *Koha* was replaced with *Marae*, and moved from a Sunday evening time slot to Sunday morning as part of a two-and-a-half hour block with *Waka Huia* and the Pacific Island magazine programme, *Tagata Pasifika*. The result was that these minority cultural groups were represented to themselves and each other rather than to mainstream society as had previously been the case with *Koha*. The change signalled a shift from public service broadcasting (PSB) to public service programming, with the broader social goals of PSB undermined by narrowcasting.

In the 1990s, as an SOE, TVNZ tended to relegate programming for older viewers and minority groups (of various cultures and interests) to non-prime-time, pursuing a similar strategy to its privately owned competitor, TV3. The shift to the CROC structure addressed this issue only marginally via charter funded content. By 2003, however, the establishment of the Maori Television Service (MTS) operating on the UHF band and funded independently through Te Mangai Paho, did make a big difference to Maori viewers; this service will be discussed further in the final section.

Funding – A New Dual System?

Over the years, state-owned television in New Zealand received funding from a variety of sources: from the public through the television licence fee; from the sale of air time for advertising; from a range of investments and entrepreneurial business activities in the 1990s; and from the government, indirectly through NZoA, and directly through charter finance and funding for the two non-commercial digital channels, TVNZ 6 and TVNZ 7 during the period 2003–2008. The licence fee, initially a substantial source of funding, as noted earlier, declined steadily as a proportion of total revenue after 1975 as a result of two channel competition and Prime Minister Robert Muldoon's refusal to its increase. The value of the licence fee fell from 43.6 per cent of total funding in 1976 to 29 per cent in 1980, to 16 per cent in 1985 (Smith 1996: 152). Advertising and business activities were increased to fill the gap.

But while advertising grew steadily as a proportion of TVNZ's total revenue after 1975, it was not until the arrival of competition and broadcasting deregulation that the corporation became a fully commercial broadcaster directed to 'maximise taxpayer's return' (Rennie 1988: i). Under the Broadcasting Act of 1989, the licence fee was redirected to the Broadcasting Commission (NZoA). The third channel hearings, which ran from August 1985 to February 1987, gave the organisation ample time to prepare for competition. Under the new CEO, Julian Mounter, three strategies were pursued. More than NZ$4 million was spent on channel branding and promotion, exclusive long term contracts were signed with major programme distributors, and TV3's plan for a personality-driven, nightly current affairs show was pre-empted by TVNZ's much-promoted *Holmes* show, fronted by former radio personality, Paul Holmes. Money was lavished on public relations and news consultants who remodelled the corporate image and the evening news bulletin in imitation of American commercial television. In the quest for cost efficiencies, the corporation was radically restructured into strategic business units with an internal market, producing a wave of redundancies as entire production departments were abolished. Addressing TVNZ staff, CEO Julian Mounter depicted the arrival of commercial competition from TV3 as war: 'The opposition is simply the enemy. There is only one rule and that is to win, win, win' (Spicer et al. 1996). TVNZ's battle for the advertising dollar proved very successful, and TV3 was in the hands of receivers only 157 days after its November 1989 launch; the new service never came close to achieving its targeted 28 per cent rating (Smith 1996: 79–80).

In preparation for restructuring, the corporation also embarked on a policy of diversification into various business activities. These were initially presented as a defensive strategy to protect against competition from foreign media conglomerates encroaching on home turf. But they also enabled the corporation to form appropriate business alliances in anticipation of industry convergence. Beginning in the late 1980s, TVNZ developed business relationships with several telecommunications companies purchasing shareholdings in Clear Communications Limited and SKY pay-TV, and Data Cast Services Limited, which at the time of purchase were deemed useful strategic links for future ventures into telecommunications as digital, interactive and broadcasting technologies converged. In addition, the corporation invested in the expanding Asian market, with a 36 per cent shareholding in Asia Business News, subsequently sold in 1995–6. A more long term commitment, TVNZ Pacific Services was set up to facilitate expansion across the Pacific in 1987, selling programming to emergent television services in Pacific Island nations such as the Cook Islands. In 1995, 'other trading revenue' amounted to 31 per cent of TVNZ's total income (TVNZ 1995: 28). The corporation's global ambitions were later modified during Chris Anderson's time as TVNZ CEO, when the internal structure was simplified. In the 1990s, the TVNZ Group included subsidiary companies based on former internal departments: South Pacific Pictures, the drama production arm; Broadcast Communications Limited (BCL), the transmission arm; Avalon Television Centre, Wellington's television studios; Moving Pictures, the outside broadcast unit; and First Scene, the set design department. Between 1995 and 1997 TVNZ also operated a network of regional television stations through a subsidiary, Horizon Pacific Limited.

Discussing TVNZ's transformation in *The Remaking of Television New Zealand: 1988–92* (1996), the authors note strategies to change internal culture such as a staff seminar series titled, 'What if I Owned the Business', along with other operational measures. Internal restructuring initiated under Mounter followed a plan proposed by consultant Chris Gedye, transforming TVNZ's administrative and production departments into strategic business units (SBUs) that were directed to be self-sufficient and to seek business where they could find it:

> Reliance would be placed on a market-based approach within the organisation through decentralisation, the use of profit centres, internal charging and results-based compensation…To ensure that the manager of each SBU was held accountable for resources consumed in the pursuit of an SBU's objectives, a system of negotiated internal charges for resources, services, or products received from, or supplied to, other SBUs was put into place. (Spicer et al. 1996: 95)

Since much production was commissioned from the independent sector, outside work became a necessity. The Natural History Unit in Dunedin survived for some time through its co-productions with overseas organisations like the Discovery Channel and NDR in Germany. Acquired by Fox Broadcasting Company in the late 1990s, Natural History New Zealand (NHNZ) is now part of Fox International Channels group in Rome (Sheeran 2009). While TVNZ retained involvement in drama production through its subsidiary, South Pacific Pictures, this was eventually sold in 1998, while another subsidiary, BCL, as previously mentioned, was sold off under the Clark Labour Government.

Despite concerns about the small size of the New Zealand market, the creation of commercial competition and the removal of restrictions on advertising brought a quantum leap in television advertising revenue, which rose from NZ$184 to NZ$455 million between 1986 and 1994 (Smith 1996: 153–4). With the advent of more channels and competition from online media, television advertising revenue dipped in the new millennium bringing new rounds of staffing cuts at TVNZ in 2007 and 2009, while the government remained insistent on receiving its dividend. TVNZ's ratings and advertising revenue have fluctuated in the 'war' with TV3, with the launch of TV4 by TV3's owner Canwest in 1997 further eroding TVNZ's appeal to younger viewers. However, TV 3 news success with the 18-49 year age group favoured by advertisers slumped in 2008, and by early 2010 TVNZ was again winning the evening news slot (Daniell 2008; Throng 2010).

Accountability

The importance given to programme ratings and advertising revenue was always in conflict with the SOE's 'social responsibility' requirement. It initially provided a sticking block for the original TVNZ board in 1989. The board members were appointed under ministerial instructions, which stated that in the context of its operation as 'a successful business', TVNZ was 'to have the predominant objective of reflecting New Zealand's identity and culture and to encourage New Zealand programming'. Endeavouring to reconcile these competing obligations, the board sought ministerial assurance that funding would be provided to accommodate these social objectives or that they could be cross subsidised by commercial activities. Subsequently rebuffed, the board was eventually persuaded to agree to a revised statement of corporate intent on the condition that TVNZ receive an annual base amount from the Broadcasting Commission (Spicer et al. 1996: 120–3). A later attempt to enforce the SOE social responsibility requirement through the courts in September 1993 failed, with the Court ruling that it was unenforceable (Comrie 1993: 6).

As a state owned enterprise with 'social obligations', the corporatised TVNZ was a remote institution, largely unaccountable to its public. The Annual Report addressed the public as shareholders rather than citizens, taking ratings as the primary measure of success, ignoring the complexities of serving pluralist needs. Under the 1989 Broadcasting Act, the Broadcasting Standards Authority was instituted to advise broadcasters on the development of codes of practice and to moderate the complaints procedure, which refers complainants to the broadcaster in the first instance. Viewer complaints procedures only permit complaints on the basis of violations of standards, not on policy related issues such as the absence of certain types of programming, or the under-representation of certain groups, or excessive levels of advertising, the issues for which TVNZ has been widely criticised. During the charter era (2003–2008), the detailed terms of the charter and the provision of charter funding provided the basis for a number of complaints, with misuse of the charter funds levelled at TVNZ on several occasions. One response to this taken under the Clark Labour Government in its last year of office was to require that charter funding be vetted by NZoA, ostensibly to ensure greater transparency; an overly bureaucratic solution that, as Peter Thompson notes, was flawed by virtue of NZoA's focus on local content (Thompson 2008).

Directed under Clause 36(c) of the Act to reflect and develop New Zealand identity and culture, to promote Maori language and culture, and to serve special interest audiences –

women, children, persons with disabilities, and minorities in the community including ethnic minorities – the agency was to become best known for its advocacy of local production. With potential audience size amongst the criteria stipulated in the Act, NZoA interpreted its role as providing New Zealand content in prime-time. This decision complicated relations with broadcasters whose consent was required for funding, and left minority interests underserved. NZoA continued to administer funding for local content during TVNZ's charter years (2003–2009), articulating its role as sustaining public service broadcasting in its five year strategy (2003–2008), arguably exacerbating TVNZ's fractured identity.

The legacy of Ministerial control inherited from radio meant that de facto political practice, the social dynamics of a small society, and the appointment of agreeable directors streamlined executive decision-making in the interests of the government of the day. Legislative requirements to 'comply with' and 'to have regard to' the general policy of the government in relation to broadcasting passed in 1961 and 1976 respectively, maintained ministerial authority at the expense of open society (Gregory 1985: 93). In 1996, the issue of political appointees on the TVNZ board drew the attention of the press when the director, Michelle Boag, became the subject of a judicial reprimand. Attention was drawn to the conflict of interests posed by her job as Public Relations Consultant for the banking corporation, Faye Richwhite, and subsequent media coverage questioned the propriety of her National Party affiliation along with that of board chairman, Norman Geary.

While the importance of editorial independence from government is acknowledged by TVNZ (TVNZ 2007: 2), accusations of interference persist. The gratuitous payment of an extra NZ$20 million dividend in 1996, the cancellation of the *Assignment* programme on the Employment Contracts Act, and extraordinary concessions made to the Prime Minister, Jim Bolger, regarding the televised pre-election debate indicate a ready compliance with government 'suggestions'. Following a pre-election television debate in which he was deemed to have performed badly, Bolger complained about the use of the 'worm', an onscreen indicator of audience support, and the seating arrangements, which he believed disadvantaged him. The programme format was subsequently adjusted without approval from the other participants (Potter et al. 1996). Although the Broadcasting Standards Authority provides an avenue for complaints, it requires that these address specific codes of practice, none of which readily encompasses government intervention like this.

Further accusations of board 'meddling' and government interference occurred under the Clark Labour Government during the television presenter pay wars from 1999 to 2005. The conflicting realities of the dual commercial/public service remit surfaced during a series of debacles surrounding the salaries of high rating presenters. In 1999, TVNZ employed the popular newsreader John Hawkesby, who had recently left TV3, only to sack him three weeks later when public disgust over the dumping of the previous incumbent, Richard Long, resulted in a dramatic fall in ratings. Having been appointed on a salary of NZ$700,000 per annum, Hawkesby subsequently sued the corporation, securing a rumoured NZ$5.8 million settlement, which ultimately resulted in the forced resignation of the National party appointed TVNZ board chairperson, Rosanne Meo (Rankin 2000; Comrie & Fountaine

2005: 106–7). Criticising the broadcaster for a culture of 'poor decision making', the Clark Government directed the board to oversee any salary negotiations above NZ$300,000. When longstanding newsreader Judy Bailey, known as 'the mother of the nation', negotiated a salary of NZ$800,000 as sole news presenter in 2004, Prime Minister Helen Clark called it, 'evidence of a culture of extravagance'. The following year Bailey's contract was not renewed and the TVNZ chief executive, veteran interviewer Ian Fraser, later resigned, blaming the board's meddling (Trevett 2005). The conflicting expectations of public service and commercial business values left TVNZ management with an unwinnable brief.

Back to the Future: Un-reinventing Public Service Television

The New Zealand government was relatively late in embracing digital terrestrial television (DTT) and finally took the decision in 2006. The government had apparently hoped broadcasters would initiate the transition themselves since the subscription sector, represented by 'Murdoch-controlled' Sky TV, had been delivering digital services since 1998 and was reaching 40 per cent of New Zealand households. Concerned about the pending obsolescence of analogue technology and committed to maintaining a universal public broadcasting service, the Clark Labour Government chose not to use Sky's existing satellite platform which would have been cheaper, instead initiating a cost benefits analysis of DTT by a global consulting firm in 2006 (Given & Norris 2010). Spectrum Strategy Consultants subsequently recommended that DTT would contribute a substantial net benefit to New Zealand provided that digital switchover (DSO) occurred before 2015 (Jameson et al. 2006). This put the government under some pressure to facilitate broadcasters' adoption of the new technology. Operating across terrestrial and satellite platforms, free digital television finally arrived in New Zealand in 2007 with the launch of Freeview, a consortium of New Zealand's free-to-air broadcasters: TVNZ, MediaWorks NZ, Maori TV and Radio NZ.

Freeview provided the strategy for encouraging digital take-up, committing each broadcaster to delivering two new digital channels within two years of the Freeview launch in return for free spectrum for the period prior to DSO, and a commitment from government for NZ$25 million towards the establishment costs. Largely driven by TVNZ, which had twice previously attempted to initiate commercial joint ventures into digital, Freeview's greatest attraction was arguably the addition of the state broadcaster's two new digital channels, TVNZ 6 and TVNZ 7, launched in 2007 and 2008 respectively, funded from a NZ$79 million grant from the government.

The distinctive features of TVNZ's two digital channels are their unique non-commercial status and the fact that 65–70 per cent of their schedules are local content. The nation's first digital channel, TVNZ 6, was launched in September 2007, screening children's programming in a 'Kidzone' block from 6 am until 6 pm when family programming screens until 8.30, which is followed by adult viewing until the midnight close-down. Launched in March 2008, TVNZ 7, originally announced as a dedicated news channel, was launched as a news, current affairs and factual service that includes arts programming and hourly news updates. By early 2010, Freeview take-up was estimated as 22 per cent and overtaking Sky TV with its High Definition service, a figure calculated on sales of television sets with FreeviewHD tuners. In addition to the new digital channels, TVNZ has also developed an online, on-demand streaming service fronted by advertising to take advantage of the expanding broadband market, offering New Zealand residents free television content from across its four channels. In March 2009, TVNZ announced its purchase of a 33 per cent share in Hybrid Television Services, a move that made it the New Zealand licensee of the TiVo digital video recorder (DVR). A set-top box combining access to both digital television and broadband internet, TiVo's DVR will enable TVNZ to offer a superior, personalisable video on-demand service, 'one whose advertising messages can never be skipped' (Given & Norris 2010: 65). The investment drew critical comment in the *National Business Review*, which noted the broadcaster's recent budget and staffing cuts, although acknowledging likely future profits post-DSO.

In October 2009, the question of the digital channels' independence arose when an episode in a TVNZ 7 programme, *Spotlight on the Economy,* was promoted on air as 'Explaining the Economy in Plain English', giving favoured positioning to the ideas of the Deputy Prime Minister, Bill English. As Minister for Finance and one of TVNZ's shareholding Ministers, English delivered a scripted upbeat account of the nation's economy to promote the episode in which he appeared, titled *The Recession – in Plain English*. Following media criticism and questions in Parliament about what was commonly seen as free political advertising, a 2008/09 House of Representatives financial review of TVNZ expressed concerns about the broadcaster's political impartiality (NZ Parliament 2009). The future of both digital channels awaits the Key government's review, with funding due to expire in 2011.

Less than a decade after Helen Clark's 1999 victory and mandate for reinventing public service broadcasting, John Key's National Government won office in 2008 with an election promise to abolish the TVNZ charter. By April 2009, the NZ$15 million allocated to charter programming had been redirected via NZoA to a Platinum Television Fund for 'high quality locally made TV programs', available to all free to air television broadcasters and in December 2009 the charter was formally abolished. It was the sixth restructuring of state owned television in 36 years. With the change of government, the extensive charter review exercise of 2007, which produced a revised TVNZ charter highlighting seven themes, was rendered redundant. Indicating a return to laissez-faire market policy, the Key Government also abandoned the Review of Regulation for Digital Broadcasting (Thompson 2009). As fulfilment of an election promise, the charter's removal arguably had public endorsement, although undoubtedly many were unaware of the broader ramifications, succinctly summarised by Green's spokesperson for broadcasting, Sue Kedgley:

Inevitably the quality of programmes on TV1 will be further eroded with the charter's demise…and many New Zealanders will start to wonder why the state should own a fully commercial channel that is hard to distinguish from any other channel…I think this is a hidden agenda – to strip TVNZ of its public broadcasting responsibilities, squeeze it like a lemon financially at a time when advertising revenues are in free fall, and then flick it off in a few years time. (Kedgley 2009)

As an SOE from 1989 to 1999, TVNZ had maximised it profits and returned dividends to government by going downmarket, chasing audiences to secure advertisers. As a prosperous commercial business during this time, the broadcaster was a potential target for privatisation, something the Clark Government's restructuring and the introduction of the charter initially promised to frustrate. In the wake of the global financial crisis, the financial year 2008/09 saw TVNZ's after-tax income drop by 89 per cent, resulting in payment of an all time low dividend of NZ$1.47 million to government, a long way from the NZ$84.52 million dividend of 2006/07 (NZ Parliament 2009; TVNZ 2008), and a potential incentive for a National government to divest itself of this state asset. On the 18th December 2009, the *New Zealand Herald* suggested the broadcaster was being prepared for sale in the event of the Key Government winning a second term.

The growth in free-to-air television channels, first via UHF and more recently via the digital platform Freeview, has vastly increased competition for audience and advertisers. While the initial growth in television advertising revenue during the 1990s outpaced TVNZ's own predictions with operating profit doubling in five years, the future prospects of free-to-air television are hard to predict as broadband television, pay services, SKY and Telstra Clear, along with new digital channels, expand and fragment the media market. With more players fighting for audience in New Zealand's very small market, programme standards and local content are at risk. The government's investment in TVNZ 6 and TVNZ 7 in 2008, as non-commercial channels with a high percentage of local programming, marked a radical break with past policy, albeit one that was intended to drive digital take-up to facilitate DSO, and also one that came at a cost to viewers, requiring the purchase of the set-top box and/ or satellite receiving dish.

The mainstream service offered by TVNZ's two main channels, TV One and TV2, is short on serious content, providing ample escapism from the trials of an increasingly complex and polarised society. However, it frames a world that has little bearing on the contemporary reality of many New Zealanders, and does little towards addressing the social rifts between rich and poor, black and white, able bodied and disabled, nationals and immigrants or other differences that divide communities. Under the 2009 amendment to the Television New Zealand Act (2003), the abolition of the charter meant that the state owned broadcaster is no longer required to have a 'significant Maori voice' or to cater for people and groups deemed to be neglected by other broadcasters. In an apparent dilution of its social obligations TVNZ is to provide 'high-quality' content that is relevant to and enjoyed and valued by New Zealand audiences, and 'reflects Maori perspectives'.

The commercial values that influence the local programming that screens on TVNZ also constrain supplementary online content that is produced to accompany it, despite the cost efficiencies offered by the online environment. In 2009, a hybrid reality TV-documentary series, *One Land*, which screened on TV1, reworked the historical reality format originated by Channel Four's *1900 House*, bringing together a white 'settler' family with two Maori families living on a traditional Maori Pa, in simulation of a community from the 1850s. While this was a project with opportunities for building cross cultural understanding which might have been further extended online, developing the digital commons, as done by public service broadcasters elsewhere, the website for *One Land* was relatively undeveloped. With both an expert in Maori culture and an historian involved in the series' production, it seems unfortunate that the research and information collected was not put to broader social use, such as linking to digital archives in public institutions or engaging greater participation from individuals and communities. Evidently the commercial imperative of the Crown-owned broadcaster inhibits such developments, which generate only a social dividend rather than a monetary one.

In 2003, the addition of a Maori UHF channel, the Maori Television Service (MTS), lifted some pressure from TVNZ regarding the provision of Maori language content. Operating on a total income of only NZ$35.7 million drawn from government revenue, Te Mangai Paho funding and advertising, MTS delivers a mix of programming including news and current affairs and low budget in-house productions. With its modest income, the service depends on considerable industry good will which raises questions about the long term sustainability of its funding model. MTS has, however, undoubtedly had a dramatic impact on programme diversity on free-to-air television. On ANZAC day 2009, MTS delivered its fourth all day broadcast, screening 18 hours of coverage, inviting viewers to share their stories with the nation and reaching an audience of 507,000. Similarly on Waitangi day, New Zealand's national day, which commemorates the signing of the 1840 Treaty by Maori and Pakeha in the Bay of Islands, MTS delivered all day coverage. MTS also broadcasts a lot of sport and, following controversy over broadcasting rights for the 2011 Rugby World Cup being held in New Zealand, became leader of the consortium bidding for the free-to-air rights. A government funded service that measures success in terms of its revitalisation of the Maori language via qualitative surveys, MTS has broken the New Zealand mould for public service broadcasting:

> The purpose of Mäori Television is to 'protect and promote Te Reo Mäori' and as such the objective is to provide a service to the public of New Zealand as opposed to that of making a financial return. (MTS 2009: 29)

While advertising is sold on MTS, the broadcaster has made the commitment to keep Te reo, its Maori language channel, non-commercial. Following the abolition of TVNZ's charter, there had been increasing enthusiasm for MTS, with former broadcaster Paul Norris describing it as, 'arguably the purest form of public service broadcasting' (Norris 2005: 46), and former CEO of Radio New Zealand and the ABC, Geoffrey Whitehead, noting in a letter to the *NZ Listener* in November 2009:

I do know Maori TV is the only channel in the country that comes anywhere near the concept of a public-service broadcaster, as defined internationally…Why do we need such a national public broadcaster? Because, as the Canadians have put it, a democracy has to have 'a public lane on the information highway'. And why isn't 'the market' doing that job? Because, as US lawyer and analyst Monroe E. Price has said, there is 'no national identity of Murdoch, no flag or loyalty to Disney'. Although 'the market' meets our wants as consumers, the state has to intervene if our needs as citizens are to be met. There are plenty of low-cost models in the Western world that have shown for decades how that can be done. All that is needed in New Zealand now is the political will to build on the practical domestic example of Maori TV. (*NZ Listener*, November 2009)

Public expression of such sentiments has been rare and New Zealand society has been relatively compliant in the transformation of television broadcasting from state owned monopoly to free market system. From its inception, public service broadcasting was defined primarily in terms of state ownership rather than public interest and, partnered with commercial funding, led to a confused and shifting set of priorities that softened public resistance to commercial involvement. When television broadcasting was deregulated in 1989 with the arrival of commercial competition, the new profit ethos imposed on TVNZ invoked little public protest, the changes widely viewed as necessary to facilitate the growth of new telecommunications technologies. New Zealand is now frequently cited as having one of the least regulated broadcasting systems in the world. There is no public input into frequency leasing, no local content obligations on broadcasters, no limits on foreign ownership (Volkerling 1996:6), levels of advertising are amongst the highest in the world, and lastly there is no mainstream non-commercial public television service. However, this could change if TVNZ 6 and TVNZ 7 continue to receive government funding after DSO in 2015/16 and increase their targets for New Zealand cultural content.

Always a particularly unstable concept in New Zealand, public service broadcasting has become even more so, now encompassing: public service programming funded via NZoA and Te Mangai Paho, delivered across six commercial channels that represent both public and private ownership; TVNZ's two non-commercial digital channels TVNZ 6 and TVNZ 7; the two UHF channels operated by the Maori Television Service (MTS) – Maori Television and Te reo, the Maori language service screening for three hours a day in the evening; and programming funded via NZoA for regional television under the name of community broadcasting. Government investment in public service programming now rests primarily with NZoA and, to a lesser extent, Te Mangai Paho, which funds Maori programming on the Maori Television Service (MTS) and on other free-to-air broadcasters. NZoA's prioritisation of prime-time local content left some public service goals neglected, most notably news and current affairs. The latter has become particularly pressing following several rounds of redundancies amongst journalists at the state owned broadcaster during 2007–9. Perhaps aspiring to address this problem, the first projects NZoA funded from its new contestable Platinum Fund for 'quality' programming were two Sunday night panel-based current affairs programmes, one on each network in different timeslots – *Q&A* on TV One and *The Nation* on TV3. The decision, along with NZoA's role in general, is problematic on two counts: firstly, being contestable by private commercial broadcasters means viewers have no clearly designated public service channel; and secondly, addressing the decline of quality of journalism via panel-based current affairs shows signals continued faith in market competition as a driver of quality, in the face of copious evidence that competition is eroding journalism standards in the digital age. Quality TV journalism, as other public service broadcasters have shown, is generally developed by long term investment in a news and current affairs department, where the practices and disciplines that constitute 'quality' in news reporting can be nurtured as a distinguishing trait of a public service institution.

Since 1990, NZoA has brokered relations between government, broadcasters and the production sector, prioritising the presence of New Zealand faces and voices in prime-time over the complex range of public interest goals identified in the charter. With the abolition of the charter in 2009, NZoA's enhanced importance as the distributor of television production funding will again see the needs of industry – broadcasters and the independent production sector – accommodated over those of the public who benefit as shareholders rather than as viewers. While MTS and the government funded digital channels, TVNZ 6 and TVNZ 7, offer hope for the future of public service television, this still depends on the political will of the Key Government and those that follow. A history as political football has left public service broadcasting in New Zealand without the cushioning of traditions or collective public memory to inspire public support.

Chapter 8

Public Service Media

Introduction

The gloom once associated with the future of public service broadcasting (Murdock 2004: 1; Tracey 1998) now clouds the future of commercial media, as competition for revenue and audience, exacerbated by the global financial crisis, heats up in the fragmenting digital marketplace. At the same time, public service broadcasters have come into their own as innovators, pioneering new modes of delivery and experimenting with interactive content, often under specific directives by government to drive digital take-up. Some of the compromises being made, however, as funding is stretched and supplemented with new commercial services, could well prove undermining in future. As they reconfigure themselves as cross-platform media content providers, public service broadcasters enter new territory with regards to their audience, their content, their relations with producers and their status in the marketplace, invoking more exacting requirements for governance and accountability, and new commercial enemies. As a result of these complexities digital innovation by public service media is becoming a growing area of study (d'Haenens et al. 2008; Lowe & Bardoel 2007; Iosifidis 2008; Isofidis 2010; Nissen 2006; Ward 2004).

The six broadcasters discussed in this book reflect the breadth of possibilities encompassed by public ownership, each possessing distinctive unique features: the BBC, the classic model of mainstream public service broadcaster, now subsidised by a highly successful, international commercial arm; Channel Four as a publisher broadcaster funded by advertising representing the cross-subsidy model; the ABC as a comprehensive and complementary non-commercial national broadcaster; the SBS as a multicultural broadcaster; American public television as the market failure model and a system offering uniquely local and educational foci; and TVNZ as a former born-again public broadcaster with a dual public-commercial remit. As a group, they also illustrate the wide-ranging new initiatives emerging across the digital and online platforms of public broadcasters: cross-platform programming; user-generated content (UGC); audience participation; the delivery of linear programming with opportunities to interact on an on-demand basis; and the generation of social networks and communities, connected to resources and activities at other public institutions.

Of the various digital platforms discussed here, the oldest is digital terrestrial television (DTT), requiring digitalization of the broadcast transmission system. Introduced across the developed world from the mid 1990s, DTT is generally seen as offering three main benefits: more efficient use of the electro-magnetic spectrum through data compression, freeing up space for more channels; improved technical quality in picture and sound resulting from a reduced signal to noise ratio; and sometimes enabling limited viewer interactivity through enhanced programming or 'Red Button' interactive television. The latter refers to television programmes specially made for viewer interactivity, which invite the viewer to respond on cue by pushing the red button on the digital remote controller. Since 2000, the spread of broadband Internet connection via various wired and wireless technologies has spawned the so-called Web 2.0 era in which it is possible to upload and download media rich content online. Alongside this development have come subsidiary mobile digital platforms onto which viewers, consumers and users can download and view/interact with Web 2.0 content – third generation (3G) mobiles and personal digital assistants (PDAs).

Reinterpreting PSB Principles

In 1985, when Alan Peacock was chairing his historic enquiry into the financing of the BBC, the Broadcasting Research Unit (BRU) was called upon to provide evidence for the Committee. Seeking to define public service broadcasting, the BRU, under the chairmanship of the renowned academic Richard Hoggart, surveyed 'broadcasters working in both the commercial and public sectors of television' and subsequently identified eight principles (Franklin 2001: 21). The 1985 BRU principles were: (i) geographic universality; (ii) catering to all tastes and interests; (iii) catering for minorities; (iv) concern for national identity and community; (v) detachment from vested interests and government; (vi) direct funding of one broadcasting system by the body of users (that is, via a licence fee system); (vii) competition in relation to good programming rather than in increasing audience numbers; (viii) guidelines which liberate programme makers rather than restrict them (Harrison 2000: 66).

This discussion adapts the eight BRU principles to accommodate the most commonly recurring elements of public broadcasting charters: universal service; independence from government and from vested interests to enable the provision of fair and impartial news and current affairs; the servicing of the interests of minorities including children, in addition to mainstream audiences; the reflection of national culture and identity; and the provision of quality programming which encompasses a preparedness to innovate and to not be driven by audience size.

Defining PSB is of course a contested field. In its first Review of Public Service Broadcasting in 2005, the UK communications regulator, Ofcom, found an 'overarching theme...competition for quality', which it defined in terms of three things: 'a competitive marketplace, plurality of PSB commissioning and production, and enough flexibility in the system for provision (and providers) of PSB to change over time, as the needs and preferences of citizens change' (Ofcom 2005). With its emphasis on market competition, this definition fits Karol Jakubowicz's view of the neoliberal position, one that is unsympathetic to the need for 'secure and dedicated financing' (Jakubowicz 2007: 41). While the BBC is widely seen as the leading model of PSB, British definitions of PSB are nevertheless at odds with those of other nations because in the UK the term is applied to all free-to-air broadcasters signalling spectrum licensing conditions. Hence UK communications industry regulator Ofcom must seek common ground across commercial and public broadcasting institutions. Other national peculiarities in definitions of PSB can also be seen in distinctions made between public broadcasting and public service broadcasting. For TVNZ General Manager of Digital Services, Eric Kearley, this distinction – which he acknowledges is not universal – is a key one: 'A public broadcaster generally, is a commercially funded broadcaster but with a clear remit from the government…whereas a public service broadcaster tends to be government funded' (Kearley 2006). On the other hand, Jakubowicz views the reaffirmation and enhancement of 'service' as critical for the effective survival and transition of PSB into the new media age (Jakubowicz 2007: 38). Such variances in positioning derive from specific national contexts (social, political and economic) and differences in cultural traditions. In this book I have chosen to take a broad view, incorporating both public and public service broadcasters in order to ascertain the impact of new digital services on public interest goals, by investigating how well traditional principles and values fit with cross platform and on-demand programme provision.

Universal coverage, the provision of a free service accessible to all, is generally considered the most important of the PSB principles because of the social value of mass audience reach as a shared public space for public discourse – a public sphere. In the digital era, free universal access is being challenged by the new on-demand services since these involve additional user-pays technology such as the Internet or a mobile phone, contributing to the digital divide – the exclusion of those who cannot pay or for other reasons are not online. One response is that on-demand, cross platform access is the *new* universality. In the social context of the digital era, when media services and the media habits of the fragmented audience are so diverse, access is no longer about scarcity, and universality needs to be addressed across the full range of media platforms in order to aggregate sufficient fragments to reach a general public. The flexible access of on-demand media offers a reinvented form of universality, one that caters for contemporary lifestyles. It can also be argued that by distributing re-versioned content such services extend the shelf-life and reach of publicly funded productions, building on word of mouth publicity, and thereby help to maximise the value of public investment. However, given the third party costs associated with these platforms, a necessary rider for the provision of absolute universality is the continued provision of free-to-air broadcasting. Commissioner for New Media at Channel Four, Adam Gee, describes his job in commissioning cross-platform programming as, 'TV plus something else. So usually TV plus web…TV plus mobile, TV plus real-life [or any combination of the above]' (Gee 2006). Andrew Owen, Managing Editor of Interactive Programmes at BBC Television, observes that Tardisodes – 'mobisodes or short clips preceding each episode' – made available online for *Dr Who* fans to download, were extremely popular during the television series broadcast, but became significantly less so when the on-air screening ended. Owen suggests that although a 'trickle of interest' in such content will persist, 'timeliness' and 'relevance' remain largely linked to broadcast television (Owen 2007). As part of what is being called '360 degree commissioning', cross platform productions thus serve PSB's goal of universality while also alerting and directing viewers to new media platforms.

Impartial news and current affairs, frequently ranked as the second most important PSB principle, is an integral aspect of the system's civic role associated with the public sphere, and is generally understood as requiring independence from the vested interests of commerce or government. News and current affairs that is fair or impartial, and of good 'quality' (well researched political reporting) goes hand in glove with universality as part of the *raison d'être* of PSB, providing readily accessible resources for an informed and active citizenship; an acknowledgement of the singular nature of the relationship between the media and democracy. Threats to the independence of PSBs remain closely linked to funding in the digital era, with new challenges arising from the new possibilities for 'monetizing' on-demand content.

PSB news, one of the content forms most widely re-versioned for cross-platform delivery, offers a tempting source of ready revenue, but the distinguishing quality that makes it valuable, public trust, is particularly vulnerable in such arrangements. As the flagship of most PSBs, trusted news is particularly crucial to channel brands. Thus the motivation to quarantine news integrity from commercial influence is arguably stronger in the digital era; TVNZ, with its dual commercial-public remit remains an interesting exception having made radical cuts to its newsroom in 2007 while planning a specialist, digital, factual/news channel for launch in 2008 (Scoop 2007). In the emerging field of Internet Protocol television (IPTV), where the volume of services is growing exponentially, brand identity is particularly critical for drawing an audience. Rather than being superseded by proliferating niche media, highly trusted PSB television brands, built on quality news services, would seem to make PSB more important than ever (Jacka 2006: 8). This key marker of difference is evident in the BBC's channel on the social-networking website, YouTube, launched initially as a means of addressing copyright breaches. The existence of this channel in the midst of user-generated clips and mash-ups signals that recognition of the value of trusted brands and professionally produced content is not incompatible with, or superseded by, contemporary enthusiasm for the democratizing potential of UGC.

Thirdly, serving minority interests – a double-sided principle – reflects the system's broader civic and cultural functions, including the representation of minorities to the mainstream and the servicing of minority groups' special interests. This dual goal has always been something of a tall order in the comprehensive schedule and another reason for claims of PSB redundancy in the 1980s. With digital terrestrial television (DTT), the Internet, IPTV, and on-demand content, the problems of serving the diverse interests of pluralist society on a single channel have been alleviated. Given political will, DTT facilitates the delivery of PSB content across multiple channels, thereby allowing broadcasters to tailor content to suit specific niche audience needs, while also enabling the cross-promotion of content of general public interest to all audiences. Addressing the need for a common junction where different audiences converge before following disparate interests, the homepages of public service media are now reprising the comprehensive remit. As a new form of common domain,

PSB portals offer some resolution to the risks posed by cultural fragmentation while also accommodating personalized media.

The fourth principle – the reflection of national culture and identity – has been particularly important for PSBs in Australia and New Zealand where cost differences between local and imported English language programming, a factor of the larger domestic markets of the UK and the US, means a hefty proportion of TV schedules is filled by imported content. This principle encapsulates various issues: serving national unity; serving as a site of contestation amongst the different cultural groups represented within a society; promoting the nation abroad; and redressing trade deficits. In the second wave of digital media, while still continuing to offer a site of contestation for the various cultural groups and values within the nation, PSBs are taking on a broader role of upholding national difference in the global marketplace. Widely interpreted as undermining the national focus of PSB in the 1980s (Born 2004: 47), this promotional role has assumed greater cultural and economic relevance post-2000 as PSBs compete with global media for a share of the fragmenting audience. Digital technology increases the economies of scale enjoyed by transnational media conglomerates delivering globally transferable content, and so serves as a disincentive for nationally based commercial broadcasters to support local production. Public broadcasters, however, are better positioned to invest in and promote national cultural product abroad through co-productions and co-ventures, and as a consequence often set industry benchmarks. Georgina Born argues that the BBC's commitment to quality children's programming with higher than average budgets on its digital channels led to Nickelodeon 'increasing its commitment to British production and the budgets of those productions' (Born 2004: 487).

Certainly the role of PSBs as producers and commissioners of 'local content' appears likely to remain a critical one given the economic and trade benefits associated with a healthy audio-visual production sector in the information age. Government subsidy of the sector also brings singular political benefits, refreshing national sentiment, a national branding exercise that helps to legitimate the role of national government in the era of globalisation (Debrett 2004: 9–10; Bell 1995: 197). The inherent tensions in reflecting national culture – the conflict between inviting national introspection and promoting the nation abroad – are also potentially diminished in the digital environment where different platforms and channels can be directed towards different needs.

The fifth principle – providing innovative 'quality' content – again reflects the system's broader civic and cultural functions. Being wide open to interpretation, 'quality' is a key challenge for public service systems in pluralist society (Nissen 2006: 65–82; Born 2004: 79). It is most often interpreted in terms of non-commercial production values – optimising money on screen, optimising research and development, and engaging in creative risk-taking – and is applied in factual and narrative programming across popular and high culture genres. That the implementation of quality as diversity and innovation is enormously advantaged by the intrinsic traits of digital media – personalisable, interactive, searchable, share-able, mobile and available on-demand – is evident in the growing popularity of UGC and social networking. Channel Four offers examples of quality as diversity in two television series that also launched cross-platform media projects. *Lost Generation* integrates a television series, *The Somme*, with a participatory online project whereby viewers' personal contributions about relatives who fought in World War One produce an interactive public archive, which connects public media with other public institutions such as libraries and museums. The second project was launched with *Medicine Men*, a four-part television series in which 'two young British doctors immerse themselves in radically different cultures in four of the most extreme places on earth'. *Medicine Chest*, the accompanying website, aims to provide a 'repository of traditional remedies and folk wisdom in the area of health and healing', drawing on the content of the TV series while also hosting 'conversations about these areas and drawing together a range of perspectives' (Channel Four 2008). Reflecting what Graham Murdock (2004) has termed the 'digital commons' – a metaphorical reference to the shared public space of medieval rural life that invokes the value of retaining public domain online – networking such as this fosters stronger community connections and serves civic education in ways previously unknown. As discussed in Chapter Two, at the BBC the *Creative Archive* project was established in 2005 as an online venture intended to open up much of the BBC's past programming for non-commercial public use and re-editing as 'mash-ups', a move described as 'the most important innovation in public service provision since its original foundation' for its 'stimulus to vernacular creativity' (Murdock 2004: 17). As part of the broader Creative Archive Group, which included the British Film Institute, Channel Four and the Open University, BBC programme content was to be made available to the public under the Creative Archive License (CAL), which drew on the spirit of the Creative Commons Licensing project, setting five rules: no commercial use; share alike; give credit; no endorsement; UK only. The BBC's Creative Archive project (CAP) originally aspired to grant access to UK licence fee payers, who would gain the right to use, re-edit and share low resolution content from specified programmes under the CAL conditions (Gerhardt 2006). After a trial release of 500 items in 2006, the Creative Archive project was placed under BBC Archive management awaiting the decision of the BBC Trust. When former programme maker, Roly Keating was appointed Archive director in 2008, Paul Gerhardt, the former the CAP project leader, expressed hope for the resolution of two concerns that had thwarted the project:

> The first is resolution of the 'boundary' question with BBC Worldwide and to pin down the necessary commercial windows for an on-demand archive. The second is to determine whether the scaled up archive plans really requires the intervention of the BBC Trust and a public value test in order to give viewers and listeners access to the programmes they have already paid for. (Gerhardt 2008)

As broadband take-up has expanded and online television initiatives have emerged, the commercial potential of the BBC's back catalogue of programming has also grown, ultimately constraining the kinds of content that will eventually be released for free use via the Creative Archive Project under the CAL conditions.

Facilitating innovation, DTT channels offer PSBs a means of testing/trialing new content on a platform where ratings are less important and greater risk can be taken. Similarly, the Internet also offers a site for trying out new concepts for a much lower cost. Precursors to YouTube and MySpace, Channel Four's *Four Docs* and the BBC's *Video Nation* pioneered social networking and UGC, yet demonstrate a clarity of purpose, richness of content and cohesiveness rarely found on commercial sites. Digital media technologies thus mean far more to PSBs than multiple channels and flexible delivery; they offer potential for renewed legitimacy, by engaging and connecting communities in new ways.

Differences in National Approach

The governments of the four countries covered in this book have taken very different approaches in their development of DTT. While the UK has been quick to exploit the benefits digital television offers PSB, elsewhere the economic and political implications have overshadowed public benefits as policy priorities.

In Australia, the two public broadcasters' ventures into digital television have been limited by policy and funding constraints. Despite the detailed submissions of the ABC and SBS, the special innovative role public service media could have played in developing the digital platform was largely ignored in the high definition versus standard digital television debate, which was primarily driven by the competing commercial interests of existing media and communications companies. The initial 1998 mandate of high definition television (HDTV) and the subsequent simulcast compromise of 2000, along with the peculiarly narrow definition of use applied to new licensees of digital spectrum via datacaster legislation, constrained delivery of new content and slowed public take-up (Given 2003: 139–49). The Howard Coalition Government's refusal to grant any additional finance for digital production prompted the ABC's 2003 cancellation of its two first digital channels established in 2002 – Fly TV for young people aged 13–18 and Kids for those at primary school (Jacka 2006: 173). Legislative changes in 2005 and 2006 led to the launch of two new digital PSB channels – ABC2, initially performing a time-shifting function, and the World News Channel by SBS, a multilingual headline service subsequently re-launched in 2008 as SBS Two. Since then, government funding for ABC3, the children's channel, and the ABC's broadband hubs has increased the potential of public service media to drive the creative and social development of digital platforms, although the digital possibilities for SBS as a multilingual provider remain curtailed by inadequate funding. Aspiring to become the drivers of digital television in Australia, ABC management initiated a strategic re-branding of the mainstream television service as ABC1, anticipating an expanding portfolio of digital channels. The announcements of a 24/7 'continuous news centre' and an Internet TV channel, ABC Playback, were made without confirmation of additional government funding (Moses 2008). While invoking budget and staff cuts, such strategies nevertheless appear to have paid off, with three channels on air by 2010 and the news channel, albeit unfunded, set to launch in mid-year.

Things are very different in the UK. Following the collapse of ITV's OnDigital service in 2002, free-to-air broadcasters launched the Freeview platform that now enables both Channel Four and the BBC to each offer a portfolio of niche channels. With UK digital uptake estimated at 88.9 per cent in the last quarter of 2008 (Ofcom 2008), this free-to-air multi-channel service has overtaken Britain's main subscription service, BSkyB digital (Ofcom 2007). A German market analyst, Datamonitor, estimates UK digital uptake as the world's highest and likely to rise to 95 per cent by 2010 (BBC 2006c).

For the cost of the set-top box (£30) viewers can get 50 free-to-air digital television channels along with 24 radio channels. The BBC and Channel Four use their new digital channels variously – time-shifting programmes that have already screened on the main channel, serving niche audiences (CBBC for school-age children and Cbeebies for pre-schoolers, Film4 for film buffs), for trialling new concepts (BBC3), for delivering less populist, 'intellectually and culturally enriching' programming (BBC4), and for cross-promoting content from the mainstream channels (BBC 2007a). Audience numbers and budgets for the new digital services are considerably smaller than those of the mainstream channels.

The special significance of the establishment of these channels is their free-to-air status. With advertising budgets moving to new media, the demise of free-to-air broadcasting has been widely forecast (Given 2003). This fear underlies the New Zealand government's about-face on digitalization, which had originally been left to the subscription sector (NZ Government 2006: 4). The government's decision to invest in the digitalization of the transmission system was undertaken on the basis of the national value of retaining a cost-free universal service that will ensure 'publicly funded programming remains available on a free and universal basis to all New Zealanders', and a cost benefit analysis that identified significant public gains estimated at over NZ$230 million after analogue switch off (Jameson et al. 2006: 157; 162). These factors also prompted the government's decision to contribute funds to TVNZ for two new non-commercial digital channels as a way of encouraging the public to purchase set-top boxes or digital receivers. As part of the digital Freeview consortium with other free to air broadcasters – MediaWorks (TV3 and TV4), Maori Television and Radio New Zealand – TVNZ now offers its two commercial channels, TV One and TV2, in addition to TVNZ 6, a family and children's channel, and TVNZ 7, a sports, news and information channel. Launched in 2007 with funding of NZ$79 million to be delivered over six years (TVNZ 2006a), a few months after job cuts to news and current affairs staff, TVNZ's venture into digital services prompted questions about the broadcaster's ability to meet its charter goals. Pragmatic compromises such as these abound in the shifting institutional dynamics of PSBs as they strategise for multiplatform reach and survival in the digital era.

Introduced in 1996 with the expectation of a digital switchover (DSO) date of 2006, the uptake of digital television in the United States has been even slower than in Australia although for different reasons, with multi-channel television services via cable and satellite a well-established reality since the 1980s. With penetration calculated at only 2.4 per cent in 2004, the Federal Communications Commission (FCC) was prompted to mandate the inclusion of DV tuners in most digital sets (Barksdale & Hundt 2005: 27). Nevertheless, American public television, a system with 348 stations, developed ambitious plans to increase accessibility and user participation through the Digital Future Initiative (DFI). Plans involved digitizing the back catalogue of analogue content and developing a 'sophisticated online on-demand distribution system' – the scale of costs for which are daunting for an organization that already raises a quarter of its revenue from voluntary viewer subscriptions (Barksdale & Hundt 2005: 25–6). A public lobby group, the Centre for Digital Democracy, has questioned both the ability of public television to resource such ambitious digital plans, and the system's commitment to localism and risk taking – decrying the use of digital channels for time-shifting at San Francisco's KQED (CDD 2006: 14–15). The debate indicates how contested every move is likely to be, yet it is hard to see other options for public television stations. Espousing the importance of the Internet in serving the traditional strengths of public television, localism and education, Richard Winefield, then Vice President for Interactive Educational Services at San Francisco's KQED observed:

> My prediction is that in ten years there won't be 300 public broadcasting stations, there may be 25 or 35 that are broadcasting stations; that the stations serving small and mid-sized markets are going to go away because they can't compete, as their content is much more regional. I am not in favour of that, but I am sure that will happen…The Internet is absolutely vital…The mission is not to run a television station; the mission is to create and deliver great content to viewers wherever they are, whenever they want it. (Winefield 2006)

While this may well eventuate for the viewer-subscription dependent public television system, circumstances differ elsewhere. Despite the revenue model of free-to-air broadcasting being under threat – as advertisers are drawn to the interactive platforms popular with the desirable youth demographic, which offer ready mechanisms for consumer data-gathering – television viewing nevertheless remains a very popular pastime (BARB 2008; BBC 2008b). The popularity of 'home cinema' and big plasma and LCD screens offers some support for speculation that HDTV might revive the communal viewing experience for specific genres – sports, wild life and travel – even as small screens and niche media proliferate and fragment the audience. For the time being, new narrowcast and on-demand platforms are extending ways of delivering media services, contributing more media rather than displacing broadcasting, which continues to retain special advantages as the mainstream site of first launch.

Diversity and Innovation Online

In the digital and online environment, the public service ethos has evolved and expanded, with the 'holy trinity' of PSB goals devised by the BBC's first director-general Lord Reith – 'to inform, educate and entertain' – complemented by Dyke's addition of 'connect' (Born 2004: 486). Digital media online potentially serves two broad purposes for PSBs: extending the scope for production through both supplementary and dedicated online content; and offering new kinds of relationships with the audience. Contributing to the 'digital commons' (Murdock 2004) the online platforms of PSBs provide a common junction where many different audiences and user groups are exposed to a wide range of ideas, services and communities. Comprehensive public portals such as these facilitate the representation of specific minority audience needs, while also cross-promoting general public interest content, ameliorating fragmentation, a key dilemma for the postmodern public sphere. Having interrogated the possibilities of the interactive mode as a new audience interface, Fiona Martin observes of ABC online:

> In a networked interactive environment, through both selective response and discursive interaction, users can render themselves visible, and to some extent less mysterious, to the institution and to each other. ABC online provides broadcasters greater insight into the lived and imagined worlds of its listeners and viewers, and the potential to engage with them as user/citizens rather than just audiences. (Martin 2002: 48)

Anticipating marketing advantages, Paul Vincent, then Manager of SBS Online, envisaged the hybrid funded, multicultural broadcaster moving into 'an era of broadband piloting of programs and program concepts', facilitating the targeting of particular audience demographics:

> I think user-generated content is going to tell us a lot about what the audience is interested in, because they will create the kind of content that they are interested in…So the talent, the direction the program takes, is all going to be researched and developed online, which is totally the bottom up version of audience feedback…Once we have upgraded all our video, broadband video capability, it's only a small step then to piloting programs in sort of closed user-groups online. Once you get to know your audience and their preferences deeply enough you can choose a focus group, a very large focus group, statistically balanced focus group, amongst your online membership and you can pilot things much more carefully than you can with the very expensive tools – that of national focus group discussions – that are around at the moment. (Vincent 2006)

As mentioned earlier, the BBC's longstanding media access project, *Video Nation*, offers an example of how the interactive mode now better serves diversity. Building on the ideas of the Mass Observation project of the 1930s, *Video Nation* began as a television access series in 1993, with 10,000 shorts made and 1300 screened in its first decade. As a site for public conversation where voices from society's margins can be heard, *Video Nation*, now a hybrid TV/Internet project, offers on-demand access to both participants and user/viewers through the always-on availability of the Internet. Complementing and extending this access, the occasional screening of participants' stories on television, in the form of short series or thematic compilations serves to keep mainstream viewers aware of these minority voices (BBC 2007b). Also previously mentioned, *Lost Generation*, another hybrid TV/Internet project initiated by Channel Four in collaboration with the Imperial War Museum, signals a different dimension to the concept of the digital commons. Inviting Britons to contribute the stories of ancestors killed in World War One through their letters and memorabilia, the project offers a site in which recent history can be brought to life in a personalised form. Offering guides to genealogy, tracing commonwealth ancestors and using war records, *Lost Generation* assists living relatives to fill in the missing gaps in the lives of their ancestors. The site simultaneously alerts the public at large to the role of public institutions such as the Imperial War Museum in documenting and archiving the nation's past. Public broadcasters' management of projects such as *Lost Generation* and *Video Nation*, that involve user-generated content (UGC), signals a shift from professionally produced programming to content that is primarily characterised by its interactivity and diverse authorship. Another example of online innovation serving diversity is *World Tales*, a multicultural and multi-platform project that invited young animators to adapt traditional folktales from around the world, as recounted by SBS Radio listeners. Viewable online in both English and the language of origin, the animated folk tales, which were five to six minutes in duration, were also used as TV interstitials (McClean 2006). As professional communicators, public broadcasters can play a mediating role, something the ABC's Head of Television, Kim Dalton, sees as central to their new functions in the digital era, bringing cohesiveness to the eclectic mix of online content through the application of PSB values:

> I think…user-generated content and the connecting potential that this media has, and the potential for the ABC to see part of what it does as actually building communities and engaging with audiences rather than just delivering content…well it poses challenges… Certainly in terms of forums that does mean a high degree of moderation. I think the other extreme on the Internet is the degree of anonymity that can exist, and with that comes the ability to completely just ignore the conventions and rules that have been built up around productive and civilised engagement…The view we take at the ABC is that… the guidelines and values that underpin our conventional services should also guide us in the online space. (Dalton 2007a)

Such values are also arguably evident in the huge amounts of background material PSB websites carry for television and radio programming, canvassing a wide range of social issues in a manner quite different from the distinctly promotional flavour of the websites of commercial television where third party tie-ins predominate. Making programme transcripts available online, for example, provides viewers with a means of verifying what was broadcast, validating public trust, while also encouraging user feedback and participation. Noting the volume and status of background content now online, David Liroff, Chief Technology Officer at WGBH Education, quotes the executive producer of the weekly public affairs documentary series, *Frontline*, who described the broadcast programme as 'the executive summary of material that the producer had assembled for the program' (Liroff 2006).

Despite the perennial struggle for funding – government appropriations have regularly been well below 20 per cent (PBS 2007) – American public television is an institution with ready access to some exceptional expertise, particularly at WGBH in Boston, the system's biggest production centre which, as noted in Chapter Six has established links with nearby Harvard and MIT. Working in the field of educational production, Howard Cutler, Executive Producer with WGBH Interactive, regards the Internet as the primary interactive platform for educational content on the basis of the depth of interactivity compared to digital television:

> It's very important for the person to be able to pause…take a different route, come back and…not have lost the continuity of the experience. So that first dimension was time. The next dimension…I would call expansion and compression, in the sense that as the producer I am not having to force everything about the subject down your throat in one fell swoop, which is usually the problem with broadcast television. I have got to get everything to you, and not only that, I have to get it to you in a limited span of time… Once I have control of time it means that then I can also give…a surface level and a deeper level and a really, really deep level. So the next level of interactivity that's palpable is that ability to layer content from the relatively superficial to the very deep. Beyond that the other things that are really important, I think for us, include what I would loosely call simulation, which merges over into gaming…that allows you to master certain kinds of understandings, which are not easily communicated by story-telling. (Cutler 2006)

Fortuitously also a much cheaper production platform, the Internet is offering American public television new opportunities to innovate and expand in the delivery of educational content and locally centred programming, the two distinguishing strengths of America's public television system (Winefield 2006). However, despite cross-platform delivery, public television's ongoing dependence on corporate sponsorship is likely to continue to frustrate those wanting a more provocative news and current affairs service from public television.

Media Content Providers

The growing take-up of broadband Internet connection, the digital revolution's second wave or Web 2.0, brings the new era of on-demand media, with television distribution via the Internet (Internet Protocol TV – IPTV) offering always-on availability and global reach along with media downloads and user generated content (Thompson 2006: 4). Unlike the first wave – the development of digital infrastructure by telephone companies, Internet service providers (ISPs), and governments – the second wave is being driven by media rich content and user take-up. As noted earlier, the term 'on-demand' encompasses media content accessed across several platforms – TV, computer, mobile phone and PDAs – that is also 'searchable, movable and share-able' (Thompson 2006: 5). Heralding a radically different relationship between content provider and viewer/user, on-demand media content is characterised by its facility for personalization, its mobility, and the possibilities for interactivity and UGC (Harrison & Wessels 2005: 835–6; Looms 2007: 99–104).

To reach the fragmenting audience, PSBs are reconfiguring themselves as media content companies to deliver 'content' as broadcasting and narrowcasting and in various digital on-demand forms – podcasts, vodcasts, really simple syndication (RSS) feeds and mobile files. With the trend towards more outsourcing of content production, PSBs are necessarily more involved in contractual negotiations of online copyright licensing, which is professionalizing relations with producers and arguably making the reflection of national culture a more diffused, mediated and business like enterprise. New applications have been developed to manage on-demand access to intellectual property rights online: the BBC's new online application, iPlayer, gives BBC license-fee payers seven days of access time to download or view online, with storage rights for 30 days. Similarly, a commercial joint venture by BBC worldwide, ITV and Channel Four, then titled Project Kangaroo – a site for viewing television content online – was planned for launch in 2009, subject to BBC Trust approval. The project was stopped in February 2009 by the Competition Commission, which considered it a 'threat to competition', advising that the three should be 'competitors not allies' (BBC 2009). When the British transmission company, Arqiva, bought the Kangaroo technology, the project was subsequently re-launched as SeeSaw, with a deal signed in December 2009 between BBC Worldwide, Channel Four and Five. Integrating advertisements at the top and sometimes in the middle of programming, SeeSaw, as a commercial IPTV application, will now compete with several other video-on-demand (VOD) providers: the US owned Hulu; YouTube, which has reached rights sharing agreements with UK broadcasters to stream full length broadcast programmes; and MSN Player. The BBC is also involved in another IPTV application, Canvas, 'an open internet-connected TV platform' that viewers can watch via their television sets if they have broadband Internet and a Freeview 2.0 set-top box. Awaiting BBC Trust approval at the time of writing, Canvas, a joint venture with Channel Four, ITV, British Telecom, TalkTalk and Five, is due to be launched in late 2010 but is likely to be challenged by BSkyB on competition policy grounds (Tryhorn 2010). Another PSB venture into IPTV is Australia's ABC iView, 'a free internet broadcasting service', launched in 2008, offering five channels of streamed on-demand television content along with an online shop, for viewing on a computer (ABC 2009a).

While the established principles of PSB remain relevant, some of the changes institutions incur in repositioning as media content companies are nonetheless fundamental. The comprehensive schedule has been a foundational tenet of public service broadcasting, reflecting the expectations that accompany public funding and universal coverage by incorporating a broad range of programming – from serious and specific to popular culture forms. This approach also served Lord Reith's idea of moral uplift, 'serving the public by forcing it to confront the frontiers of its own taste' (Smith 1976: 63). The comprehensive schedule offered a variety of genres and topics in prime-time, and in constructing a general mass audience served as a vehicle for the public sphere. With the spread of narrowcasting, the comprehensive remit became increasingly anachronistic as the audience fragmented. Since the 1980s in the UK and US, and the mid 1990s in Australia, increases in the numbers of commercial competitors for specialist minority audiences prompted mainstream PSB channels to pursue a populist approach in an effort to shore up dwindling audience numbers (Born 2004: 64; Biltereyst 2004: 344; Murdock 2005: 190). In the US and across Europe, pay channels such as Discovery, National Geographic and Nickelodeon have drawn away some of the traditional audiences of public broadcasters – those for documentary and children's programming. Diminishing its potential to contribute public value and driving the marketisation of the media, audience fragmentation has been a considerable threat to PSB (Murdock 2005: 190).

In the era of Web 2.0, the cost efficient, readily updatable, searchable and interactive qualities of the Internet offer new ways for PSBs to reach niche audiences in response to this threat. At the same time, the unique qualities of online content are also attracting commercial players and bringing PSBs new challenges from the marketplace. The basis of that attraction is articulated in Chris Anderson's concept of the 'long tail', which identifies a new viability for niche products that can now be cheaply displayed online, and readily matched to consumers via search engines and sophisticated filters that track and aggregate consumer habits (Anderson 2006: 108–15). But the concept also evokes enhanced value for licence fee payers according to how the BBC's Creative Archive develops, as then joint project director, Paul Gerhardt, explained:

> I think the way that the long tail argument has been framed is to emphasise the commercial value of products, which can be relatively old but still have a retail value many years because of the ability of the audience to find them and to revalue them…Exactly the same argument applies to the public value of the BBC. So to give you an example, it could be that an old costume drama by the BBC, let's say from the 1970s about Elizabeth I could have very, very little value in terms of the production, or even in terms of acting. However, it may well be that the costumes that were made for that production were some of the best expressions of costume design. So it's the ability to take that and re-evaluate that program in terms of its costume design if nothing else, and to take from that program two or three scenes that exemplify the high quality of production of the costume design, that's what I would call the application of the long tail for the Archive. In other words, the opportunity for a small group of people to place a high value on one particular item within that content. (Gerhardt 2006)

One telling example of how the enhanced capacity of public service media to deliver personalized educational goals more creatively is also drawing more competition for PSBs, as content companies, is the case of BBC Jam. Launched in January 2006 after a rigorous approval process by the BBC Governors, the Department for Culture Media and Sport, and the European Commission, BBC Jam was designed to assist school age children with their homework 'to support key areas of the school curricula across the UK'. It broke new ground in servicing PSB educational goals online and had 170,000 registered users when the BBC Trust suspended it in March 2007. The Trust acted after commercial competitors complained to the European Commission that the service was not 'complementary and distinctive' as was required, and was 'damaging their business' (BBC 2007c). An additional complexity in the suspension of BBC Jam was that half of the production budget went to independent producers (Kiss 2007: 1). In January 2008, the Trust decided 'the public interest is best served by BBC Jam remaining suspended and formally closing when its service expires on 30 September 2008' (BBC 2008). One irate blogger, Johnson, noted:

> Since the UK licence fee payer has invested this huge amount of money, whether willingly or not, in the BBC's educational output, it seems odd of the BBC Trust to refuse to let them see – and benefit from – what they've already paid for…How can there possibly be public value in suppressing excellent educational resources? It feels like burning books. (Johnson 2008)

This episode reflects the new rules under which the BBC must compete; as competition hots up, increased outsourcing is no longer sufficient response to accusations that PSBs have an unfair advantage. The Public Value test which now governs new 'services' undertaken by the BBC is jointly implemented by the industry regulator, Ofcom, and the BBC Trust, and sets out to balance public value (as assessed by the BBC Trust) against the 'market impact' on potential commercial competitors (assessed by Ofcom), with the final result arbitrated by the Trust:

> Only if the Trust is satisfied that any likely adverse impact on the market is justified by the likely public value of the change, will the proposal go forward for consultation. At the end of the consultation, the BBC Trust will then make its decision. (BBC 2008a)

Another element in the reinvention of PSBs as media content providers is the electronic programme guide (EPG); an off-shoot of digital television, EPGs now enable viewers to compile their own schedules. While self-scheduling is undoubtedly an advance for viewers as consumers, it alters PSB's address to viewers as citizens – once thought integral to the public sphere function. Viewers can now readily omit news and current affairs programming. Constituting a key concern for PSBs, the shift of youth audiences to new media has prompted concerted engagement with the challenge of being more attractive and relevant to youth in the quest for audience renewal. Packaging PSB news bulletins for on-demand accessibility

– as podcasts or vodcasts, or as content for mobile phones – is one strategy for drawing younger viewers back to public service media (BBC 2004: 67). Investment in on-demand developments – various forms of downloads for later listening/viewing on the run – have been criticised because they are not universal and exclude viewers who are not online. On the other hand, fears of a generation growing up under-informed about current affairs offers a public service justification for this investment, and frames on-demand media content as the new universality for PSBs in the digital era, offering everywhere availability rather than simply access.

To Inform, Educate, Entertain and Network

Anticipating the impact of the 'truly fragmented, self pleasing audience', Kim Dalton describes contemporary developments as the 'tipping point' for network television, seeing it as an opportunity for Australia's ABC to both ride and drive changes in how people watch TV programmes. Asserting the ABC's continuing importance to the national conversation, Dalton describes its role in the digital era as, 'a place where people can meet, visually and virtually, to discuss, debate and make sense of their world in a trusted safe environment' (Dalton 2007b: 2–3). Noting tension between freedom and safety in reference to civic engagement online, SBS Manager of Policy and Research, Georgie McClean, questions how the role of PSB moderators should be defined:

> Online obviously offers entirely new opportunities for engagement…for people to contribute to…debates around major issues of public concern…It's something that I think is going to be a challenge for public broadcasters, just to find a way of doing that… without it just being sort of lost in the commercial world…there is a space for us to actually maintain a different…calibre and quality of service online without it just being a free for all…[but] what sort of levels of monitoring and filtering do we have to have… in order to maintain our key editorial standards that differentiate us from any chat forum online? (McClean 2006)

The era of globally available, on-demand media content represents a considerable challenge for national media – both commercial and public service – particularly for policies intended to protect national culture, although public service media generally enjoys some advantages in this regard being publicly funded. Although they continue to attract very high levels of public trust around the world, and as public media content companies serve a vital new social role as developers of cohesive portals to reliable information online, PSBs are facing opposition from a new field of competitors – multimedia producers and software developers – and new pressures for more rigorous systems of performance measurement and accountability. Tomas Coppens and Frieda Saeys (2006) note the trend towards public service contracts in Europe, where various efforts have been made to pin down what quality stands for and to measure broadcasters' performances, with a view to making funding contingent on delivery of goals. At Australia's ABC, the battle over accountability focused on 'balance', with a new position, Director of Editorial Policies, created in December 2006, whilst the BBC's 2006 charter, as already noted, has bought the introduction of a Public Value Test against which market impact must be measured. Ultimately whether such new measures prove advantageous or corrosive will depend on political and public will to protect and maintain these fields of national culture and communication.

In the online environment where information is often anonymous and un-verifiable, public service broadcasters acquire special prestige by virtue of their independence and public accountability. While the old PSB principles may be shifting, they continue to validate public service institutions as the best positioned to deliver independent news and current affairs content, to contribute cultural and programming diversity and to service national conversations about identity. Public service broadcasters' reinvention as multiplatform media content providers marks more than just the delivery of re-versioned content across more platforms. Identifying key markers of difference, Gregory Ferrell Lowe and Jo Bardoel note of European PSBs: 'The decisive issues have always been primarily *social*' (2007: 10). In the digital era, however, technology and economics necessarily play a larger role. The nature of on-demand content – personalizable, shareable and interactive – inviting new kinds of relationships with viewers, brings a raft of new complexities: UGC and the shared authorship of online fora; it also means less producing and more commissioning, which brings new constraints in the licensing of intellectual property online; and additionally opens up the possibility and the need for new revenue streams, with potentially damaging consequences. Whether or not developments such as the ABC's recently announced portfolio of online channels, which includes plans to sell ABC content online (ABC 2008b), poses any threat to the national broadcaster's independence of voice will ultimately depend on future government funding. The ABC strategy is intended to serve both its status as a mainstream media player and the government's plans for high-speed broadband roll out (Moses 2008) by helping to drive user take-up. It is indicative of the gamble PSBs are taking around the world in riding the wave of on-demand media; increasing their financial burden despite existing funding constraints, foreshadowing hybrid funding possibilities and thereby risking non-commercial distinctiveness to initiate innovations.

Chapter 9

Trust and Public Service Media

Introduction

Past arguments supporting public service broadcasting (PSB) have drawn on the notion of spectrum scarcity, the importance of the public service principles as articulated in charters, along with the need to redress areas of market failure in the broadcasting sector. In the new millennium, the defence of public service media relies increasingly on the capacity of publicly owned systems to drive digital uptake, serving the digital economy and the expansion of the information society, an argument that has offered financial justification for public investment in PSBs. This argument assumes that digital television is in the public interest, a claim some dispute, pointing to the cost born by consumers in contrast to the gains for government – the 'digital dividend' arising from the auctioning of freed up spectrum after DSO. However, arguments for the relevance and social value of public service media organisations in the digital era need look no further than their status as trusted brands. Fulfilling a purpose no others can, public service media represent islands of safe, reliable, impartial, 'quality' content in the uncertain, unreliable sea of digital online media. Long a key point of difference for public broadcasters, trustworthiness has assumed new significance in a global media marketplace characterised by conglomeration, corporate and government spin, and non-accountable citizen and social networking media.

As public service media organisations renegotiate relationships with the audience via multi-platform delivery, it seems pertinent to question how these changes might affect public trust, which is integral to the role of providing crucial resources for citizenship. However, drawing on the high level of trust generally invested in public media as a defence for continued public investment holds almost as much peril as promise for the future of public media. This new phase as cross platform providers presents both opportunity and conundrum for PSB management – how to leverage trust as an asset without damaging it? The discussion of trust in this final chapter explores the value and benefits of public service media as trusted institutions, along with the risks of exploiting trust for brand advantage in the media marketplace.

A Crisis of Trust

Surveys of public attitudes around the world indicate that 'generalised trust' in other people has been in decline for decades. Public trust in social institutions is worse, with survey results invariably ranking politicians and journalists towards the bottom (BBC 2007d: 9). Although a certain level of scepticism of officialdom and those in power might be deemed 'healthy', many social commentators have linked the parlous state of public trust to the erosion of citizenship and democracy evident through poor voter turnout, with cynicism viewed as likely to induce apathy and disengagement from civic life (Putnam 2000). While any measurement of trust raises the credibility issues associated with survey research and opinion polling, that trust is viewed as an indicator of benevolence means it generally tends to be seen as a good thing. However, as often noted while trust is associated with honesty, it is not the prerogative of the good: criminals are just as likely to trust one another as those of law-abiding disposition. In the media, public trust is something that offers an important point of difference for public service broadcasters (PSBs), because the public generally accord high scores for trustworthiness 'to institutions perceived to be independent and existing mainly for the good of others rather than for the interests of the organization itself' (Bakir & Barlow 2007: 4). Traditionally this trustworthy status has incurred the paradoxical obligation of preparedness to risk trust by representing diverse viewpoints and providing commentary free from the influence of government or commercial vested interests. This has often resulted in public broadcasters being accused of leftwing bias since it has led to coverage of dissenting views unavailable elsewhere.

The characteristics of trustworthiness identified by Bakir and Barlow are reflected in the charters of PSBs – independence from vested interests, delivering news that is fair and impartial, reflecting national culture and identity, serving diversity through representing minority voices, and addressing audiences and interests not served by commercial media – and indicate why public media are deemed to hold a trust advantage. As Biltereyst observes, there is a close connection between trust and traditional PSB ethos and values – impartiality, independence, quality, diversity, integrity, truth and accuracy (Biltereyst 2004: 342). This is signalled by the high trust in public broadcasters in surveys of public attitudes around the world (Inglis 2002: 588; Lowe & Bardoel 2007: 20–1). The focus of interest in this final chapter is how public service broadcasters' transition to public service media will impact on their trusted status, and thus on the capacity of the public system to provide the variety of resources required for cultural and political citizenship in pluralist democracies (Murdock 1999).

Reflected in polls and surveys taken of public attitudes over the last few decades, the decline in public trust is commonly described as a crisis, generally with reference to trust in public institutions (Bakir & Barlow 2007; Beck et al. 1994; Gore 2007; Keen 2007; O'Neill 2002; Paxman 2007; Putnam 2000; Thompson 2007; 2008), and has been attributed to various factors: recurring reports of official mismanagement and corporate fraud; the reframing of social progress in contemporary technological societies in terms of risk management, foregrounding inherent risks such as those to health, the environment, national security and the economy (Beck et al. 1994); reduced social capital as a result of declining social networking (Putnam 2000); and a new drive for quantifiable accountability that has had the side-effect of inducing a culture of suspicion and distrust (O'Neill 2002c: 4–5).

In their book, *The Age of Suspicion*, Vian Bakir and David Barlow identify two broad debates about trust in the media: the role of the media in relation to the process and practice of citizenship; and the extent to which the media enable the public to 'talk back' to power, thus making the state accountable. They also observe that it is only when citizens are empowered through the debates of a 'free' media that they can make the state accountable (Bakir & Barlow 2007: 19). Certainly trusted media are widely viewed as an important prerequisite for an informed citizenry and a democratic society (Archer 2007; Splichal 2006; Murdock 2007; Beecher 2008).

The proliferation of online media has contributed to the crisis of trust and plays a part in both debates identified by Bakir and Barlow – citizenship and holding government accountable. As regards the first – citizenship – by increasing competition for audience/market share, online media is fuelling conglomeration amongst commercial players as existing businesses leverage their 'first mover' advantage through mergers and acquisitions, raising the bar for new entrants. Conglomeration in media ownership concentrates the editorial influence of vested interests, eroding the diversity of voices heard across the news media. These developments underline two specific concerns: the dearth of serious political journalism as news media providers become more entertainment focused to cope with a fragmenting audience/readership and dwindling advertising share; and the demise of investigative journalism, a resource hungry enterprise once valued by media organisations for the status it imbued, but which is no longer cost efficient (Schlesinger 2006; Turner 2005: 156–61; Hirst & Harrison 2007: 238–59; 334–55). There is also considerable evidence to indicate that reductions in newsroom budgets and increased workloads have made editors more dependent on public relations copy, and made journalists more vulnerable to manipulation by government and corporate communications staff (Louw 2005). Together with shifts in audience habits, these changes are being widely interpreted as signalling the decline of the professional news media (Greenslade 2008).

On the other hand, web logs, or blogs, referred to en masse as the blogosphere, along with online citizen media which celebrate unmediated freedom of opinion and the personalizing of public issues, are being heralded as having a key role in the future of journalism. One forecast from *The Guardian's* Roy Greenslade envisages stripped-down, hybrid news organizations where the reportage of amateur 'citizen' journalists is edited by professionals (ABC 2008a). Malaysia's Malaysiakini.com and South Korea's OhMyMedia.com offer impressive examples of how citizen media is extending diversity across the media sector by democratising access and inviting participation. But while offering democratizing advantages alongside traditional hard news helps to keep professionals in touch and honest, citizen media is problematic as a dominant news model. During London's July 2007 Underground bombing, mobile phone reports from citizen-journalists on the spot proved unreliable. This reflects that the efforts of those working outside the media without pay or institutional resources is unlikely to match the work of trained journalists with reputations and livelihoods to lose (Hirst & Harrison 2007: 258). Thus the high volume of news services online may well enhance rather than challenge the perceived public value of the news services of PSBs.

Defining Trust

Trust is a slippery concept to define; Bakir and Barlow describe it as a 'complex phenomenon, compromising many subtleties', with three features at its core – rationality, faith and confidence. The association with rationality originates in Enlightenment thinking, with trust being an integral part of the recognized benefits – individualist and collective – of a logical social order. Freeing the individual from the paralysis of indecision, trust as faith comes into play when fair judgements or assessments are inhibited by circumstance. The association of trust with confidence is less clear, requiring differentiation from hope. Only those who have considered all alternatives trust with confidence rather than hope (Bakir & Barlow 2007: 10; 110).

Exploring the value of trust, Bakir and Barlow ask the question, 'What does trust do?' and identify five functions: serving as social glue; generating social capital and thereby lubricating economic and political cooperation; managing social complexity – facilitating effective communication and administration in technologically and culturally complex societies; acting as a solution for risk; and serving as a prerequisite for forming self identity. The idea of trust as social glue has been endorsed by sociologists from Simmel (1908) to Durkheim (1964), the central argument being that without trust people would be unable to arrive at the shared goals that form the basis of any community (Bakir & Barlow 2007: 12).

The second function – social capital – which refers to community networks and their role in building 'civic engagement', both draws on and builds trust. In his work on the topic, Robert Putnam assesses social capital as strengthening shared ethical values that reduce the need for legal regulation and simplify bureaucracy, lubricating cooperation, bringing tangible economic and social benefits. Social capital is attributed with political significance at both macro institutional and micro community levels; when it is high, 'citizens express confidence and trust not only in each other but also in public institutions, which in turn encourages citizens to work to improve the state's democratic accountability' (Putnam 2000). Putnam identifies 'generalised reciprocity' as the most valuable benefit of social capital:

A society characterised by generalized reciprocity is more efficient than a distrustful society, for the same reason that money is more efficient than barter. If we don't have to balance every exchange instantly, we can get a lot more accomplished. Trustworthiness lubricates social life. Frequent interaction among a diverse set of people tends to produce a norm of generalised reciprocity. Civic engagement and social capital entail mutual obligation and responsibility for action. (Putnam 2000: 21)

Describing trust as contributing 'complexity reduction', Luhmann (1979) allocated an important function to trust in contemporary, multicultural and technocratic society, disrupting assumptions that its social value was defunct, which had cast it as 'an obsolete resource typical of traditional society' (Bakir & Barlow 2007: 13). Social trust, as opposed to the impersonal, contractual, fiduciary trust of trusteeship, plays an important part in democratic societies with the electorate required to imbue trust in the government it elects.

Trust takes on a new significance as the corollary to 'risk', now a popular frame for analysing the contemporary, globalised world. The proliferation and scale of risk in contemporary society thus amplifies the importance and contingent nature of trust. Ulrich Beck's concept of the risk society, which is helpful in elucidating this, hinges on the way in which society is now organized around the management of manufactured risks:

> The concept of risk reverses the relationship of past, present and future. The past loses its power to determine the present. Its place as the cause of present-day experience and action is taken by the future, that is to say something non-existent, constructed and fictitious. We are discussing and arguing about something which is not the case, but could happen if we were not to change course. Believed risks are the whip used to keep the present-day moving along at a gallop. (Beck 2000: 214)

In *Risk Society*, Beck (1992) identified risk as a key attribute of the reflexive phase of late capitalism; society loses confidence in how things are judged as rational and safe having recognized the underlying industrial causes – that private enterprise escapes financial responsibility – and the role Science plays in legitimising the situation. This means that the issue of trust in authorities is constantly being raised invoking what Lash (1994) has called 'active trust', where official accounts are up for contestation, where trust is always contingent. Social psychological research has found that competence and honesty are critical in winning trust. Thus some argue that the public distrust targeted communications that avoid engagement or consultation (Bakir & Barlow 2007: 15). This suggests a key position for the media as brokers of public trust.

Trust and the Media

The relationship between public trust and contemporary media is now an established focus of research (Biltereyst 2004; Bakir & Barlow 2007; Putnam 2004). Theories about the social significance of trust, taking a broader view, offer deeper understanding of how trust is constructed and how this has changed over time, and so shed more light on what changes in public trust in the media might mean for the future. Drawing on the ideas of Anthony Giddens and Scott Lash, Biltereyst observes the close association of 'trust' and 'authority' in traditional societies, noting a definitional change in 'post-traditional modern society':

> Formulaic truth was replaced by modernist belief in the corrigibility of knowledge, while trust in abstract systems was more difficult to generate. Especially in the conditions of late modernity, mechanisms of trust shifted while expertise was contested...In late modern

society, with its circumstances of uncertainty, multiple choices and possible lifestyles, the need to trust is intrinsically linked to growing doubt and risk. (Biltereyst 2004: 349)

Trust has been theorised as both arising from common value systems and contributing to the establishment of common goals, serving as 'social glue' (Bakir & Barlow 2007: 12). Research on social capital also explores the role of trust in this regard, signalling the importance of social networks as trust-building mechanisms that enable society to function effectively. Like Lash, Giddens uses the term 'active trust', applying it rather differently as being 'at the origin of new forms of social solidarity' and as 'necessarily geared to the other'. This active engagement of trust invokes a role commonly played by public service media – broadcasting diverse special interest programming, thereby contributing to bridging cultural difference by eroding suspicion of the 'other' and actively building trust across different cultural groups (Giddens 1994: 186). These functions commonly associated with trust, in tandem with key attributes of digital media technology – interactivity and multichannel possibilities – do offer public service media a distinct point of difference with commercial media, a means of proving public value.

Apart from the general decline of social trust, diminishing public trust in the media can be attributed to some specific factors. As already mentioned, increasing conglomeration in ownership, initially arising from media deregulation, became a pattern around the world in the 1980s and 1990s. The so-called phenomenon of Web 2.0 – media rich online content enabled by the spread of broadband Internet connectivity – has brought a new wave of conglomeration. Eroding the diversity of voices heard across the mainstream news media, as old media moguls acquire new media companies (such as News Limited's purchase of MySpace) and as new media giants digest one another (Google's acquisition of YouTube), the trend is also accelerating the demise of both serious political journalism – as news becomes more entertainment-focused – and investigative journalism (Schlesinger 2006; Turner 2005: 156–61; Hirst & Harrison 2007: 238–59; 334–55). On the other hand, the blogosphere and online citizen media, which celebrate unmediated freedom of opinion, appear to be the future of journalism and to offer new means for making governments accountable. But while offering democratizing advantages, helping to keep news professionals in touch and honest, citizen media, as noted earlier, is problematic as a dominant news model. The unstable qualities of the digital domain destabilise trust: ease of reproduction and malleability foster a 'culture of copy' and 'sharing' that transgresses mainstream notions of authenticity/ legitimacy; the spread of conversational opinion and rumour online via blogs and social networks displaces factual reporting as news (Keen 2007: 64; 96); speed of delivery online drives hourly news updating, leaving corrections unacknowledged; 'amateur' journalists write un-curtailed by professional obligations to ethics or the law (Hirst & Harrison 2007: 240–61); easy anonymity shields those with fraudulent intent; embedded hyperlinks and frames facilitate the blurring of editorial and advertising content; online consumer profiling applications such as cookies and spyware intrude on personal privacy; while online security threats from malware of various kinds routinely thwarts protection software. Lastly, as also noted earlier, there is the rise of the public relations (PR) sector and the role of public relations professionals as mediators of political news (Louw 2005), a development in which opinion polling and controlled access to politicians and political information via media management limits election coverage and political reporting, variously termed 'plebiscitary democracy' and 'government by focus group' (Scammell 1995; Schlesinger 2006). This has been suggested as a key reason underlying a general declining public trust of government (Bakir & Barlow 2007: 5). With adversarial interviewing, the broadcast media's stock rebuttal of PR manipulation, viewers are increasingly short changed on political analysis.

That PSB is not immune to this crisis of trust was evident in Britain during and after the 2004 Hutton Enquiry, which, as discussed in Chapter Two, investigated BBC reporting on the Blair Government's dossier of reasons for invading Iraq following the suicide of Dr David Kelly, later identified as the source for the BBC story. Lord Hutton's Report, which criticized the BBC, subsequently resulted in the resignation of both the BBC chairman and director-general. However, as British broadcaster, Steve Barnett reports, 'opinion polls in the wake of Hutton consistently showed that voters trusted the BBC a great deal more than the government' (Barnett 2006: 61), indicating heightened public cynicism regarding government 'spin'. Between 2005 and 2007, a series of scandals kept public trust in British broadcasting in the media spotlight (BBC 2007). Driving BBC management into a state of prolonged angst about public trust, the scandals indicate both the new dangers of proprietary relationships (unfair charging, albeit unintentional, in on-air, premium phone line competitions), and the perils of trying to compete with commercial populism (reflected in provocative out-of-sequence editing of an impromptu comment by the Queen in an on-screen promotion for a documentary, *A Year With the Queen*).

Anxiety about PSBs and public trust is not confined to Britain. Around the world the heightened emphasis public service broadcasters are placing on accountability and mechanisms for building trust is evident in the emergence of new systems of governance and performance measurement – strategies employed to justify public funding. Coppens and Saeys discuss negotiation of periodical contracts with specific mandatory tasks for PSBs (Coppens & Saeys 2006: 261). Such measures seek to legitimise public funding by 'proving' delivery of charter goals. In Australia, the ABC instituted a Director of Editorial Policy in 2006 to oversee 'balance' in response to prolonged government accusations of bias, or 'bullying' as it has also been described (Lawrence 2007: 6). Despite trust-building objectives, institutional timidity is a natural outcome of such measures, emerging through reduced creative risk taking (since ratings are increasingly important too), and in self-censorship with the abandonment of fearless scrutiny of power elites. Both broadcaster Quentin Dempster (2005; 2008a) and academic Robert Manne (2007) have written about timidity at the ABC, with Dempster describing the emergence of a 'careful blandness' in ABC news and current affairs, as discussed earlier in Chapter Four.

Writing about the Howard Government's 'culture war' with the ABC – most evident in Senator Alston's 59 accusations of bias against ABC Radio National – Robert Manne argued that subsequent 'nervousness on questions of political and ideological sensitivity' ultimately damaged ABC Iraq war coverage. Timidity under pressure could well erode public trust in the ABC as the provider of news and current affairs with 'no fear or favour' – in the words of a 2006 on-air promotion. In his December 2007 article for *The Monthly*, Manne details how the 'culture wars' against a presumed left wing bias have changed the range of voices heard on political issues on ABC television, with many articulate left wing experts now excluded from the airwaves (Manne 2007).

Another PSB trend that has implications for trust is the increased push for outsourcing of production, which necessarily leads to a reduction in in-house production staff. The anecdotal evidence of filmmakers in Australia and New Zealand with experience of producing both in-house and as independents, is that in-house production frequently offers more creative freedom and opportunities to innovate than the freelance environment, where funders require recipients to accommodate overseas market needs – to facilitate sales and a return on the public investment (Debrett 2006: 148–9; 184–5). The support network of experienced colleagues as mentors is an important benefit of in-house production.

In Australia, successive governments have promoted outsourcing and the downscaling of in-house production on the basis of increasing efficiency, a claim that ABC staff-elected director, Kirsten Garrett, strenuously disputed with the ABC board in the 1990s, noting the absence of facts to back it up when independent production companies' notional quotes for ABC-produced programmes were given as evidence (Dempster 2000: 246–7). When Bob Mansfield proposed the ABC outsource all production bar news and current affairs in his 1997 Report, he conceded he had no evidence to prove its greater efficiency, highlighting instead the savings to be made in reduced infrastructure through the sell-off of ABC buildings. Calculating comparative efficiency is complicated, as Glenn Withers (2002) relates in his discussion of ABC funding in which he ranks ABC efficiency high alongside commercial competitors and other public broadcasters. Other audits, like the Howard Government's 2006 KPMG Report from which the public only ever received leaked information, suggest little reason to assume inefficiency at the ABC.

Head of ABC television, Kim Dalton, explains his drive for increased production outsourcing as bringing more money to ABC production by leveraging external investment funding thereby increasing hours of local content on screen (Dalton 2008). Those opposing increased outsourcing note this money is tied to conditions, the need to achieve overseas sales, to produce a product that can be sold off-shore, and that this is thus not the best way to reflect the nation's culture to its public. Other threads in this argument are: the role of ABC in-house production as a training ground for the industry with many in the production sector having learned their craft at the ABC; and the enhanced value of copyright ownership in the digital era with its multiple possibilities for distribution, which makes public ownership of television programmes through in-house production cost-efficient and in the public interest, with royalties reinvested in future productions.

Increased outsourcing thus has implications for public trust, often preferencing the needs of the local commercial film/television sector to reach global markets over the national public interest PSBs are directed to serve. The latter involves the delivery of resources for cultural citizenship – programming that informs various sectors of society about each other (Murdock 1999). Keeping a careful balance between in-house production (where the public service ethos is supported through collegial *corps d'ésprit*) and outsourcing (which broadens and diversifies the production base) is important for retaining public trust. It is also the case that the history of the ABC, as with other PSBs, rebounds with incidents where staff have defended the broadcaster's editorial independence and institutional public service ethos against management pragmatism (Inglis 2006b; Dempster 2000). Thus the ABC's scale as an employer and its status as a comprehensive mainstream service (rather than simply addressing market failure) are also relevant to its trustworthiness.

These key areas where PSBs have traditionally taken greater risks than commercial media, are now threatened by new policy trends: a renewed emphasis on policing journalistic 'balance' in response to political pressure, which appears to have increased self-censorship and timidity; and the move, apparently in response to financial pressure, towards increased outsourcing of drama and documentary production, which threatens to subjugate public interest values to commercial ones.

Of the contemporary push for stronger mechanisms for ensuring accountability, philosopher Onora O'Neill noted in her third Reith Lecture on trust:

> Serious and effective accountability, I believe, needs to concentrate on good governance, on obligations to tell the truth and needs to seek intelligent accountability. I think it has to fantasise much less about Herculean micro-management by means of performance indicators or total transparency. If we want a culture of public service, professionals and public servants must in the end be free to serve the public rather than their paymasters. (O'Neill 2002c: 5)

Risk taking is integral to the role of public service media with directives to be innovative and reflect cultural diversity routinely included in charter goals. Also invoking a degree of risk, separate requirements in the editorial policies for news and current affairs stipulate the need for journalists to be impartial and questioning. As ABC legal adviser, Bruce Donald, argues, good journalists need to be prepared to risk a defamation suit to do their jobs properly (ABC 1995).

New Media, PSBs and Trust

At Australia's ABC, managing director, Mark Scott, sees the new multiplatform structure enabling the broadcaster 'to connect with more Australians in more ways more often' (Scott 2009). He compares this to 'hosting the conversation', identifying a new role for the ABC: 'being the town square where a range of voices can be heard and exchanged with each other, not just listen to us broadcasting to them'. Analysing ABC Online's capacity to serve this role, Toija Cinque has noted the importance of 'a (post) modern form of citizenry' arising from a variety of online activities:

> This development allows ABC Online innovative ways to promote an informed citizenry through access to educational and informational services…The promotion of an informed citizenry by the ABC is arguably imperative in a new media environment for three reasons: (1) an informed and educated citizenry is best served by the new technology providing accurate and independent information that the public broadcaster can offer; (2) new technologies are increasingly seen as an essential part of democratic practice and education; and (3) the goal of promoting an informed citizenry is not met elsewhere in commercial oligopolies. (Cinque 2007: 92)

The interactive potential of digital platforms contributes a new line of accountability for public service media: a rejuvenated and transparent 'publicness' through social networking; the delivery of diverse specialised content through sites such as Art Post, where Australian artists can post profiles and images of their work; and sites for public debate such as Unleashed and ABC Fora, where 'ordinary' Australians can participate in discussions with commentators with specialist knowledge or experience, and make their opinions known.

However, these new on-demand media contain a number of anomalies for public service broadcasters. The previously discussed unstable nature of digital technologies and the anonymity available on online platforms foster non-accountability, cyber-crime and surveillance, which do not invite trust. Yet these qualities also justify the involvement of public service media as multiplatform providers – to establish a trusted place online. The interactive potential of social networking also offers greater user/audience accountability and cost-efficient accommodation of pluralist needs, serving a community building role. But as part of a PSB portal such content requires moderation and careful judgement as to what is legitimate in terms of user comment/content and external hyperlinks. For many, such moderation goes against the grain of the democratising potential of online communication, echoing the gatekeeper role of 'old media', despite its goal of protecting users from potential abuse. Web moderation, as Cinque observes, also slows user-interactivity and is generally not done on commercial websites, which are naturally faster as a result. Establishing online moderation as a trustworthy characteristic thus requires careful education about the nature of online media. Properly negotiated with users, moderation offers a means of building social trust in public service media but raises the bar in terms of intervention.

Various sites on ABC Online have had conflicting policies regarding the use of external hyperlinks taking viewers beyond the ABC portal, signalling some ambivalence about the function and purpose of ABC Online – safe haven or town square? While it is not impossible to integrate both in the same access protocol, Cinque observes differences in approach should be transparent (Cinque 2007: 97). Clarification of this kind is also important in insuring continued trust in PSBs as institutions committed to risk-taking – both in creative production and public interest journalism. In March 2009, the ABC launched specific 'relaxed' guidelines for user generated content along with three levels of moderation – pre-moderation, post moderation and reactive moderation – measures that are intended to clarify the trustworthiness of ABC content online for different audiences and user groups.

The global reach and easy access of the Internet as a distribution platform in the Web 2.0 era brings an additional threat to public trust in public media. While most PSBs have a long history of commercial licensing arrangements, the potential scope and scale of such operations in the digital era enhances the threat of commercial 'back-doorism', potentially undermining public trust in the independence and freedom of public service media from commercial vested interests.

Conclusion

While the opportunities arising from online and digital technology in terms of engaging citizenry appear something of a new dawn for PSB, the possibilities for commercial revenue, coupled with political and financial pressures, have potential to undermine that most valuable asset – public trust – that is necessary for those opportunities to be realised.

At the BBC, it was interestingly scandals induced by populist content, the out-of-context editing of the Queen rather than the Hutton Enquiry, which diminished public trust in the organisation (Thompson 2008), perhaps because politicians and government rank so low in most surveys of public trust. For Channel Four, falling public trust was associated with the pursuit of audiences, as controversy turned to international scandal when racist comments made in the *Celebrity Big Brother* series in 2007 went to air. Having opted to interpret difference in terms of provocative and controversial content, deemed attractive to the youth audience, Channel Four later outlined plans for a public service direction in *Next on Four*. Similarly snarled in the possibilities of increasing commercial revenue, SBS television's introduction of spot advertising and pursuit of audience ratings in the youth demographic angered the Federation of Ethnic Community Councils of Australia, representatives of the original audience for the service, who made their feelings known through the government's ABC/SBS Review in 2008, along with others calling for a return to a multicultural service. In the United States, public television, Hoynes notes, has pursued exploitation of the system's 'trusted brand', which is increasingly 'traded for revenue streams in the form of corporate sponsorships and strategic partnerships', a fund raising strategy that runs the risk of undermining 'the very trust and loyalty that makes their brand so valuable' (Hoynes 2003: 124–8). For TVNZ, in 2009 it is the very absence of any public service remit, with its charter now abandoned, that is likely to not only undermine trust but also to renew government threats of privatisation. The hope for TVNZ as a public broadcaster now appears to lie with its two digital non-commercial channels, TVNZ 6 and TVNZ 7, which may continue to receive funding on the basis of the incentive they provide for digital take-up. Linked to a sense of shared ownership trust imbues affection which builds across time, something TVNZ's repeated restructurings have thwarted.

With the proliferation of media around the globe, trustworthiness has increased in value as a distinguishing attribute, but has also arguably become more ambiguous and difficult to define as a characteristic of public service media as it is employed towards various ends. Trust is currently employed to reinforce and prove institutional trustworthiness through greater accountability – via new strictures on editorial 'balance' and rejuvenation of the internal public complaints processes (Simons 2008). That this can be overdone and become counter-productive is suggested by various commentaries on experiences at the ABC. Following a decade of government accusations of bias or 'bullying' (Lawrence 2007), these new mechanisms were seen as being motivated by a perceived need to keep governments on side (Dempster 2000: 56–61; 314–5). Trust is also integral to the projection of 'quality' as a marker of public service programming – reliable, well researched and crafted – and a factor in drawing users to engage with complementary content online, subsequently driving digital take-up. Undoubtedly, however, it is the reputation of public service news as well researched, impartial and independent that best invites trust in an organisation. In addition, the active time and place shifting of audiences online requires a re-thinking of how to interpret editorial policies to accommodate the diverse needs of different audience groups for on-demand content – the need to both stimulate and protect children, and to serve citizens through inviting open engagement with online information and resources. On-demand online content subverts the old time-based censorship categories where parental guidance was clearly signalled onscreen as the clock ticked on to the adult viewing time zone. Always-on digital media has created new problems for parents that PSBs as traditional deliverers of educational content designed for different age and ability levels are best equipped to address.

Balancing three imperatives – providing reliable, safe content for young people, being accountable and transparent, while incorporating the risk-taking inherent in charter goals (being innovative and delivering impartial and independent news and current affairs) – are all necessary to preserve public trust. Given the implications of the crisis in public trust for citizenship and democracy, the need for resilient public service media seems more important than ever before. As commercial media retreat from public service commitments, government acknowledgement of the multiple functions served by public media is welcome. Many governments have seen public media as a strategy to drive user take-up of DTT and to a lesser extent broadband. Many governments have seen public service media as a strategy to drive user take-up of DTT and to a lesser extent broadband; while this assists the status of PSBs as mainstream players, enabling technological innovations, it nevertheless represents something of a gamble, raising costs and foreshadowing increased government interference.

As an asset that is inherently at risk, trust requires careful management by PSBs in the era of unstable online domains, particularly given the new tolerance for hybrid funding and public private partnerships. With terrorism and global warming as two compelling global issues that require complexity reduction, trusted media organisations are more important than ever as vehicles for the public sphere, contributing broader public understanding of cultural minorities, a necessary precursor to social tolerance, and delivering impartial information and analysis free from vested interests. As cross platform providers, public service media are far better placed to achieve the 'individuated and collective' vision (Born 2004: 516) that they historically tackled as broadcasters, bringing together the institutional nurturing of the creative expression of talented individuals and the commitment to a broader, open debate that can now engage directly with citizens online. How these various public media organisations undertake that challenge will depend on how the winds of political and economic fortune blow. In March 2010, as this book was going to print, the BBC's director-general, Mark Thompson, announced the outcomes of the BBC Strategy Review which outlined moves to halve the content of BBC Online and cut its staffing and budgets by a quarter, along with similarly radical cuts to other services. The review also proposed that every web page should contain an external link unless not editorially appropriate, a move that potentially challenges the trustworthiness of the site. The changes echo the strategy pursued by an earlier director-general, John Birt, under the hostile Thatcher government, and are presumably intended to signal an organisational will for improved efficiency in hopes of pre-empting more radical reform by an incoming Conservative government should the Labour party lose the May 2010 election. The proposed cuts followed ongoing complaints from the private sector, particularly from the Murdoch controlled BSkyB, that the BBC's expansion in the digital era constitutes unfair competition. Ultimately the ability of PSBs to stare down the private sector's increasingly strident claims of market distortion will depend on public support, which hinges on public trust and on keeping faith with the audience by upholding charter goals, maintaining a delicate balance between leading and following public opinion and taste, something that the asynchronous platforms of interactive digital media have made much more attainable.

References

ABC (1995), *The ABC All-Media Law Handbook*, Australia.

ABC (2006), 'The World Today: 15 March', in E. Hall (ed.), *ABC Radio National*, Australia: ABC.

ABC (2007), 'The State of Children's Television', *Media Report*, http://www.abc.net.au/rn/mediareport/stories/2007/2108989.htm. Accessed 14 January 2008.

ABC (2007a), '2007 ABC TV Highlights', *Media Release*, http://www.abc.net.au/corp/pubs/media/s2107690.htm. Accessed 2 June 2008.

ABC (2007b), 'ABC Bolsters Its Commitment to International Broadcasting', *Media Release*, 7 February 2007, http://www.abc.net.au/corp/pubs/media/s1842867.htm. Accessed 6 March 2010.

ABC (2008), 'Wired for the Future', *Media Watch*, http://www.abc.net.au/mediawatch/transcripts/s2235826.htm.

ABC (2008b), 'Australian Broadcasting Corporation Submission to the Department of Broadband, Communications and the Digital Economy Discussion', in *ABC and SBS: Towards the Digital Future*, http://www.abc.net.au/corp/pubs/reportsindex.htm. Accessed 20 June 2009.

ABC (2008c), 'ABC Designs For The Future', *Media Watch*, http://www.abc.net.au/mediawatch/transcripts/s2365258.htm. Accessed 25 May 2009.

ABC (2009), 'Fifty Years of Science Television', *Catalyst*, http://www.abc.net.au/catalyst/team/about.htm. Accessed 20 January 2009.

ABC (2009a), 'What is ABC iView?', http://www.abc.net.au/tv/iview/. Accessed 6 June 2009.

ABC (2009b), 'ABC Funding Boost', *Media Release*, 12 May 2009, http://www.abc.net.au/corp/pubs/media/s2568522.htm. Accessed 6 June 2009.

ABC Commercial (2009c), 'About Content Licensing', http://www.abccontentsales.com.au/contentlicensing/. Accessed 14 January 2009.

Abrash, B. (2006), *Beyond Broadcast: Reinventing Public Media in a Participatory Culture*, Boston: Harvard Law School.

Adams, K. (1973), *The Broadcasting Future of New Zealand: Report of the Committee on Broadcasting*, Wellington: New Zealand Government Printer.

Alvarado, M. (2004), 'Public service television: Challenge, adaptation and survival', in J. Sinclair and G. Turner (eds.), *Contemporary world television*, London: BFI, pp. 7–11.

Anderson, C. (2006), *The long tail: When the future of business is selling less of more*, New York: Hyperion.

Ang, I., Brand, Jeff, Noble, Greg and Sternberg, Jason (2006), *Connecting Diversity: Paradoxes of Multicultual Australia*, Sydney: SBS.

Ang, I., Hawkins, G., and Dabboussy, L. (2008), *The SBS Story*, Sydney: UNSW Press.

Annan, Lord (1977), *Report of the Committee of Inquiry into the Future of Broadcasting*, London: British Parliament.

Anon (2003), 'Stirring the melting pot'. *Sydney Morning Herald*, 11 November, http://www.smh.com.au/articles/2003/11/10/1068329493892.html. Accessed 21 February 2009.

APT (2009), 'About American Public Television – our mission and history', http://www.aptonline.org/aptweb.nsf/vAboutAPT/Index-Our+Mission+&+History. Accessed 5 June 2009.

Archer, J. (2007), 'The Erosion of Trust in Australian Public Life', in D. Barlow and V. Bakir (eds.), *Communication in the Age of Suspicion: Trust and the Media*, Houndsmill, Basingstoke: Palgrave Macmillan, pp. 39–50.

Atkinson, J. (1989), 'Mass Communication, Economic Liberalisation and the New Mediators', *Political Science*, 41: 2, pp. 85–108.

Atkinson, J. (1994), 'The Americanisation of One Network News', *The Australasian Journal of American Studies*, 13: 1, pp. 1–26.

Atkinson, J. (1994a), 'The State, The Media and Thin Democracy', in A. Sharp (ed.), *A Leap in the Dark*, Auckland University Press.

Atkinson, J. (1999), 'Broadcasting Cross Pressures: Reflections on a Failed Experiment', http://www.arts.auckland.ac.nz/online/politics328/BCxpressures.htm. Accessed 4 May 2005.

Atkinson, J. (2002), *Putting Humpty Together Again: Will the Charter Change Richard and Judy?* Third Annual Chapman Lecture, 20 May, Maidment Theatre: University of Auckland.

Aufderheide, P. (2001), 'Public television now and later', in Horace Newcombe (ed.), *The Encyclolpedia of Television*, http://www.centerforsocialmedia.org/publictelevisionnowandlater.htm. Accessed 3 February 2009.

Bakir, V. and Barlow, D (eds.) (2007), *Communication in the Age of Suspicion*, Houndsmill, Basingstoke: Palgrave Macmillan.

Balas, G. R. (2003), *Recovering a Public Vision for Public Television*, Rowman & Littlefield Publishers, Inc.

Balding, R. (2005), 'Making History', *The Australian Financial Review*, 10 November.

Banerjee, I. and Seneviratne, K. (eds.) (2006), *Public Service Broadcasting in the Age of Globalisation*, Singapore: Asian Media Informational and Communication Centre (AMIC) and The School of Communication and Information (SCI) Nanyang Technological University, Singapore.

BARB (2009), 'Annual percentage share of viewing (Individuals) 1981–2008', http://www.barb.co.uk/facts/annualShareOfViewing?_s=4. Accessed 28 September 2009.

Barksdale, J. and Hundt, R. (2005), *Digital future initiative: Challenges and opportunities for public service media in the digital age*, A report by the DFI Panel, Washington: PBS Foundation.

Barnett, S. (2006), 'Can the BBC Invigorate our Political Culture?', in J. Lloyd and J. Seaton (eds.), *What can be done? Making the Media and Politics Better*, Oxford: Blackwell Publishing, pp. 58–69.

Barnouw, E. (1990), *Tube of Plenty*, New York: Oxford.

Barwise, P. (2006), 'The BBC Licence fee bid: What does the public think?', London: BBC, http://faculty.london.edu/pbarwise/reportsandmonographs.htm. Accessed 26 December 2009.

Bazalgette, P. (2002), 'No Birt, No BBC', *The Observer*, 27 October, http://www.guardian.co.uk/2002/oct/27. Accessed 22 December 2009.

BBC (1996), *BBC Annual Report 1995/96*, London: BBC.

BBC (2002), 'Secret State Timeline', 17 October 2002, http://news.bbc.co.uk/2/hi/programmes/true_spies/2336987.stm. Accessed 28 September 2009.

BBC (2004), 'Building Public Value: Renewing the BBC for the Digital World', London: BBC Media Centre.

BBC (2005), 'The BBC Under Pressure', http://www.bbc.co.uk/historyofthebbc/resources/pressure/strike.shtml. Accessed 15 September 2009.

BBC (2006), *BBC Annual Report*, London: BBC.

BBC (2006a), *The Future of the BBC: Building Public Value*, London: BBC.

BBC (2006c), 'UK "will lead digital TV uptake"', http://news.bbc.co.uk/2/hi/entertainment/5275718. stm. Accessed 11 March 2007.

BBC (2006d), 'Ministers agree TV licence deal', http://news.bbc.co.uk/2/hi/6201935.stm. Accessed 27 September 2009.

BBC (2006e), 'How the Governors are appointed', http://www.bbcgovernorsarchive.co.uk/about/appointed.html. Accessed 27 September 2009.

BBC (2007), 'At a glance: Shows in TV Scandal', *BBC News*, 5 October, http://news.bbc.co.uk/1/hi/entertainment/6915136.stm. Accessed 11 February 2008.

BBC (2007b), 'BBC Trust Suspends BBC Jam', *Press Release*, http://www.bbc.co.uk/bbctrust/news/press_releases/14_03_2007.html. Accessed 6 June 2009.

BBC (2007c), 'Fair Trading Guidelines', http://www.bbc.co.uk/info/policies/commercial_guides/text/fairtrading_guidelines1106.html. Accessed 24 January 2007.

BBC (2007d), 'From Seesaw to Wagon Wheel: Safeguarding Impartialiy in the 21st Century', London: BBC Trust.

BBC (2007e), 'BBC Apologises over Queen Clips', http://www.bbc.co.uk/2/hi/6294472.htm. Accessed 4 October 2009.

BBC (2008), 'BBC Jam and Future BBC Learning Strategy', http://www.bbc.co.uk/bbctrust/framework/bbc_service_licences/jam.html. Accessed 6 June 2009.

BBC (2009), 'Broadcasters' Kangaroo Tied Down', http://news.bbc.co.uk/1/hi/entertainment/7869181. stm. Accessed 6 June 2009.

BBC (2009a), *BBC Trust Annual Report – 2008/9*, London: BBC Trust.

BBC (2009b), 'BBC Executive Annual Report 2008/09', http://www.bbc.co.uk/annualreport/download_trust.shtml. Accessed 30 December 2009.

BBC (2009c), *BBC Mission and Values*, http://www.bbc.co.uk/info/purpose/public_purposes/index. shtml. Accessed 13 September 2009.

BBC (2009d), 'Fair Trading Guidelines', http://www.bbc.co.uk/info/policies/fairtrading/. Accessed 15 September 2009.

BBC (2009d), 'BBC Worldwide', http://www.bbcworldwide.com/about-bbc-worldwide. Accessed 16 September 2009.

BBC (2009e), 'History of the BBC', http://www.bbc.co.uk/historyofthebbc/resources/pressure/falklands.shtml.

BBC (2009f), 'BBC Trust', http://www.bbc.co.uk/bbctrust/our_work/new_services/index.shtml. Accessed 27 September 2009.

BBC (2009e), 'Record audiences for BBC's digital services', 9 December, http://www.bbc.co.uk/pressoffice/pressreleases/stories/2009/12_december/09/vision.shtml. Accessed 28 December 2009.

BBC (2010), 'The BBC's £7 billion Boost to Economy, Jobs and Businesses', http://www.bbc.co.uk/blogs/aboutthebbc/. Accessed 21 January 2010.

Beasley, V. (c1995), 'Anita Hill – Clarence Thomas hearings', *TV Archives*, http://www.museum.tv/archives/etv/H/htmlH/hill-thomash/hill-thomas.htm. Accessed 3 July 2009.

Beck, U., Giddens, A. and Lash, S. (1994), *Reflexive Modernization: Politics, Tradition and Aesthetics in the Modern Social Order*, Cambridge: Polity Press.

Beck, U. (2000), 'Risk Society Re-visited', in B. Adams, Ulrich Beck and Joost van Loon (eds.), *The Risk Society and Beyond: Critical Issues for Social Theory*, London: Sage, pp. 212–24.

Beecher, E. (2008), 'Beecher v Devine: The threat to public trust journalism', *Crikey*, 12 September 2008.

Bell, A. (1995), '"An Endangered Species": Local Programming in the New Zealand Television Market', *Media, Culture & Society*, 17, pp. 181–200.

Biltereyst, D. (2004), 'Public Service Broadcasting, Popular Entertainment and the construction of Trust', *European Journal of Cultural Studies*, 7: 3, pp. 341–62.

Birt, J. (2002), *The Harder path: The autobiography*, London: Time Warner.

Blanchard, S. and Morley, D. (eds.) (1982), 'What's This Channel Four?', London: Comedia Publishing.

Bonner, F. (2003), *Ordinary television*, London: Sage.

Born, G. (2003), 'Strategy, positioning and projection in digital television: Channel Four and the commercialization of public service broadcasting in the UK', *Media Culture & Society*, 25: 6, pp. 779–82.

Born, G. (2004), *Uncertain vision: Birt, Dyke and the reinvention of the BBC*, London: Secker & Warburg.

Born, G. (2006), 'Digitising Democracy', in J. Lloyd and J. Seaton (eds.), *What Can be Done? Making the Media and Politics Better*, Oxford: Blackwell Publishing, pp. 102–23.

Boycott, R. and Etherington-Smith, M. (2008), *25 x4: Channel 4 at 25*, London: Cultureshock Media.

Boyd-Bell, R. (1985), *New Zealand Television: The First Twenty Five Years*, Auckland: Methuen.

Boyd-Bell, R. (1996), *Lecture at UNITEC Institute of Technology*, 18 August.

Bradshaw, B. (2009), *Address to the Royal Television Society*, Paper presented at the Royal Television Society.

Briggs, A. (1985), *The BBC: The First Fifty Years*, Oxford: Oxford University Press.

British Government (1980), Broadcasting Act 1980, London: Government Printer.

Brown, A. and Picard, R. G. (2005), *Digital Terrestrial Television in Europe*, Lawrence Erlbaum Associates Inc.

Brown, M. (2007), *A Licence to be Different: The Story of Channel 4*, London: BFI.

Brown, S. (2009), 'Strengthening Multiculturalism and Building Social Inclusion', *FECCA Conference*, 29–30 October, Shepparton, Victoria, http://www.sbs.com.au/shows/aboutus/tab-listings/curr-tab/i//tab/Speeches. Accessed 20 February 2010.

Bunz, M. (2009), 'BBC and British Library to take joint approach to building digital archive', http://www.guardian.co.uk/media/2009/dec/11/bbc-british-library-digital-archives. Accessed 21 January 2010.

Burns, M. (2002), 'Nostalgia for the Future: Nation, Memory and technology at ABC Online', *Southern Review*, 35: 1, pp. 63–73.

Burns, M. (2003), *ABC Online: Becoming the ABC*, Brisbane: Griffith University Press.

Butterworth, R. (1989), 'Media', in D. Novitz, B. Wilmot (eds.), *Culture and identity in New Zealand*, Wellington: GP Books.

Campbell, G. (1996), 'Too Tender to Touch', *New Zealand Listener*, 7 September.

Carnegie Commission (1967), *Public Television: A Programme for Action – The Report and Recommendations of the Carnegie Commission on Educational Television*, New York: Harper and Row Publishers.

Carter, S. (2009), *The Digital Britain Report*, London: HMS, http://www.culture.gov.uk/what_we_do/broadcasting/5631.aspx. Accessed 27 December 2009.

Cassidy, D. (2007), 'What Each Party Will Do With SBS: Election 2007', http://saveoursbs.org/archives/127. Accessed 14 April 2009.

Cassidy, D. (2008), 'Minister responds to petition', http://saveoursbs.org/archives/316. Accessed 14 April 2009.

Cassidy, D. (2008a), 'SBS sells itself short', *Online Opinion*, 13 March.

CDD (2006), 'Back to the Future: Public Boradcasting in the Digital Age. Centre for Digital Democracy', http://www.democraticmedia.org/BB/BBfront.php. Accessed 3 February 2008.

Chadwick, P. (2007), *Sources and Conflicts: Review of the adequacy of ABC editorial policies relating to source protection and to the reporting by journalists of events in which they are participants*, Sydney: ABC.

Channel Four (1984), *Annual Report*, London: Channel Four.

Channel Four (2006), 'Arrangements Under Schedule 9 of the Communications Act 2003', http://www.channel4.com/about4/overview.html. Accessed 12 March 2009.

Channel Four (2007), *Channel 4 Response to the Ofcom consultation: A new approach to public service content in the digital media age – the potential role of the Public Service Publisher*. http://www.ofcom.org.uk/consult/condocs/pspnewapproach/summary. Accessed 21 February 2010.

Channel Four (2007b), 'The Great Global Warming Swindle', http://www.channel4.com/science/microsites/G/great_global_warming_swindle. Accessed 2 August 2009.

Channel Four (2008), 'Channel 4 submission to the BBC Trust's review of BBC services for younger audiences', http://www.bbc.co.uk/bbctrust/assets/files. Accessed 24 January 2010.

Channel Four (2009), '2008 Annual Report', http://www.channel4.com/about4/annualreport.html. Accessed 20 February 2010.

Chapman, R., McD. (1986), 'Broadcasting and Related Telecommunications in New Zealand: Report of the Royal Commission of Inquiry', Wellington: New Zealand Government.

Cinque, T. (2007), 'ABC Online: A Vortal for New Opportunities?', *Australian Journal of Communication*, 34: 3.

Coatman, J. (1951), 'The BBC Government and Politics', *Public Opinion Quarterly*, Summer, pp. 287–98.

Cocker, A. (1995), 'Oh What the Hayek! Public Exasperation, Exclusion and Elite Capture; the Formulation of New Zealand's Broadcasting Policy, Unpublished paper delivered to the *New Zealand Political Studies Association Conference*, 30 August-1 September, Victoria University.

Collins, R. (1992), 'Public Service Broadcasting and Freedom', *Media Information Australia*, 66.

Collins, R. (2002), 'The Future of Public Service broadcasting in the United Kingdom', Paper presented at the *The Future of public broadcasting in a changing media society*, IPMZ, University of Zurich.

Collins, R. (2005), 'Taking the high ground: The struggle for ideas in the UK broadcasting policy', http://www.open.ac.uk/socialsciences/staff/rcollins/info.html. Accessed 15 January 2007.

Commonwealth of Australia (1991), 'Special Broadcasting Service Act', Canberra: Government Printer.

Commonwealth of Australia (2008), 'Report of the Australia 2020 Summit', 31 May. http://www.australia2020.gov.au/final_report/index.cfm. Accessed 28 February 2010.

Comrie, M. (1993),. *TVNZ Capturing and Keeping a Deregulated Broadcast Market*, Palmerston North: Massey University.

Comrie, M. and McGregor, J. (1992), *Whose News*, Palmerston North: Dunmore Press.

Comrie, M. and Fountaine, Susan. (2005), 'Retrieving public service broadcasting: treading a fine line at TVNZ', *Media, Culture & Society*, 27: 1, pp. 101–18.

Conroy, S. (2009), *Budget 2009: More Australian stories from ABC and SBS*, Canberra: DBCDE.

Coppens, T. and Says, Frieda (2006), 'Enforcing performance: new approaches to governing public service broadcasting', *Media, Culture & Society*, 28: 2, pp. 261–84.

CPB (2008), *Corporation for Public Broadcasting Annual Report 2007–08*, Washington: CPB.

CPB (2010), 'CPB Responds to Administration's Proposed FY 2011 Budget', *Media Release*, 2 February, http://www.cpb.org/presroom/release.php?prn=802. Accessed 7 February 2010.

Cunningham, S. (2006), 'What Price a Creative Economy?', *New Matilda*, http://www.newmatilda.com//policytoolkit/policydetail.asp?NewsletterID=230&PolicyID=435&email=1. Accessed 30 June 2006.

Cunningham, S. and Turner, G. (1993), *The Media in Australia: Industries, Texts, Audiences,* St Leonards, NSW: Allen & Unwin.

Dalton, K. (2007a), Author's interview by telephone, 5 August, Melbourne.

Dalton, K. (2007b), 'Public Service Media', Paper presented at the *Communications Policy and Research Forum*, http://www.abc.net.au. Accessed 29 September 2007.

Daniell, S. (2008), 'Battle of the Box', *NZ Listener,* 213: 3545, http://www.listener.co.nz/issue/3545/features/10877/printable/battle_of_the_box.html. Accessed 14 February 2010.

Davies, P. (2009), 'Black Saturday', A lecture to Media Studies students at La Trobe University, 20 October .

Davis, G. (1988), *Breaking up the ABC,* Sydney: Allen & Unwin.

Dawson, E. (2006), 'A dramatic decline', *New Matilda,* 2006, pp. 1–3, http://www.newnatilda.com/home/articledetail.asp?NewsletterID=177&ArticleID=1283&email=1. Accessed 18 January 2006.

Dawson, E. (2008), 'Not So Special Anymore: The Demise of SBS Television', Paper presented at the *Democratic Audit of Australia.*

Dawson, E. (2008 pending), *Public Broadcasting and Multiculturalism: the Special Broadcasting Service (SBS) 1978–2008,* Monash, Melbourne.

Day, M. (2006), 'Field day for the Flat-Earthers: Under the ABC's Bias Police', *The Australian,* http://www.theaustralian.news.com.au/story/0,20867,20605106-12280,00.html.

DBCDE (2008), *ABC and SBS: Towards a digital future,* http://www.dbcde.gov.au/media_broadcasting/consultation_and_submissions/abc_sbs_review. Accessed 21 February 2009.

DCITA (2006), *Ready, get set, go digital: A digital action plan for Australia,* http://www.ag.gov.au/cca. Accessed 10 March 2007.

DCMS (2003), 'Review of the BBC's Royal Charter', http://www.bbccharterreview.org.uk/publications/pub_home.html. Accessed 22 September 2009.

Debrett, M. (2004), 'Branding Documentary: New Zealand's Minimalist Solution to Cultural Subsidy', *Media Culture & Society,* 26: 1, pp. 5–23.

Debrett, M. (2005), 'Extreme Makeover: The recurring motif of New Zealand broadcasting policy', *Media International Australia incorporating culture and policy,* 117, pp. 76–85.

Debrett, M. (2006), 'Documentary Subsidy in Australia and New Zealand: The future of the social project', Unpublished Ph.D. Thesis, Melbourne: La Trobe University.

DeGeorge, K. (2005), 'What Next? Public Broadcasting at a Crossroads', *City Newspaper,* http://www.rochester.gyrosite.com. Accessed 12 January 2007.

D'Haenens, L., Sousa, H., Meier, W. A. and Trappel, J. (2008), 'Editorial', in *Convergence: the International Journal of Research into New Media Technologies,* 14: 3, pp. 243–7.

Deloitte, U. (2008), 'Loves me, loves me not…perspectives on the UK television sector', *Research Report,* London: Media Guardian, Edinburgh International Television Festival and Deloitte & Touche.

Dempsey, D. (1995), 'SBS puts Creative Nation funding to work', *The Age,* 12 October, p. 6.

Dempster, Q. (2000), *Death Struggle: How Boardrom Power Play is Killing the ABC,* Crows Nest, NSW: Allen & Unwin.

Dempster, Q. (2005), 'The Slow Destruction of the ABC', in R. Manne (ed.), *Do Not Disturb: Is the Media Failing Australia?,* Melbourne: Black Inc, pp. 101–20.

Dempster, Q. (2006), 'Technological Betrayal', *New Matilda,* 23 June.

Dempster, Q. (2006), 'Public broadcasting: Lights out at the ABC', *New Matilda,* http://www.newmatilda.com. Accessed 12 April 2006.

Dempster, Q. (2007), 'Come Clean on Commercialisation', *News and Views: Newsletter of Friends of the ABC,* Spring 2007, p. 8.

Dempster, Q. (2008), 'Say no to ads on any ABC content', *The Australian*, 12 September, http://www.theaustralian.news.com.au/story/0,25197,24335110-13243,00.html.

Dempster, Q. (2008a), 'The price of creative independence at the ABC', *New Matilda,* 10 November.

Docherty, D., Morrison, D. and Tracey, M. (1988), *Keeping Faith: Channel Four and Its Audience*, London: John Libbey.

Dhondy, F. (2002), 'The death of multiculturalism?', *The Guardian*, 8 November, http://www.guardian.co.iuk/nov/08/broadcasting.channel4. Accessed 29 January 2010.

Dovey, J. (2000), *Freakshow: first person media and factual television*, London: Pluto Press.

Drinnan, J. (1996), 'Horizon Losses Arisin', *Onfilm,* June 1996.

Duncan, A. (2007), *Next on 4*, http://www.channel4.com/about4/next_on4.html. Accessed 2 August 2009.

Eccleshall, R. (1984), *Political Ideologies*, London: Routledge.

Edgerton, G. (1996), 'Quelling the "Oxygen of Publicity": British Broadcasting and "The Troubles" During the Thatcher Years', *Journal of Popular Culture*, 30: 1, pp. 115–32.

Edwards, B. (1992), 'The Cootchie Coo News', in M. Comrie and J. McGregor (eds.), *Whose News*, Palmerston North: Dumore Press.

Edwards, B. (1998), 'The dumbing of TV', *Sunday Star-Times,* 5 April.

Ellis, John. (2008), 'What did Channel 4 do for us? Reassessing the early years', *Screen*, 49: 3, pp. 331–42.

ETRP (1980), *Programming for the Multicultural/Multilingual Television Service – Objectives and Policies,* Canberra: Commonwealth of Australia.

Ewins, T. (2006), 'Public Private Partnerships no "magic pudding"', *New Matilda,* 1 December.

FABC (2008), 'Where's the $48.1 million?', http://www.fabc.org.au/vic/index.html. Accessed 20 March 2009.

FABC (2009), 'More funds for the ABC', *News and Views: , Newsletter of Friends of the ABC*, 30: 2.

FAIR (2010), 'Goodbye Moyers, Hello Bush Institute?', http://fair.org/index.php?page=3993&printer_friendly. Accessed 4 February 2010.

Farnsworth, J. (1992), 'Mainstream or Minority: Ambiguities in State or market arrangements for New Zealand Television', in J. Deeks and N. Perry (eds.), *Controlling Interests*, Auckland: Auckland University Press.

FCC (1995), 'Decision regarding WTTW Home Shopping Channel complaint from the Coalition for Democracy in Public Television', 94070142 C.F.R. Federal Communications Commission.

FCC (2010), 'Digital Television Statistics', http://www.dtv.gov/dtv-stats.htm#sources_of_information. Accessed 6 February 2010.

FECCA (2008), 'FECCA's SBS Policy: For consideration with the SBS Triennial Funding Submission 2009–2012', Federation of Ethnic Communities Councils of Australia.

FECCA (2008), 'FECCA's Submission to the ABC and SBS Towards a Digital Future', Discussion Paper 2344, Melbourne: Federation of Ethnic Communities Councils of Australia.

Finlayson, T. (1996), 'The Documentary in NZ Television', Paper presented at the *Public Lecture*, 21 August, Auckland University.

Flew, T. (2006), 'The Social Contract and Beyond in Broadcast Media Policy', *Television and New Media,* 7: 3, pp. 282–305.

Foster, N. (c 1995), 'Film on Four: British Film Series', *The Museum of Broadcast Communication*, http://www.museum.tv/archives/etv/F/htmlF/filmonfour. Accessed 29 July 2009.

Frank, R. E. and Greenberg, M. (1982), *Audiences for Public Television*, Beverly Hills, CA: Sage.

Franklin, B. (2001), *British Television policy: a reader*, London: Routledge.

Friedland, L. (1995), 'Public Television as Public Sphere: The case of the Wisconsin collaborative project', *Journal of Broadcasting and Electronic Media,* 39, pp. 147–76.

Fürisch, E. (2003), 'Between credibility and commodification: Nonfiction entertainment as a global media', *International Journal of Cultural Studies,* 6: 4, pp. 131–53.

Gabert, S. (1996), 'Get a Load of the Competition', *The Independent,* August / September 1996.

Gerhardt, P. (2008), 'Welcome News for the BBC', *Archives for Creativity,* http://www.archivesforcreativity.com/blog.aspx#4011. Accessed 10 February 2010.

Georgiou, P. (2008), 'The Limits of Tolerance – Diversity, Identity and Cohesion', Paper presented at *The Marion Adams Memorial Lecture,* http://www.australiansall.com.au/the-limits-of-tolerance-%E2%80%93-diversity-identity-and-cohesion/#bio. Accessed 14 March 2009.

Gibson, O. (2007), 'BBC pays £50,000 in First Ever Fine After Blue Peter Competition Deceived Viewers', *Media Guardian Online,* http://www.media.guardian.co.uk/0,,2122574,00.html. Accessed 3 February 2008.

Gibson, O. (2008), 'No relaunch for £150m BBC Jam', *The Guardian,* 28 February, http://www.guardian.co.uk/media/2008/feb/28/bbc.digitalmedia. Accessed 6 June 2009.

Giddens, A. (1990), *The consequences of modernity,* Cambridge: Polity Press.

Giddens, A. (1994), 'Risk, Trust, Reflexivity', in Ulrich Beck, Anthony Giddens and Scott Lash (eds.), *Reflexive Modernization: Politics, Tradition and Aesthetics in the Modern Social Order,* Cambridge: Polity Press, pp. 184–97.

Giddens, A. (1999), *The Third Way: The Renewal of Social Democracy,* Cambridge: Polity Press.

Given, J. (2002), 'A Digital Agenda', *Southern Review,* 35: 1, pp. 21–41.

Given, J. (2003), *Turning Off the Television,* Sydney: UNSW Press.

Given, J and Norris, P. (2010), 'Would the Real Freeview Please Stand Up?', *International Journal of Digital Television,* 1: 1, pp. 51–68.

Gordon-Smith, M. (2002), 'Governing Public Service Broadcasters', *Southern Review,* 35: 1, pp. 87–106.

Gore, A. (2007), *The assault on reason,* New York: Penguin Press.

Goulden, H., Hartley, John and Wright, Trevor (1982), 'Consciousness Razing', in S. Blanchard and D. Morley (eds.), *What's this Channel Four?,* London: Comedia.

Graf, P. (2004), 'Independent Review of BBC Online', http://www.culture.gov.uk/global/publications/archive_2004/BBC_Online_Review.htm. Accessed 20 August 2009.

Greenslade, R. (2008), 'Future of Journalism Conference', *ABC News,* Australia: ABC.

Gregory, R. J. (1985), *Politics and Broadcasting; Before and Beyond the NZBC,* Palmerston North: Dunmore Press.

Grenard, P. (1982), 'Ethnic Television', *The Bulletin,* 3 August, p. 52.

Guardian (2007), 'Black Viewers Desert Channel 4', *Guardian.co.uk, TV&Radio Blogs,* http://www.guardian.co.uk/culture/tvandradioblog/2007/oct/11. Accessed 24 January 2010.

Haley, W. (1949), 'Parliamentary institutions and broadcasting', *Parliamentary Affairs,* 11: 2, pp. 108–17.

Hall, S. (1981), *Turning On Turning Off,* North Ryde, Sydney: Cassell.

Hansard. (1985), *"20: 20 Vision",* http://hansard.millbanksystems.com/commons/1985/feb/21/2020-vision-programme. Accessed 28 August 2009.

Harrison, D. (2009), 'New faces coming soon for the boards of the ABC and SBS', *The Age,* 24 February.

Harrison, J. (2000), *Terrestrial TV news in Britain: The culture of production,* Manchester: Manchester University Press.

Harrison, J. and Wessells, B. (2005), 'A New Public Service Communication Environment? Public Service Values in the Reconfiguring Media', *New Media & Society*, 7: 6, pp. 834–53.

Hart, J. A. (2010), 'The transition to digital television in the United States: The endgame', *International Journal of Digital Television*, 1: I, pp. 7–29.

Harvey, S. (1989), 'Deregulation, Innovation and Channel Four', *Screen*, 30: 1 & 2.

Harvey, S. (1994), 'Channel 4 Television: From Annan to Grade', in S. Hood (ed.), *Behind the screens: The Structure of British Broadcasting in the 1990s*, London: Lawrence & Wishart, pp. 102–32.

Harvey, S. (2006), 'Ofcom's first year and neo-liberalism's blind spot: attacking the culture of production', *Screen*, 47: 1, pp. 91–105.

Hawke, J. (1995), 'Privatising the Public Interest: The Public and the Broadcasting Services Act', in Jennifer Craik, Julie James Bailey and Albert Moran (eds.), *Public Voices: Private Interest – Australia's Media Policy*, St Leonards, NSW: Allen & Unwin, pp. 44–6.

Hayek, F. (1960), *The Constitution of Liberty*, London: Routledge & Kegan Paul.

Helm, D., Green, Damian, Oliver, Mark, Terrington, Simona, Graham, Andrew, Robinson, Bill, Davies, Gavyn, Mayhew, Jeremy and Bradley-Jones, Luke (2005), *Can the Market Deliver? Funding Public Service Television in the Digital Age*, Eastleigh, UK: John Libbey.

Herrick, L. (1996), 'Some Great News on the Horizon', *Sunday Star*, 4 April.

Hess, John and Zimmerman, Patricia (1999), 'Transnational/National Digital Imaginaries', *Mesh*, 13: 33.

Hirst, M. and Harrison, J. (2007), *Communication and new media: from broadcast to narrowcast*, (First ed.), Melbourne: Oxford University Press.

HMSO (1988), *Broadcasting in the Nineties: Competition, Choice and Quality. The Government's Plans for Broadcasting Legislation. (White Paper)*.

Holmwood, L. (2007), 'BBC Halts Phone-in Contests', *Media Guardian Online*, 18 July, http://www.media.guardian.co.uk/bbc/story/0,,2129300,00.html. Accessed 30 March 2008.

Howe, D. (2009), 'Does Aunty Really Deserve More Money?', *New Matilda*, 23 January.

Hoynes, W. (1995), *Public Television for Sale*, Colorado: Westview Press.

Hoynes, W. (2002), 'Why Media Mergers Matter', *Open Democracy Website*. Accessed 29 May 2006.

Hoynes, W. (2003), 'Branding Public Service: The "New PBS" and the Privatization of Public Television', *Television & New Media*, 4: 2, pp. 117–30.

Hoynes, W. (2005), 'The Real Challenge for Public Television', *Common Dreams News Center*, Accessed 29 May 2006.

Hoynes, W. (2002), 'Political Discourse and the "new PBS"', *Harvard International Journal of Press/Politics*, 7: 4, pp. 34–56.

Hundal, S. (2009), 'Differences over Diversity', *The Guardian*, 12 January, http://www.guardian.co.uk/media/2009/jan/12/bbc-asian-programmes-unit. Accessed 30 March 2009.

Hutchison (2006), *Submission to the Department of Communications, Information Technology and the Arts in response to the Issues Paper "Meeting the Digital Challenge – Reforming Australia's media in the Digital Age", issued March 2006*, Hutchison Telecommunications (Australia) Limited and Hutchison 3G Australia Pty Limited.

Hutton, J. B. (2004), *Investigation into the circumstances surrounding the death of Dr David Kelly*, London: Ministry of Justice.

Ickes, L. R. (2006), *Public Broadcasting in America*, New York: Novinka Books.

Ickes, L. R. (2006), *Public Broadcasting in America*, New York: Nova Science.

Inglis, K. S. (2002), 'Changing Notions of Public Service Broadcasting', *Southern Review*, 35: 1, pp. 9–20.

Inglis, K. S. (2006a), *This is the ABC: The Australian Broadcasting Commission 1932–1983*, Vol. 1, Melbourne: Black Inc.

Inglis, K. S. (2006b), *Whose ABC? The Australian Broadcasting Corporation 1983–2006*, (First ed.), Vol. 2, Melbourne: Black Inc.

Ingram, D. (2009), 'The Zampatti Makeover', *New Matilda*, 9 December, http://newmatilda.com/print/7351. Accessed 22 February 2010.

Ingram, D. (2009b), 'Can the Ethnic Lobby Save SBS?', *New Matilda*, 2 June, http:newmatilda.com/print/6091. Accessed 2 June 2009.

Iosifidis, P. (2007), *Public Television in the Digital Era*, Houndsmills, Basingstoke: Palgrave.

Iosifidis, P. (2010), *Reinventing Public Service Communication: European Broadcasters and Beyond*, London: Palgrave MacMillan.

Isaacs, J. (1989), *Storm Over Four: A Personal Account*, London: Weidenfield and Nicholson.

Jacka, E. (2006), 'The ABC and the 2006 Federal media reforms', *Media International Australia incorporating culture and policy*, 120, pp. 5–9.

Jacka, L. (2002), 'Digital Spaces, Public Places', *Southern Review*, 35: 1, pp. 1–8.

Jacka, L. (2004), *Arts by Stealth? ABC and the Arts*, Redfern, NSW: Community and Public Service Union on behalf of members in ABC Radio.

Jacka, L. (2006), 'The ABC and Public Value – Public Service Broadcaster in the Age of Competition', in Indrajit Banerjee and Kalinga Seneviratne (eds.), *Public Service Broadcasting in the Age of Globalisation*, Singapore: Asian Media, Informational and Communication Centre (AMIC) and The School of Communication and Information (SCI) Nanyang Technological University, Singapore, pp. 165–86.

Jacka, L. (2006a), 'The future of public broadcasting', in S. Cunningham and G. Turner (eds.), *The Media and Communications in Australia*, (Second Ed.), Crows Nest, NSW: Allen & Unwin, pp. 344–56.

Jacka, L. (2006b), 'The ABC and the 2006 Federal Media Reforms', *Media International Australia incorporating Culture and Policy*, 120, pp. 5–9.

Jakubowicz, A. (1989), 'Speaking in Tongues: Multicultural Media and the Constitution of the Socially Homogeneous Australian', in H. Wilson (ed.), *Australian Communications and the Public Sphere*, Melbourne: MacMillan, pp. 105–27.

Jakubowicz, A. and Newell, K. (1995), 'Which World? Whose/Who's Home?', in Julie James Bailey, Jennifer Craik and Albert Moran (ed.), *Public Voices: Private Interests – Australia's Media Policy*, St Leonards, NSW: Allen & Unwin.

Jakubowicz, K. (2007), 'Public Service Broadcasting in the 21st Century. What Chance for a New Beginning?', in G. F. Lowe and J. Bardoel (eds.), *From Public Service Broadcasting to Public Service Media*, Goteborg, Sweden: Nordicom, pp. 29–50.

Jameson, J., Papadimitriou, M., Bradley-Jones, L., and Aslam. S. (2006), 'Cost benefit analysis of the launch of digital free to air television in New Zealand', New Zealand Ministry for Culture and Heritage, 15th June, http://www.mch.govt.nz/publications/digital-tv. Accessed 4 November 2007.

Jivani, A. (1990), 'Making a Difference: The Impact of Channel Four', in Janet Willis and Tana Wollen (eds.), *The Neglected Audience*, London: BFI.

Johns, B. (1991), 'SBS: Coping with the Strange Idea', in D. Goodman, D. O'Hearn, C. Wallace-Crabbe (eds.), *Multicultural Australia: The challenges of change*, Newham, Victoria: Scribe.

Johnson, K. (2008), 'BBC Jam and licence fee payers', http://johnsonk.wordpress.com/2008/0605/bbc-jam-and-the-rights-of-the-licence-fee-payers. Accessed 20 October 2008.

Jolly, R. (2007), 'Special Broadcasting Service (SBS): Operations and Funding', http://www.apo.org.au/node/16176. Accessed 15 March 2009.

Khan, U. (2009), 'Popularity of BBC iPlayer', http://www.telegraph.co.uk/technology/news/4143794/Popularity-of-BBC-iPlayer-leads-to-renewed-concerns-internet-could-grind-to-a-halt.html. Accessed 22 December 2009.

Kalantzis, M. (2003), 'Immigration, multiculturalism and racism', in Susan Ryan and Troy Bramston (eds.), *The Hawke Government: A critical retrospective*, Annandale, NSW: Pluto Press Australia.

Katz, H. (1989), 'The Future of Public Broadcasting in the US', *Media, Culture & Society*, 11: 2, pp. 195–205.

Keane, J. (1991), *The Media and Democracy*, Cambridge: Polity Press.

Kedgley, S. (2009), 'Government Plans to Sink TVNZ in unchartered waters', *Media Release*, http://www.greens.org.nz/press-releases/govt-plans-sink-tvnz-unchartered-waters. Accessed 10 September 2009.

Keen, A. (2007) *The Cult of the Amateur*, London; Boston: Nicholas Brealey.

Kellner, D. (1990), *Television and the Crisis of Democracy*, Boulder, Colarado: Westview Press.

Kiss, J. (2007), 'BBC Jam closure angers new media producers', *Guardian Unlimited Online*, 15 March, http://www.guardian.co.uk/print0,,329746476-103690,00.html. Accessed 12 November 2007.

Kolar-Panov, D. and O'Regan, T. (1994), 'SBS-TV: Symbolic Politics and Multicultural Policy in Television Provision', in T. O'Regan (ed.), *Australian Television Culture*, St Leonards, NSW: Allen & Unwin, pp. 121–42.

Kolar-Panov, and O'Regan, T. (1994a), 'SBS-TV: A Television Service', in T. O'Regan (ed.), *Australian Television Culture*, St Leonards, NSW: Allen & Unwin, pp. 143–68.

Kumar, K. (1982), 'Holding the Middle Ground', in J. Curran, Michael Gurevitch and Janet Woolacott (ed.), *In Mass Communication and Society*, London: Edward Arnold.

Küng-Shankleman, L. (2000), *Inside the BBC and CNN: Managing Media Organisations*, London ; New York: Routledge.

Lambert, S. (1982), *Television with a Difference*, London: BFI.

Lash, S. (1994), 'Expert Systems or Situated Interpretation? Culture and Institutions in Disorganised Capitalism', in U. Beck, A. Giddens and S. Lash (eds.), *Reflexive Modernization: Politics, Tradition and Aesthetics in the Modern Social Order*. Cambridge: Polity Press, pp. 198–215.

Lashley, M. (1992), *Public Television: Panacea, Pork Barrel or Public Trust?*, Westport: Greenwood Publishing.

Lawrence, C. (2007), 'Bullying the ABC', *New and Views: Newsletter of Friends of the ABC*, Spring 2007, p. 8.

Ledbetter, J. (1997), *Death of Public Broadcasting*, Verso.

Leong, K. (1983), 'The Emergence of Multicultural T.V. in Australia', *Australian Journal of Communication*, 4.

Lewis, A. F. (1995), 'Public Television as Public Sphere: The Case of the Wisconsin Collaborative Project', *Journal of Broadcasting & Electronic Media*, 39: 39, pp. 147–76.

Lewis, S. (2006), 'Keating, Neville and Joyce: Demand to Protect Diversity of Media', *The Australian*, 24 July, http://www.fabc.org.au/vic/index.html. Accessed 7 August 2006.

Long, M. (1995), 'Representing SBS and Australia to the World', *Media Information Australia*, 76.

Looms, P. (2007), 'Public Service Media: All Things to All People – On All Platforms Anytime?', in C. S. Nissen (ed.), *Making a Difference: Public Service broadcasting in the European Landscape*, Eastleigh, UK: John Libbey.

Louw, E. (2005), *The media and political process*, London: Sage.

Lowe, G. F. and Bardoel, J. (2007), *From Public Service Broadcasting to Public Service Media*, Goteborg, Sweden: Nordicom.

MacDonald, B. (1993), *Broadcasting in the United Kingdom*, London: Mansell.

McDonald, D. (2006), 'The Renewal of a Tradition: International Broadcasting and the ABC', Paper presented to the *Asia Society*, AustralAsia Centre: CEO update luncheon.

McDonnell, J. (1991), *Public Service Broadcasting: A Reader*, London: Routledge.

McGregor, J. (1996), *Dangerous Democracy*, Palmerston North: Dunmore Press.

Madge, T. (1989), *Beyond the BBC*, London: Macmillan Press.

Malik, S. (2008), '"Keeping it real": the politics of Channel 4's multiculturalism, mainstreaming and mandates', *Screen*, 49: 3, pp. 343–53.

Manne, R. (ed.) (2005), *Do Not Disturb: Is the Media Failing Australia?*, Melbourne: Black Inc.

Manne, R. (2007), 'New Teeth for Aunty: Reinvigorating the National Broadcaster', *The Monthly*, December.

Marriner, C. and Needham, K. (2003), 'ABC takes the buzz out of digital', *The Sydney Morning Herald*, 26 May, http://www.smh.com.au/articles/2003/05/26/1053801337923.html. Accessed 27 February 2010.

Martin, F. (2002), 'Beyond Public Service Broadcasting? ABC and the User-Citizen', *Southern Review*, 35: 1, pp. 42–62.

Meade, A. (2009), 'Funding plea issued for the ABC and SBS', *The Australian*, 11 May, http://www.theaustralian.com.au/business/media/funding-plea-issued-for-abc-and-sbs/story-e6frg996-1225710735874. Accessed 27 February 2010.

Meech, P. (1990), 'The British Media in Transition', *Innovation*, 3: 2.

Meehan, E. R. (2005), *Why TV Is Not Our Fault: Television Programming, Viewers, and Who's Really in Control Series: Critical Media Studies: Institutions, Politics, and Culture*, Rowman & Littlefield Publishers, Inc.

Meijer, I. C. (2005), 'Impact or Content? Ratings v Quality in Public Broadcasting', *European Journal of Communication*, 20: 1, pp. 27–53.

Miller, T. (2008), 'The New World Makeover', *Continuum: Journal of Media and Cultural Studies*, 25: 4, pp. 585–90.

Moe, H. (2008), 'Public Service Online? Regulating Public Broadcasters' Internet Services – A comparative Analysis', *Television and New Media*, 9: 3, pp. 220–38.

Monbiot, G. (2007), 'Don't let truth stand in the way of a red-hot debunking of climate change: The science might be bunkum, the research discredited. But all that counts for Channel 4 is generating', *The Guardian*, 13 March, http://www.guardian.co.uk/commentisfree/2007/mar/13/science.media. Accessed 2 August 2009.

Moore, T. (2008), 'Opening up the ABC', Electronic Version, *New Matilda*, http://www.newmatilda.com. Accessed 21 April 2008.

Moran, A. (ed.) (1992), *Stay Tuned: an Australian Broadcasting Reader*, Sydney: Allen & Unwin.

Moran, A. (1992), 'Changing ABC television Programming', in A. Moran (ed.), *Stay tuned: an Australian television reader*, Sydney: Allen & Unwin, pp. 120–3.

Morgan, G. (2005), 'Morgan Poll: Australians Sceptical of the Media', *Morgan Poll*, http://www.roymorgan.com/news/polls/2005/3952/. Accessed 19 February 2008.

MORI (2005), 'Trust in Online Resources Poll', 10 February 2005, http://www.ipsos-mori.com/polls/2004/cie.shtml. Accessed 19 February 2008.

Moses, A. (2008), 'ABC Jumps in Digital Hyper Drive', *The Age*, 12 March.

MTS (2009), 'Maori Television 2009 Annual Report', http://corporate.maoritelevision.com/Default.aspx?tabid=170. Accessed 20 January 2010.

Mulgan, G. (1990), *The Question of Quality*, London: BFI.

Murdoch, J. (2009), 'The Absence of Trust', Paper presented at the *MacTaggart Lecture*.

Murdock, G. (1990), 'Television and Citizenship: In Defence of Public Broadcasting', in A. Tomlinson (ed.), *Consumption, Identity and Style: Marketing, Meanings and the Packaging of Pleasure*, London: Routledge, pp. 77–101.

Murdock, G. (1992), 'Citizens, Consumers and Public Culture', in Michael Skovmand and Kim Chistian Schroeder (eds.), *Media Cultures: Reappraising, Transnational Media*, London: Routledge.

Murdock, G. (1994), 'Corporate Dynamics and Broadcasting Futures', in Meryl Aldrich and Nicholas Hewitt (eds.), *Controlling Broadcasting: Access Policy in North America and Europe*, London: Manchester University Press.

Murdock, G. (1999), 'Rights and Representations: Public Discourse and Cultural Citizenship', in J. Gipstrud (ed.), *In Television and Common Knowledge*, London; New York: Routledge, pp. 7–17.

Murdock, G. (1999), 'Rights and Representations: Public Discourse and Cultural Citizenship', in J. Gipstrud (ed.), *Television and Common Knowledge*, London: Routledge, pp. 7–17.

Murdock, G. (2004), 'Building the Digital Commons: Public Broadcasting in the Age of the Internet', Paper presented at *The 2004 Spry Memorial Lecture*, 22 November, University of Montreal: Montreal.

Murdock, G. (2005), 'Public broadcasting and democratic culture', in J. Wasko (ed.), *A companion to television*, Malden, MA: Blackwell, pp. 174–98.

Murdock, G. (2005), 'Public Broadcasting and Democratic Culture: Consumers, Citizens and Communards', in J. Wasco (ed.), *The Companion to Television*, New York: Blackwell.

Murdock, G. (2007), 'Digital Technologies and Moral Economies', in Virginia Nightingale and Tim Dwyer (eds.), *New Media Worlds: Challenges for Convergence*, South Melbourne, Victoria: Oxford University Press, pp. 325–43.

Naughton, P. (2005), 'Shaken by the Hutton Enquiry', *The Times*, 2 March, http://business.timesonline.co.uk/tol/business/industry_sectors/media/article417291.ece. Accessed 26 September 2009.

Neill, R. (2008), 'Identity Crisis: Has SBS Lost its Way?', *The Australian*, 5 July, http;//www.theaustralian.news.com.au/story/0,25197,23952152-5.

Newspoll. (2007), *ABC Appreciation Survey: Summary Report*, Sydney: ABC.

Nissen, C. S. (2006), 'No Public Service without Public and Servie – Content provisions between the Scylla of populism and the Chrybdis of elitism', in Christian S. Nissen (ed.), *Making a Difference: Public Service Broadcasting in the European Media Landscape*, Eastleigh, UK: John Libbey Publishing, pp. 65–82.

NLA (c1994), 'Film, Television and Radio', *National Library of Australia*, http://www.nla.gov.au/creative.nation/filmtv.html. Accessed 27 February 2010.

Noam, E. M., Groebel, J and Gerbarg, D. (eds.) (2004), *Internet Television*, Mahwah, N.J.: Lawrence Erlbaum Associates Inc.

Nolan, D. (2005), 'Ask not who runs Aunty, but how Aunty is run', *The Age*, 8 March, http://www.culture-communication.unimelb.edu.au/publications/abc-nolan.html. Accessed 12 May 2009.

NZ Government (2006), 'Digital Television Strategy', http://www.mch.govt.nz/publications/digital-tv/index.htm#strategy. Accessed 20 November 2007.

NZ Government (1976), *Broadcasting Act*, Wellington: Government Printer.

NZ Government (1986), *State Enterprises Act 4(1)*, Wellington: Government Printer.

NZ Government (2009), '2008/09 Financial Review of Television New Zealand Limited: Report of the Finance and Expenditure Committee, House of Representatives', http://www.parliament.nz/en-NZ/PB/SC/BusSum/0/2/f/00DBSCH_FIN_9378_1-2008-09-financial-review-of-Television-New-Zealand.htm. Accessed 14 February 2010.

NZoA (1995), *Annual Report 1995*, Wellington: New Zealand on Air.

NZPA (2009), 'TVNZ Charter to Go Because it Doesn't Work – Key', *NZ Herald,* 23 March, http://www.nzherald.co.nz/television/news/print.cfm?c_id=33. Accessed 31 August 2009.

O'Malley, T. (1994), *Closedown? The BBC and Government Broadcasting Policy, 1979–92,* London: Pluto.

O'Neill, O. (2002), 'The Philosophy of Trust – Introduction', *Reith Lectures,* London: BBC.

O'Neill, O. (2002a), 'Spreading Suspicion – Lecture 1', *Reith Lectures,* London: BBC.

O'Neill, O. (2002b), 'Trust and Terror – Lecture Two', *Reith Lectures,* London: BBC.

O'Neill, O. (2002c), 'Called to Account – Lecture 3', *Reith Lectures,* London: BBC.

O'Neill, O. (2002d), 'Trust and Transparency – Lecture 4', *Reith Lectures,* London: BBC.

O'Neill, O. (2002e), 'License to Deceive – Lecture 5', *Reith Lectures,* London: BBC.

O'Regan, T. (1994), *Australian Television Culture,* St Leonards, NSW: Allen & Unwin.

Ofcom (2006), *Digital PSB: Public Service Broadcasting Post Digital Switchover,* http://www.ofcom.org.uk. Accessed 4 August 2007.

Ofcom (2007), *Channel 4 Group Financial Review – Terms of Reference,* http://www.ofcom.org.uk. Accessed 4 August 2007.

Ofcom (2007), *Adjudication of Ofcom Content Sanctions Committee – Channel Four,* London: Ofcom.

Ofcom (2008), *Digital Television Update,* London: Ofcom.

Onfilm. (1996), 'Film & TV Politics', *Onfilm,* September.

Otago Daily Times (2009), 'TVNZ charter doesn't work – Key', *Otago Daily Times,* 23 March, http://www.odt.co.nz/48597/tvnz-charter-to-go-because-it-does-not-work-key. Accessed 6 June 2009.

Otago Daily Times (2009), 'The Charter Doesn't Worked – Key', http://www.odt.co.nz/48597/tvnz-charter-to-go-because-it-does-not-work-key. Accessed 24 September 2009.

Ouellette, L. (2009), 'Reinventing PBS: Public Television in the Post-Network, Post-Welfare Era', in A. D. Lotz (ed.), *"Beyond Prime Time": Television Programming in the Post-Network Era,* New York: Routledge, pp. 180–200.

PACT (2009), 'Pact welcomes decision to include older children's content in Channel 4's remit', *Media Release,* 20 November, https: //www.pact.co.uk/homepage/press_releases. Accessed 22 January 2010.

Padovani, C. and Tracey, M. (2003), 'Report on the Conditions of Public Service Broadcasting', *Television and New media,* 4: 2, pp. 131–53.

Patterson, R. (1992), 'SBS-TV: Forerunner of the Future', *Media Information Australia,* 66.

Paxman, J. (2007), 'McTaggart Lecture – Never mind the scandals: what's it all for?', *Media Guardian Edinburgh Television Festival,* Edinburgh.

PBS (2009a), 'PBS Corporate Facts', http://www.pbs.org/aboutpbs/aboutpbs_corp. html. Accessed 5 June 2009.

PBS (2009b), 'About PBS Programming', http://www.pbs.org/aboutpbs/aboutpbs_prog.html. Accessed 5 June 2009.

PBS (2010a), 'Series Overview', http://www.pbs.org/wnet/expose/about.html. Accessed 8 February 2010.

PBS (2010b), 'We Shall Remain', http://www.pbs.org/wgbh/amex/weshallremain/in_thefilms/about. Accessed 4 February 2010.

Peacock, A. (2004), *Public Service Broadcasting Without the BBC?,* London: The Institute of Economic Affairs.

Peacock, A. (ed.) (1986), *Report of the Committee on Financing the BBC,* London: HMSO.

Pearce, M. (2000), 'Perspectives on Australian Broadcasting Policy', *Continuum: Journal of Media and Cultural Studies,* 14: 3, pp. 367–82.

Potter, T., Clifton, Jane and Rooney, Edward (1996), 'PM Lashes Holmes over Worm', *Sunday Star Times,* 29 September.

Powell, M., Spicer, Barry and Emanuel, David. (1996), *The Remaking of Television New Zealand 1984–1992,* Auckland University Press.

Putnam, R. (2000). *Bowling alone: the collapse and revival of American community,* New York: Simon & Schuster.

Quinn, K. (2009), 'Sunday Arts Cut Short as ABC Shunts Culture Online'. *The Age,* 2 October, http://www.theage.com.au/news/entertainment/tv--radio/sunday-arts-cut-short-as-abc-shunts-culture-online/2009/10/01/1253989995518.html.

Rankin, K. (2000), 'John Hawkesby: World Famous in New Zealand', *Scoop. co.nz,* 3 February, http://www.scoop. co.nz/stories/HL0002/S00015.htm. Accessed 11 September 2009.

Rennie, H. (1988), 'Report of the Steering Committee on the restructuring of the Broadcasting Corporation of New Zealand on State Owned Enterprise Principles', Wellington: New Zealand Government Printer.

Robinson, J. and Brown, M. (2009), 'A Chill Wind', *The Guardian,* 31 August, http://www.guardian.co.uk/media/2009/aug/31/james-murdoch-attacking-bbc-ofcom.

Robinson, J. and Brown, M. (2009b), 'RTS Cambridge Convention: Trouble at the top', *The Guardian,* 21 September, http://www.guardian.co.uk/media/2009/sep/21/rts-cambridge-bbc-itv. Accessed 1 February 2010.

Rothschilds, H. (2008), 'Labour of Love', in Rosie Boycott and Meredith Etherington-Smith (eds.), *25 x 4: Channel Four at Twenty Five,* London: Channel Four, pp. 394–8.

Rowland, W. (1993), 'Public Service Broadcasting in the United States: Its mandate, Institutions and Conflicts', in R. K. Avery (ed.), *Public Service Broadcasting in a Multichannel Environment,* White Plains, N.Y.: Longman.

Rowland, W. D. J. (2002), 'Public Broadcasting in the United States', in *Encyclopedia of Communication and Information,* New York: Macmillan Library Reference USA.

Rubin, N. (2009), 'Preserving Digital Public Television: Not Just an Archive, but a New Attitude to Preserve Public Broadcasting', *Library Trends,* 57: 3, pp. 393–412.

Rudd, K. (2007), 'Letter to FABC', http://www.fabc.org.au/vic/index.html. Accessed 30 May 2009.

Salter, D. (2006), 'Disconnect in the Fourth Estate', *The Monthly,* 7 December.

SBS (1990), *Corporate Plan 1990–93,* Sydney: SBS.

SBS (1994), *Annual Report 1993–94,* Sydney: SBS.

SBS (1994a), *Codes of Practice,* Sydney: SBS.

SBS (1995), 'SBS Online', http://www.sbs.com.au. Accessed 30th July 1995.

SBS (2006), *Annual Report 2005–2006: Television and Online Content,* Sydney: SBS.

SBS (2007), *SBS scores best ever ratings in 2007,* Sydney: SBS.

SBS (2008), *Annual Report 2007–08,* Sydney: SBS.

SBS (2008b), *SBS's plans for the future,* Sydney: SBS.

SBS (2008c), 'Main Submission to the ABC SBS Review', http://www.dbcde.gov.au/consultation_and_submissions/abc_sbs_review/_submissions/s/2993. Accessed 12 February 2009.

SBS (2009), 'About Us', http://www20.sbs.com.au/sbscorporate/index.php?id=1178. Accessed 29 April 2009.

Scammell, M. (1995), *Designer Politics: How Elections are Won,* Houndsmill, Basingstoke; London: Macmillan Press Ltd.

Schlesinger, P. (2006), 'Is There a Crisis in British Journalism?', *Media, Culture & Society,* 28: 2, pp. 299–307.

Schulze, J. (2009), 'ABC's diplomatic note in row with Sky', *The Australian*, 6 March, http://www. theaustralian.com.au/news/abcs-diplomatic-note-in-row-with-sky/story-0-1111119047732. Accessed 6 March 2009.

Scoop (2007), 'TVNZ Proposes to Gut Journalism', 12 April, http://www.scoop. co.nz/stories/PO0704/ S00152.htm. Accessed 30 July 2008.

Scott, K. (2006), 'Honesty and Trust in America Survey', http://www.zogby.com/lichtman%20 Final%20Report%205-22-06.pdf.

Scott, M. (2007), 'The ABC in the Digital Age: Towards 2020', http://www.abc.net.au/corp/pubs/ documents/2020_ABC_in_the_Digital_Age.pdf. Accessed 20 February 2009.

Scott, M. (2008), 'The ABC in the Digital Age: Towards 2020', Paper presented at the *2020 Summit*, Canberra, http://www.abc.net.au/corp/pubs/media/s2219354.htm. Accessed 24 June 2008.

Scott, M. (2009), 'A Global ABC: Soft Diplomacy and the World of International Broadcasting', *Bruce Allen Memorial Lecture 2009*, http://www.abc.net.au/corp/pubs/documents. Accessed 20 February 2010.

Seligman, A. B. (1997), *The Problem of Trust*, Princeton, N. J.: Princeton University Press.

Service, P. B. (2009), 'About PBS Programming', http://www.pbs.org/aboutpbs/aboutpbs_prog.html. Accessed 29 September 2009.

Shapiro, S. P. (1987), 'The social control of personal trust', *American Journal of Sociology*, 93: 3, pp. 623–58.

Sheeran, G. (2009), 'Why Natural History keeps repeating', *Sunday Star Times*, 16 August, http://www. stuff.co.nz/sunday-star-times/business/2754239/Why-Natural-History-keeps-repeating.

Simons, M. (2005), 'Inside the ABC', in R. Manne (ed.), *Do Not Disturb: Is the Media Failing Australia?*, Melbourne: Black Inc.

Simons, M. (2008), 'Aunty to review complaints process, but not for Gerard Henderson', *Crikey*, 9 April, http://www.crikey.com.au/Media-Arts-and- Sports/20080409-Aunty-to-review-complaints-process-but-not-for-Gerard-Henderson-.html. Accessed 20 April 2008

Simons, M. (2009), 'A-Pac Hits the Airwaves, Beats ABC to the Punch', *Crikey*, 20 January.

Simons, M. (2009b), 'ABC Opens its Archives – Slowly', *The Content Makers: Margaret Simons on the Media*, http://blogs.crikey.com.au/contentmakers/2009/01/05/abc-opens-its-archives-slowly. Accessed 27 February 2010.

Smith, A. (1976), *The Shadow in the Cave*, London: Quartet Books Ltd.

Smith, P. (1996), *Revolution in the Air*, Auckland: Longman.

Somerset-Ward, R. (1993), *Public Television: The Ballpark's Changing*, Washington: Twentieth Century Fund Inc.

SPAA (2009), 'ABC Funding Increase Welcome', http://www.spaa.org.au/displayindustryarticle. cfm?articlenbr=39296. Accessed 28 February 2010.

Sparks, C. (1995), 'The Survival of the State in British Broadcasting', *Journal of Communications*, 45: 4, pp. 140–59.

Spicer, B., Powell, M., and Emanuel, D. (1996), *The Remaking of Television New Zealand: 1988–92*, Auckland: Auckland University Press.

Splichal, S. (2006), 'Public Media in Service of Civil Society and Democracy', in C. S. Nissen (ed.), *Making a Difference: Public Service Broadcasting in the European Landscape*, Eastleigh, UK: John Libbey Publishing, pp. 17–34.

Starks, M. (2007), *Switching to digital television: UK public policy and the market*, Bristol, UK: Intellect.

Starr, J. (2004), 'An Alternative View of the Future of Public Television', *CIPB Online*.

Starr, J. (2000), *Air Wars: the fight to reclaim public broadcasting*, Boston, MA: Beacon Press.

Stewart, D. E. and Moss, L. (1983), 'Communication Policy in New Zealand: Overseas Influence and Local Neglect', in Patricia Edgar and Syed A. Rahim (eds.), *Communication Policy in Developed Countries*, London: Kegan Paul.

Streeter, T. (1983), 'Policy discourse and broadcast practice: the FCC, the US broadcast networks and the discourse of the marketplace', *Media, Culture & Society,* 5, pp. 247–62.

Sweney, M. (2009), 'Let Channel 4 make its own shows, says shadow culture secretary Jeremy Hunt', *The Guardian*, 7 January, http://www.guadian.co.uk/media/2009/jan/07/channel-4-jeremy-hunt. Accessed 22 January 2010.

Sweney, M. and Holmwood, L. (2009), 'Big Brother axed by Channel 4', http://www.guardian.co.uk/media/2009/aug/26/big-brother-dropped-channel-4. Accessed 1 February 2010.

Synovate (2007), *New Zealanders' Perceptions of the Importance and Contribution of Public Broadcasting*, Wellington: Ministry for Culture and Heritageo.

Tanner, L. (2004), 'Future Broadcasting: Speech to Australian Fabian Society', Paper presented at the *Fabian Society Autumn Lectures 2004*.

Thompson, J. B. (2000), *Political Scandal: Power and Visibility in the Media Age*, Cambridge: Polity.

Thompson, M. (2006), 'The future's creative', *Television*, 4–8 May, Royal Television Society, London.

Thompson, M. (2007), 'Trust and Values', *BBC blogs*, http://www.bbc.co.uk/blogs/theeditors/2007/09/trust_and_values.html. Accessed 20 February 2008.

Thompson, M. (2008), 'The trouble with trust', *BBC blogs*, http://www.bbc.co.uk/blogs/theeditors/2008/01/the_trouble_with_trust.html. Accessed 15 March 2008.

Thompson, P. (2002), 'A Sorry State? Public Service broadcasting in Contemporary New Zealand', *Southern Review,* 35: 1, pp. 120–35.

Thompson, P. (2003), 'The CROC with no Teeth? Television in the post-TVNZ Charter context', *NZ Political Review,* 12: 1, pp. 18–27.

Thompson, P. (2004), '"Unto God or Unto Caesar?": Television after the TVNZ Charter', *Communication Journal of New Zealand*, 5: 2, pp. 60–91.

Thompson, P. (2005), 'Calling the tune without paying the piper: The political- economic contradictions of funding the TVNZ Charter', Paper presented at the refereed stream of the *2005 ANZCA Conference: 'Communication at Work'*, 4–7 July, University of Canterbury: Christchurch.

Thompson, P. (2007), 'Review of Public Submissions on the Redraft of the TVNZ Charter', Auckland Working Party: TVNZ Charter Review.

Thompson, P. (2008), 'Survival of the TVNZ Charter Depends on Definitions', *Scoop,* 10 July, http://www.scoop. co.nz/stories/HL0807/S00080.htm. Accessed 8 September 20009.

Thompson, P. (2009), 'National's Broadcasting Policy: Expedient Fictions, Inconvenient Truths', http://www.scoop. co.nz/stories/HL0904/S00090.htm. Accessed 8 September 2009.

Thompson, P. (2009a), 'The Demise of the TVNZ Charter: The arguments the Government wants us to ignore', http://www.scoop. co.nzstories/HL0903/S00356.htm. Accessed 31 August 2009.

Throng (2010), 'Top TV Shows – AGB Nielsen Media Research', 31 January – 6 February, http://www.throng.co.nz/blog/agb-nielsen. Accessed 15 February 2010.

Tingle, L. (1997), 'ABC Cuts Strategy Exposed'. *The Age*, 23 January.

Tracy, M. (1998), *The Decline and Fall of Public Service Broadcasting*, London: Oxford University Press.

Trevett, C. (2005), 'Fraser Quits TVNZ over meddling'. *New Zealand Herald*, 31 October, http://www.nzherald.co.nz. Accessed 11 September 2009.

Tryhorn, C. (2010), 'SeeSaw: Your Questions Answered', *The Guardian*, 17 February, http://guardian.co.uk/media/2010/feb/17/seesaw-your-questions-answered/print. Accessed 3 March 2010.

Turner, G. (2005), *Ending the Affair: The Decline of Television Current Affairs in Australia*, Sydney: UNSW Press.

TVNZ (1995), *Annual Report*, Auckland: TVNZ.

TVNZ (2007), *A successful past: an exciting future*, Auckland: TVNZ

TVNZ (2007a), *Annual Report 2006/07*. Auckland: TVNZ.

TVNZ (2008), *Annual Report*. Auckland: TVNZ.

TVNZ (2009), *Media Release*, 26 March, http://tvnz.co.nz/view/page/816457/2590540. Accessed 6 September 2009.

Volkerling, M. (1996), *A New Broadcasting Policy for New Zealand: A Discussion Paper*, Wellington: Screen Producers and Directors Association of New Zealand (SPADA).

Ward, D. (2004), *Public Service Broadcasting. Change and Continuity: A Special Issue of Trends in Communication*, Mahwah, N. J.: Lawrence Erlbaum Associates Inc.

Wellings, S. (2007), 'Mary Kostakidis walks out on SBS'. *The Sydney Morning Herald*, 21 August, http://www.smh.com.au/news/tv--radio/stan-and-mary-show-storm/2007/08/21/1187462225475.html.

Whitehead, G. (1988), *Inside the ABC*, Ringwood, Victoria: Penguin Books.

Whittle, S. (2004), 'Public Service Broadcasting in the New Media Age', in David Ward (ed.), *Public Service Broadcasting: Change and Continuity: A Special Issue of Trends in Communication*, Mahwah, N. J.: Lawrence Erlbaum Associates, Inc.

Williams, R. (1996), *Normal service won't be resumed: the future of public broadcasting*, St Leonards, NSW: Allen & Unwin.

Willis, J. and Wollen, T. (1990), *The Neglected Audience*, London: BFI.

Wilmoth, P. (1993), *Glad All Over: The Countdown Years, 1974–1987*, Ringwood,Victoria: McPhee Gribble.

Wishart, I. (2000), *Beating Big Brother: How People Turned Off the TV Tax!*, Orewa, Auckland: The Anti TV Licence Campaign.

Withers, G. (2002), 'Funding Public Service Broadcasters', *Southern Review*, 35: 1, pp. 107–19.

Wray, R. (2010), 'Lords: privatize BBC Worldwide', *The Guardian*, 25 January, http://www.guardian.co.uk/media/2010/jan/25/lords-report-privatise-bbc-worldwide. Accessed 26 January 2010.

Young, S. (2002), 'New Media: Brave New World or Same Old Same Old?', *Southern Review*, 35: 1, pp. 74–86.

Interviews

Australia

Kim Dalton, Head of Television, ABC. Author's recorded telephone interview, 5 August 2007, La Trobe University, Melbourne, Australia.

Courtney Gibson, Head of Content Creation, ABC Television. Author's recorded telephone interview, 7 February 2008, La Trobe University, Melbourne, Australia.

Murray Green, Director of International Corporate Strategy and Governance, ABC. Author's recorded telephone interview, February 2008, La Trobe University, Melbourne, Australia.

Georgie McClean, SBS Manager of Policy and Research. Author's interview, 20 October 2006, La Trobe University, Melbourne Australia.

Mark Scott, Managing Director, ABC. Author's recorded telephone interview. January 2009, La Trobe University, Melbourne, Australia.

Paul Vincent, then Manager of SBS Online. Author's telephone interview, 23 November 2006, La Trobe University, Melbourne, Australia.

Michael Ward, Head of Policy for Television, ABC. Author's recorded telephone interview, March 2008, La Trobe University, Melbourne, Australia.

New Zealand

Joe Atkinson, Senior Lecturer, Political Studies, University of Auckland. Author's recorded interview, 29 September 2006, University of Auckland, Auckland, New Zealand.

Eric Kearley, Director New Media, TVNZ. Author's recorded interview, 28 September 2006, TVNZ Network Centre, Hobson St., Auckland, New Zealand.

Richard Harman, Executive Producer, Front Page Ltd. Author's recorded interview, 6 October 2006, Auckland New Zealand.

Alistair Mathewson, General Manager, Interactive, TVNZ. Author's recorded interview, 2 October 2006, TVNZ Network Centre, Hobson St., Auckland, New Zealand.

David Murphy, Executive Producer New Media, TVNZ. Author's recorded interview, 6 October 2006, TVNZ Network Centre, Hobson St., Auckland, New Zealand.

Peter Thompson, Senior lecturer, Department of Communications, Unitec. Author's recorded interview, 5 October 2006, Mount Albert, Auckland, New Zealand.

United Kingdom

Tony Ageh, Controller BBC Online. Author's recorded interview, 29 August 2006, BBC, Broadcast Centre, Media Village, 201 Wood Lane, London, United Kingdom.

Maxine Baker, filmmaker, broadcaster and lecturer. Author's recorded interview, 1 September 2006, National Film and Television School, London, United Kingdom.

Robert Beveridge Lecturer: Media Policy, Media Regulation, Journalism & Government, Department of Media Studies, Napier University, and a director with the Voice of the Listener and Viewer. Author's recorded interview, 27 August 2006, Edinburgh, United Kingdom.

David Booth, Head of Scheduling and Strategy for Digital Channels. Author's recorded interview, 1 September 2006, Channel Four, Horseferry Road, London, United Kingdom.

Rahul Chakkara, Controller BBCi. Author's recorded interview, 22 August 2006, BBC Broadcast Centre, Media Village, 201 Wood Lane, London, United Kingdom.

Nick Cohen, Commissioning Editor for BBCi. Author's recorded interview, 29 August 2006, BBC, Broadcast Centre, Media Village, 201 Wood Lane, London, United Kingdom.

Adam Gee, Commissioner for New Media at Channel 4. Author's recorded interview, 24 August 2006, Channel 4, London.

Paul Gerhardt, joint project director, BBC Creative Archive. Author's recorded interview, 29 August 2006, BBC, London.

Marc Goodchild, Executive Producer: Innovation Development (Cross platform development). Author's recorded interview, 30 August 2006, BBC, Broadcast Centre, Media Village, 201 Wood Lane, London, United Kingdom.

Sylvia Harvey, Professor of Broadcasting Policy at the Centre for Media Policy, Regulation and Ethics at the University of Lincoln. Author's recorded interview, 3 August 2006, Lincoln.

Steve Hewlett, media consultant, Media Guardian television columnist and Visiting Professor in Journalism and Broadcasting at University of Salford. Author's recorded interview, 16 August 2006, London, United Kingdom.

David Levy, BBC Controller: Public Policy. Author's recorded interview, 4 August 2006, BBC Media Centre, 201 Woodlane, White City, London, United Kingdom.

Graham Murdock, Reader in Sociology of Culture, Loughborough University. Author's recorded interview, 2 September 2006, London, United Kingdom.

Andrew Owen, Managing Editor, Interactive Programmes, BBC Television. Author's recorded interview, 17 August 2006, BBC Television Centre, Wood Lane, White City, London, United Kingdom.

Steve Perkins, Head of Public Service Broadcasting Content, Ofcom. Author's recorded interview, 30 August 2006, Ofcom, 2 Suffolk Bridge Road, London, United Kingdom.

Sarah Thane, Former Ofcom staffer and broadcaster. Author's recorded interview, 29 August 2006, The Reform Club, London, United Kingdom.

Kate Vogel, Commissioning Editor, Channel Four. Author's recorded interview, 1 September 2006, Channel Four, Horseferry Road, London, United Kingdom.

United States

Howard Cutler, Executive Producer with WGBH Interactive. Author's recorded interview, 13 September 2006, WGBH, Boston.

Anne Gleason, Vice President of Marketing and New Media. Author's interview, 18 September 2006, WTTW Chicago, United States of America

William Hoynes, Professor of Sociology and Director of Media Studies, Vassar College. Author's recorded interview, 8 September 2006, Poughkeepsie, United States of America.

Evie Kintzer, Legal Adviser, WGBH. Author's recorded interview, 13 September 2006, WGBH, 114 Western Ave., Cambridge, Boston, United States of America.

David Liroff, Chief Technology Officer, WGBH. Author's recoded interview, 12 September 2006, WGBH, 114 Western Ave., Cambridge, Boston, United States of America.

Tim Olson, Vice President of New Media, KQED. Author's recorded interview, 21 September 2006, KQED, San Francisco, United States of America.

Nan Rubin, Community Producer, Thirteen (aka WYNET). Author's recorded interview, 6 September 2006, New York.

Scott Sanders, member of CIPB, Chicago Chapter. Author's interview, 15 September 2006, Chicago, United States of America.

Dan Schmidt, President and CEO, WTTW, United States. Author's interview, 18 September 2006, Chicago United States of America.

Dan Soles, President of Broadcasting, WTTW. Author's interview, 18 September 2006, WTTW, Chicago, United States of America.

Annie Valva, Director, Research and Development, WGBH Educational Foundation. Author's recorded interview, 11 September 2006, WGBH, 114 Western Ave., Cambridge, Boston, United States of America.

Richard Winefield, then Vice-President for Interactive Educational Services at San Francisco's KQED. Author's recorded interview, 21 September 2006, KQED San Francisco.

Index